The Identity of the New Testament Text

The Identity of the New Testament Text

Revised Edition
WILBUR N. PICKERING

THOMAS NELSON PUBLISHERS
Nashville

Revised edition

Library of Congress Cataloging in Publication Data

Pickering, Wilbur N
   The identity of the New Testament text.

   References: p. 235.
   Includes index.
   1. Bible. N.T.—Criticism, Textual.   I. Title.
BS2325.P52   1980   225.4   80-17369
ISBN 0-8407-5744-1 (pbk.)

My wife, Ida Lou, joins me in dedicating
this book to the memory of
JOHN ARTHUR TRAVIS

TABLE OF CONTENTS

CONTENTS

CONTENTS

FOREWORD

Few questions are of more importance than the one suggested by the title of this book. The "identity" of the original text of the New Testament is a matter of considerable moment to every Bible-believing Christian. After all, the New Testament is a unique book and, as breathed out by God's Holy Spirit, is genuinely inspired and inerrant in its original autographs.

But many centuries and a multitude of copies have intervened since the original writing of the New Testament. Unlike the inspired autographs these copies are not free from error and must be carefully compared and evaluated in order to determine the original readings. The specialized branch of study which undertakes to do this is called "textual criticism."

It is about textual criticism that the author is writing. And he writes knowledgeably. The literature of the field has been well examined by him and, even more important, its prevailing theories have been searchingly appraised. The conclusion he reaches is that, since the late nineteenth century, these theories have been misdirected and have rendered the search for the original text a very poor service indeed.

This conclusion is long overdue, and it is encouraging to see the publication of a modern book which proclaims it. As a matter of fact, the discernment of the writer is enhanced by his deep commitment to the full authority and total reliability of the New Testament Scriptures. This commitment has not been shared by many of the textual critics whose ideas he criticises. It is hardly surprising, therefore, that some of these ideas have not really been consistent with true faith in the inspiration of God's Word.

But *The Identity of the New Testament Text* is not a mere pamphlet dogmatically affirming a position which cannot be adequately defended from the available data of textual criticism. There *are* pamphlets like that, but this is not one of them. On the contrary, the writer competently sifts the data of this highly technical field to reach conclusions that should be genuinely reassuring to every Bible believer.

It is not necessary to agree with every syllable of this book to perceive that it brings a potent indictment against contemporary textual theories. But it does more than that. It seeks also to point the way toward a more valid approach to a field of study which cannot be ignored by any serious student of the New Testament Scriptures.

Zane C. Hodges

The
Identity
of the
New Testament
Text

1
INTRODUCTION*

Because this book will be read by people representing a broad spectrum of interest and background, I will begin with a brief review of the textual problem.

That there is a problem concerning the identity of the Greek text of the New Testament is made clear by the existence of a number of competing editions in print. By competing I mean that they do not agree with one another as to the precise wording of the text. Such disagreement is possible because no two of the ancient Greek manuscripts (handwritten copies) known to us are identical in wording, and we are dependent upon those copies because the Apostles' Autographs, or original documents, are no longer in existence. (They were probably worn out by about A.D. 200, if not before.)

In short, we are faced with the problem of recovering the original wording of the text from the surviving manuscripts, no two of which entirely agree. In this task we may also appeal to copies of the ancient Versions (translations into Syriac, Latin,

*A good deal of the research underlying this book was done in connection with the master's thesis I submitted to the Dallas Theological Seminary in 1968 entitled "An Evaluation of the Contribution of John William Burgon to New Testament Textual Criticism." My thesis was subsequently published in edited form in *True or False?*, ed. D. Otis Fuller, (Grand Rapids: Grand Rapids International Publishers, 1972)—the full text of the thesis appears in the 2nd edition, 1975. I have re-used some of the material in the thesis by permission of both entities.

Coptic, etc.) and to the surviving writings of the early church Fathers where they quote or refer to New Testament passages.

There are over 5,000 extant (known) Greek manuscripts (hereafter MSS, or MS when singular) of the New Testament. They range in size from a scrap with parts of two verses to complete New Testaments. They range in date from the second century to the sixteenth. They come from all over the Mediterranean world. They contain several hundred thousand variant readings (differences in the text). The vast majority of these are misspellings or other obvious errors due to carelessness or ignorance on the part of the copyists. However, many thousands of variants remain which need to be evaluated as we seek to reconstruct the precise original wording of the text. How best to go about such a project? This book seeks to provide an answer.

Of course, I am not the first to attempt an answer. Numerous answers have been advanced over the years. They tend to form two clusters, or camps, and these camps differ substantially from each other. In very broad and over-simplified terms, one camp generally follows the large majority of the MSS (between 80 and 90 percent) which are in essential agreement among themselves but which do not date from before the fifth century A.D., while the other generally follows a small handful (often less than ten) of earlier MSS (from the third, fourth and fifth centuries) which not only disagree with the majority, but also disagree among themselves. The second camp has been in general control of the scholarly world for the last 100 years.

The most visible consequence and proof of that control may be seen in the translations of the New Testament into English done during these 100 years. Virtually every one of them reflects a form of the text based upon the few earlier MSS. In contrast to them, the King James Version reflects a form of the text based upon the many later MSS. Thus, the fundamental difference between the New Testament in the American Standard Version, Revised Standard Version, New English Bible, Today's English Version, New American Standard Bible, New International Version, etc., on the one hand, and in the King James Version on the other is that they are based on different forms of the Greek text. (There are over 5,000 differences between those two forms.[1])

To the extent that you may be aware of these matters you may well have accepted as reasonable the statements usually made to the effect that the very considerable improvement in our stock of available materials (Greek manuscripts and other witnesses) and in our understanding of what to do with them (principles of textual criticism) has made possible a closer approximation to the original text in our day than was achieved several hundred years ago. The statements to be found in the prefaces of some versions give the reader the impression that this improvement is reflected in their translations. For example, the preface to the Revised Standard Version, p. ix, says:

> The King James Version of the New Testament was based upon a Greek text that was marred by mistakes, containing the accumulated errors of fourteen centuries of manuscript copying. . . . We now possess many more ancient manuscripts of the New Testament, and are far better equipped to seek to recover the original wording of the Greek text.

And the preface to the New International Version, p. viii, says:

> The Greek text used in the work of translation was an eclectic one. No other piece of ancient literature has so much manuscript support as does the New Testament. Where existing texts differ, the translators made their choice of readings in accord with sound principles of textual criticism. Footnotes call attention to places where there is uncertainty about what constitutes the original text.

But if you have used a number of the modern versions you may have noticed some things that perhaps intrigued, bewildered, or even distressed you. I am thinking of the degree to which they differ among themselves, the uncertainty as to the identity of the text reflected in the many footnotes regarding textual variants, and the nature and extent of their common divergence from the King James Version.

The bulk of the differences between the modern versions is presumably due to differences in style and translation technique. However, although they are in essential agreement as to the Greek text used, as opposed to that underlying the King James Version, no two of them are based on an identical Greek text. Nor have the translators been entirely sure as to the precise wording of the text—while some versions have few notes about textual variation, others have many, and even in these cases by no means all the doubts have been recorded.[2] In short, no one in the world today really knows the precise original wording of the Greek text of the New Testament.

Such a realization may beget an incipient uneasiness in the recesses of your mind. Why isn't anyone sure, if we have so many materials and so much wisdom? Well, because the present "wisdom," the "sound principles of textual criticism" currently in vogue, may be summed up in two maxims: choose the reading that best explains the origin of the competing variants, and choose the variant that the author is more/most likely to have written.

No wonder Bruce Metzger[3] says, "It is understandable that in some cases different scholars will come to different evaluations of the significance of the evidence."[4] A cursory review of the writings of textual scholars suggests that Metzger's "in some cases" is decidedly an understatement. In fact, even the same scholars will vacillate, as demonstrated by the "more than five hundred changes" introduced into the third edition of the Greek text produced by the United Bible Societies as compared with the second edition (the same committee of five editors prepared both).[5] Further, it is evident that the maxims above cannot be applied with certainty. No one living today knows or can know what actually happened. It follows that so long as the textual materials are handled in this way *we will never be sure* about the precise wording of the Greek text.[6]

It is not surprising that scholars working within such a framework say as much. For example, Robert M. Grant, a well-known biblical scholar, says:

The primary goal of New Testament textual study remains the recovery of what the New Testament writers wrote. We have already suggested that to achieve this goal is well-nigh impossible. Therefore we must be content with what

Reinhold Niebuhr and others have called, in other contexts, an "impossible possibility."[7]

And Kenneth W. Clark, another well-known textual scholar and professor, commenting on P[75]:

> . . . the papyrus vividly portrays a fluid state of the text at about A.D. 200. Such a scribal freedom suggests that the gospel text was little more stable than the oral tradition, and that we may be pursuing the retreating mirage of the 'original text.'[8]

Thirty years ago Grant had said, "it is generally recognized that the original text of the Bible cannot be recovered."[9]

At this point I get uncomfortable. If the original wording is lost and gone forever, whatever are we using? The consequences of such an admission are so far-reaching, to my mind, that a thorough review of the evidence is called for. Do the facts really force an honest mind to the conclusion expressed by Grant? In seeking an answer to this question I will begin with the present situation in New Testament textual criticism and work back. The procedure which dominates the scene today is called "eclecticism."[10]

2

ECLECTICISM

In late 1974, Eldon Jay Epp, a respected contemporary textual scholar, wrote:

> The "eclectic" method is, in fact, *the* 20th century method of NT textual criticism, and anyone who criticizes it immediately becomes a self-critic, for we all use it, some of us with a certain measure of reluctance and restraint, others with complete abandon.[1]

Thus, the RSV (Revised Standard Version), NEB (New English Bible) and NIV (New International Version) are confessedly based upon an eclectic text.

The two great translation efforts of these years—RSV and NEB—each chose the Greek text to translate on the basis of the internal evidence of readings. F. C. Grant's chapter in the expository pamphlet on the RSV made this clear. The translators, he says, followed two rules: (1) Choose the reading that best fits the context; (2) Choose the reading which explains the origin of the other readings. Professor C. H. Dodd informed me that the British translators also used these two principles—Hort's Intrinsic Probability and Transcriptional Probability. One of the RSV translators while lecturing to the New Testament Club at the University of Chicago replied to a question concerning the Greek text he used by saying that it depended on where he was working: he used Souter at the office and Nestle at home. One of the British translators in admitting the unevenness of the textual quality of the NEB translation explained that the quality depended on the ability of the man who made the first draft-translation of a book.

Whether in early Christian times or today, translators have so often treated the text cavalierly that textual critics should be hardened to it. But much more serious is the prevalence of this same dependence on the internal evidence of readings in learned articles on textual criticism, and in the popularity of manual editions of the Greek New Testament. These latter with their limited citations of variants and witnesses actually reduce the user to reliance upon the internal evidence of readings. The documents which these rigorously abbreviated apparatuses cite cannot lead the user to dependence upon external evidence of documents. These editions use documents (to quote Housman) "as drunkards use lampposts—, not to light them on their way but to dissimulate their instability."[2]

The statement in the preface to the NIV has already been noted: "The Greek text used in the work of translation was an eclectic one."

The introduction to the recent Greek text put out by the United Bible Societies, pp. x-xi (1966), says:

By means of the letters A, B, C, and D, enclosed within "braces" { } at the beginning of each set of textual variants, the Committee has sought to indicate the relative degree of certainty, arrived at on the basis of internal considerations as well as of external evidence, for the reading adopted as the text. The letter A signifies that the text is virtually certain, while B indicates that there is some degree of doubt. The letter C means that there is a considerable degree of doubt whether the text or the apparatus contains the superior reading, while D shows that there is a very high degree of doubt concerning the reading selected for the text.

A review of their apparatus and its lack of pattern in the correlation between degree of certainty assigned and external evidence makes clear that it is eclectic. In Acts 16:12 they have even incorporated a conjecture! It will be remembered that this text was prepared specifically for the use of Bible translators. The TEV (Today's English Version) is translated directly from it, as is the *Version Popular*, etc. The text-critical conclusions of G. D. Kilpatrick, a thorough-going eclecticist, are finding expression in *A Greek-English Diglot for the Use of Translators*, issued by the British and Foreign Bible Society. And so on. Enough evidence has been given to show that eclecticism is a major, if not controlling, factor on the textual scene today.

What Is It?

Wherein does "eclecticism" consist? Metzger explains that an eclectic editor "follows now one and now another set of witnesses in accord with what is deemed to be the author's style or the exigencies of transcriptional hazards."[3]

E. C. Colwell[4] spells it out:

Today textual criticism turns for its final validation to the appraisal of individual readings, in a way that involves subjective judgment. The trend has been to emphasize fewer and fewer canons of criticism. Many moderns emphasize only two. These are: 1) that reading is to be preferred which best suits the context, and 2) that reading is to be preferred which best explains the origin of all others.

These two rules are nothing less than concentrated formulas of all that the textual critic must know and bring to bear upon the solution of his problem. The first rule about choosing what suits the context exhorts the student to know the document he is working on so thoroughly that its idioms are his idioms, its ideas as well known as a familiar room. The second rule about choosing what could have caused the other readings requires that the student know everything in Christian history which could lead to the creation of a variant reading. This involves knowledge of institutions, doctrines, and events. . . . This is knowledge of complicated and often conflicting forces and movements.[5]

(What living man really possesses these qualifications? And how can such rules be applied when neither the identity nor circumstances of the originator of a given variant is known?)

More recently Colwell seems to be less enchanted with the method.

The scholars who profess to follow "the Eclectic Method" frequently so define the term as to restrict evidence to the Internal Evidence of Readings. By "eclectic" they mean in fact free choice among readings. This choice in many cases is made solely on the basis of intrinsic probability. The editor chooses that reading which commends itself to him as fitting the context, whether in style, or idea, or contextual reference. Such an editor relegates the manuscripts to the role of supplier of readings. The weight of the manuscript is ignored. Its place in the manuscript tradition is not considered. Thus Kilpatrick argues that certain readings found only in one late Vulgate manuscript should be given the most serious consideration because they are good readings.[6]

J. K. Elliott, a thorough-going eclecticist like Kilpatrick, says of transcriptional probabilities:

By using criteria such as the above the critic may reach a conclusion in discussing textual variants and be able to say which variant is the original reading. However, it is legitimate to ask: can a reading be accepted as genuine if it is supported by only one ms.? There is no reason why an original reading should not have been preserved in only one ms. but obviously a reading can be accepted with greater confidence, when it has stronger support. . . .

Even Aland with his reservation about eclecticism says: "Theoretically the original readings can be hidden in a single ms. thus standing alone against the rest of tradition," and Tasker has a similar comment: "The possibility must be left open that in some cases the true reading may have been preserved in only a few witnesses or even in a single relatively late witness."[7]

Among what Elliott calls "positive advantages of the eclectic method" is the following:

> An attempt is made to reach the true or original text. This is, of course, the ultimate aim of any textual critic, but the eclectic method, by using different criteria and by working from a different standpoint, tries to arrive at the true reading, untrammeled by discussion about the weight of ms. support. . . .[8]

No wonder Epp complains:

> This kind of "eclecticism" becomes the great leveller—all variants are equals and equally candidates for the original text, regardless of date, residence, lineage, or textual context. In this case, would it not be appropriate to suggest, further, that a few more conjectural readings be added to the available supply of variants on the assumption that they must have existed but have been lost at some point in the history of the textual transmission?[9]

What shall we say of such a method; is it a good thing?

What About It?

An eclecticism based solely on internal considerations is unacceptable for several reasons. It is unreasonable. It ignores the over 5,000 Greek MSS now extant, to say nothing of patristic and versional evidence, except to cull variant readings from them. In Elliott's words, it "tries to arrive at the true reading untrammeled by discussion about the weight of ms. support." It follows that it has no principled basis for rejecting conjectural emendations. It has no history of the transmission of the text. Therefore the choice between variants ultimately depends upon guesswork. This has been recognized by Colwell.

> In the last generation we have depreciated external evidence of documents and have appreciated the internal evidence of

readings; but we have blithely assumed that we were reject-ing "conjectural emendation" if our conjectures were sup-ported by some manuscripts. We need to recognize that the editing of an eclectic text rests upon conjectures.[10]

F. G. Kenyon[11] called conjectural emendation "a process precarious in the extreme and seldom allowing anyone but the guesser to feel confidence in the truth of its results."[12] Al-though enthusiasts like Elliott think they can restore the origi-nal wording of the text in this way, it is clear that the result can have no more authority than that of the scholar(s) involved. Textual criticism ceases to be a science and one is left wonder-ing what is meant by "sound principles" in the NIV preface.

Clark and Epp are right in calling eclecticism a secondary, tentative, and temporary method.[13] As A.F.J. Klijn[14] says, "This method arrives at such varying results that we wonder whether editors of Greek texts and translations can safely fol-low this road."[15] This procedure seems so unsatisfactory, in fact, that we may reasonably wonder what gave rise to it.

What Is Its Source?

Eclecticism grew out of the Westcott and Hort (hereafter W-H) theory of textual criticism. Epp gives a useful summary statement of that theory, for our immediate purpose:

> . . . the grouping of manuscripts led to the separation of the relatively few early manuscripts from the mass of later ones, and eventually the process reached its climactic point of development and its classical statement in the work of Westcott and Hort (1881–1882), and particularly in their (ac-tually, Hort's) clear and firm view of the early history of the NT text. This clear picture was formed from Hort's isolation of essentially three (though he said four) basic textual groups or text-types. On the basis largely of Greek manuscript evi-dence from the middle of the 4th century and later and from the early versional and patristic evidence, two of these, the so-called Neutral and Western text-types, were regarded as

competing texts from about the middle of the 2nd century, while the third, now designated Byzantine, was a later, conflate and polished ecclesiastical text. . . . This left essentially two basic text-types competing in the earliest traceable period of textual transmission, the Western and the Neutral, but this historical reconstruction could not be carried farther so as to reveal—on historical grounds—which of the two was closer to and therefore more likely to represent the original NT text.[16]

. . . the question which faced Westcott-Hort remains for us: Is the original text something nearer to the Neutral or to the Western kind of text? . . . Hort resolved the issue, not on the basis of the *history of the text,* but in terms of the presumed *inner quality* of the texts and on grounds of largely subjective judgments of that quality.[17]

Hort, following the "ring of genuineness," preferred the readings of the "Neutral" text-type (today's Alexandrian) and especially those of Codex B, while some subsequent scholars have preferred the readings of the "Western" text-type and of Codex D, on the same basis. Although Hort professed to follow external evidence—and he did in fact follow his "Neutral" text-type, by and large—his prior choice of that text-type was based on internal (subjective) considerations.[18] Still, the general impression was given that the W-H theory was based on external (manuscript and historical) evidence.

But various facets of the theory came under attack soon after it appeared in 1881, and with the conflicting voices came confusion. It is this confusion that has given rise to eclecticism. Thus, Elliott frankly states:

In view of the present dilemma and discussion about the relative merits of individual mss., and of ms. tradition, it is reasonable to depart from a documentary study and to examine the N.T. text from a purely eclectic standpoint.[19]

In R.V.G. Tasker's words, "The fluid state of textual criticism today makes the adoption of the eclectic method not only desirable but all but inevitable."[20] Metzger cites dissatisfaction "with the results achieved by weighing the external evidence for variant readings" as the cause.[21] Epp blames "the lack of a definitive theory and history of the early text" and the resultant "chaotic situation in the evaluation of variant readings in the NT text."[22] Colwell also blames "manuscript study without a history."[23] The practice of pure eclecticism seems to imply either despair that the original wording can be recovered on the basis of external evidence, or an unwillingness to undertake the hard work of reconstructing the history of the text, or both.

But most scholars do not practice *pure* eclecticism—they still work essentially within the W-H framework. Thus, the two most popular manual editions of the Greek text today, Nestle-Aland and UBS (United Bible Society), really vary little from the W-H text.[24] The recent versions—RSV, NEB, etc.—also vary little from the W-H text.

Why is this? Epp answers:

One response to the fact that our popular critical texts are still so close to that of Westcott-Hort might be that the kind of text arrived at by them and supported so widely by subsequent criticism is in fact and without question the best attainable NT text; yet every textual critic knows that this similarity of text indicates, rather, that we have made little progress in textual *theory* since Westcott-Hort; that we simply do not know how to make a definitive determination as to what the best text is; that we do not have a clear picture of the transmission and alteration of the text in the first few centuries; and, accordingly, that the Westcott-Hort kind of text has maintained its dominant position largely by default. Gunther Zuntz enforces the point in a slightly different way when he says that "the agreement between our modern editions does not mean that we have recovered the original text. It is due to the simple fact that their editors . . . follow one narrow section of the evidence, namely, the non-Western Old Uncials."[25]

Clark agrees with Zuntz: "All are founded on the same Egyptian recension, and generally reflect the same assumptions of transmission."[26] Clark also gives a sharper focus to one aspect of Epp's answer.

> . . . the Westcott-Hort text has become today our *textus receptus*. We have been freed from the one only to become captivated by the other. . . . The psychological chains so recently broken from our fathers have again been forged upon us, even more strongly. . . .
>
> Even the textual specialist finds it difficult to break the habit of evaluating every witness by the norm of this current *textus receptus*. His mind may have rejected the Westcott-Hort term "neutral," but his technical procedure still reflects the general acceptance of the text. A basic problem today is the technical and psychological factor that the Westcott-Hort text has become our *textus receptus*. . . .
>
> Psychologically it is now difficult to approach the textual problem with free and independent mind. . . . However great the attainment in the Westcott-Hort text, the further progress we desiderate can be accomplished only when our psychological bonds are broken. Herein lies today's foremost problem with the critical text of the New Testament.[27]

In spite of the prevailing uncertainty and dissatisfaction, when it comes right down to it most textual critics fall back on W-H—when in doubt the safe thing to do is stay with the party line.[28]

Elliott, mentioned earlier, deliberately tried to set the party line aside, and the result is interesting—his reconstruction of the text of the Pastoral Epistles differs from the *Textus Receptus* 160 times, differs from W-H 80 times, and contains 65 readings that have not appeared in any other printed edition. A review of his reasoning suggests he did not altogether escape the psychological grip of W-H, but the result is still significantly different from anything else that has been done.[29]

Elliott's effort underscores, by contrast, the extent to which UBS, NEB, etc. still hew to the W-H line. To really understand what is going on today we must have a clear understanding of the W-H critical theory and its implications. Its importance is universally recognized.[30] J. H. Greenlee's statement is representative. "The textual theory of W-H underlies virtually all subsequent work in NT textual criticism."[31]

So, to a discussion of that theory I now turn.

3
THE WESTCOTT-HORT
CRITICAL THEORY

Although Brooke Foss Westcott identified himself fully with the project and the results, it is generally understood that it was mainly Fenton John Anthony Hort[1] who developed the theory and composed the Introduction in their two-volume work.[2] In the following discussion I consider the W-H theory to be Hort's creation.

At the age of 23, in late 1851, Hort wrote to a friend:

> I had no idea till the last few weeks of the importance of texts, having read so little Greek Testament, and dragged on with the villainous *Textus Receptus*. . . . Think of that vile *Textus Receptus* leaning entirely on late MSS.; it is a blessing there are such early ones.[3]

Scarcely more than a year later, "the plan of a joint [with B. F. Westcott] revision of the text of the Greek Testament was first definitely agreed upon."[4] And within that year (1853) Hort wrote to a friend that he hoped to have the new text out "in little more than a year."[5] That it actually took twenty-eight years does not obscure the circumstance that though uninformed, by his own admission, Hort conceived a personal animosity for the *Textus Receptus*,[6] and only because it was based entirely, as he thought, on late manuscripts. It appears Hort did not arrive at his theory through unprejudiced intercourse with the facts. Rather, he deliberately set out to construct a theory that would vindicate his preconceived animosity for the Received Text.

Colwell has made the same observation: "Hort organized his entire argument to depose the Textus Receptus."[7] And again,

> Westcott and Hort wrote with two things constantly in mind; the Textus Receptus and the Codex Vaticanus. But they did not hold them in mind with that passive objectivity which romanticists ascribe to the scientific mind.[8]

As the years went by, Hort must have seen that to achieve his end he had to have a convincing history of the text—he had to be able to explain why essentially only one type of text was to be found in the mass of later manuscripts and show how this explanation justified the rejection of this type of text.

The Basic Approach

Hort started by taking the position that the New Testament is to be treated like any other book.[9]

> The principles of criticism explained in the foregoing section hold good for all ancient texts preserved in a plurality of documents. In dealing with the text of the New Testament no new principle whatever is needed or legitimate.[10]

This stance required the declared presupposition that no malice touched the text.

> It will not be out of place to add here a distinct expression of our belief that even among the numerous unquestionably spurious readings of the New Testament there are no signs of deliberate falsification of the text for dogmatic purposes.[11]

Such a position allowed him to bring over into the textual criticism of the New Testament the family-tree method, or genealogy, as developed by students of the classics.

Genealogy

Here is Hort's classic definition of genealogical method:

The proper method of Genealogy consists . . . in the more or less complete recovery of the texts of successive ancestors by analysis and comparison of the varying texts of their respective descendants, each ancestral text so recovered being in its turn used, in conjunction with other similar texts, for the recovery of the text of a yet earlier common ancestor.[12]

Colwell says of Hort's use of this method:

As the justification of their rejection of the majority, Westcott and Hort found the possibilities of genealogical method invaluable. Suppose that there are only ten copies of a document and that nine are all copied from one; then the majority can be safely rejected. Or suppose that the nine are copied from a lost manuscript and that this lost manuscript and the other one were both copied from the original; then the vote of the majority would not outweigh that of the minority. These are the arguments with which W. and H. opened their discussion of genealogical method. . . . They show clearly that a majority of manuscripts is not *necessarily* to be preferred as correct. It is this *a priori* possibility which Westcott and Hort used to demolish the argument based on the numerical superiority of the adherents of the Textus Receptus.[13]

It is clear that the notion of genealogy is crucial to Hort's theory and purpose. He felt that the genealogical method enabled him to reduce the mass of manuscript testimony to four voices—"Neutral," "Alexandrian," "Western," and "Syrian."

Text-types and Recensions

To sum up what has been said on the results of genealogical evidence proper, as affecting the text of the New Testament, we regard the following propositions as absolutely certain. (I) The great ancient texts did actually exist as we have described them in Sections II and III. . . . (III) The extant documents contain no readings (unless the peculiar Western non-interpolations noticed above are counted as exceptions), which suggest the existence of important textual events unknown to us, a knowledge of which could materially alter the interpretation of evidence as determined by the above history.[14]

The "great ancient texts" are the four named above. Although Hort's "Neutral" and "Alexandrian" are now generally lumped together and called "Alexandrian," and Hort's "Syrian" is now usually named "Byzantine," and the literature refers to an added text-type, "Caesarean," the notion of at least three major text-types or recensions dominates the field to this day. Here is another basic tenet of Hort's theory.

Having, ostensibly, justified the handling of the mass of later manuscripts as one witness or text, Hort now moved to demonstrate that this supposed text was an inferior, even inconsequential, witness. The first proof put forward was "conflation."

Conflation

Once manuscripts are assigned to different text-types on the basis of characteristic variants shared in common, almost any early manuscript that one chances to pick up is observed to exhibit variants thought to be diagnostic or characteristic of alien text-types. Such a situation has been called "mixture." "Conflation" is a special kind of mixture. In Hort's words,

The clearest evidence for tracing the antecedent factors of mixture in texts is afforded by readings which are themselves mixed or, as they are sometimes called, 'conflate,' that is, not simple substitutions of the reading of one document for that of another, but combinations of the readings of both documents into a composite whole, sometimes by mere addition with or without a conjunction, sometimes with more or less of fusion.[15]

Hort urged the conclusion that a text containing conflate readings must be posterior in date to the texts containing the various components from which the conflations were constructed.[16] Then he produced eight examples[17] where, by his interpretation, the "Syrian" (Byzantine) text had combined "Neutral" and "Western" elements. He went on to say:

To the best of our belief the relations thus provisionally traced are never inverted. We do not know of any places where the α group of documents supports readings apparently conflate from the readings of the β and δ groups respectively, or where the β group of documents supports readings apparently conflate from the readings of the α and δ groups respectively.[18]

It was essential to Hort's purpose of demonstrating the "Syrian" text to be posterior that he not find any inversion of the relationships between the three "texts." (An "inversion" would be either the "Neutral" or the "Western" text containing a conflation from the other plus the "Syrian.") So he claimed that inversions do not exist.

Hort's statement and interpretation have been generally accepted.[19] Vincent Taylor calls the argument "very cogent indeed."[20] Kirsopp Lake calls it "the keystone of their theory."[21] Here is another tenet crucial to Hort's theory and purpose. For a second and independent proof of the posteriority of the "Syrian" text he turned to the ante-Nicene Fathers.

"Syrian" Readings Before Chrysostom

After a lengthy discussion, Hort concluded:

Before the middle of the third century, at the very earliest, we have no historical signs of the existence of readings, conflate or other, that are marked as distinctively Syrian by the want of attestation from groups of documents which have preserved the other ancient forms of text. This is a fact of great significance, ascertained as it is exclusively by external evidence, and therefore supplying an absolutely independent verification and extension of the result already obtained by comparison of the internal character of readings as classified by conflation.[22]

Elsewhere he considered that Chrysostom (who died in 407) was the first Father to characteristically use the "Syrian" text.[23]

The importance of this argument to Hort's theory has been recognized by Kenyon.

Hort's contention, which was the corner-stone of his theory, was that readings characteristic of the Received Text are never found in the quotations of Christian writers prior to about A.D. 350. Before that date we find characteristically 'Neutral' and 'Western' readings, but never 'Syrian.' This argument is in fact decisive; . . .[24]

Lake, also, considered it to be decisive.[25]

Hort's purpose would appear to have been achieved, but for good measure he advanced a third argument against the "Syrian" text, one based on internal evidence.

Internal Evidence of Readings

Such "evidence" is based on two kinds of probability—intrinsic and transcriptional. Intrinsic probability is author-oriented—what reading makes the best sense, best fits the context, and conforms to the author's style and purpose? Transcriptional probability is scribe or copyist oriented—what reading can be attributed to carelessness or officiousness on the part of the copyist? Aside from inadvertent mistakes, presumed deliberate changes have given rise to two important canons of criticism—*brevior lectio potior*, the shorter reading is to be preferred (on the assumed propensity of scribes to add material to the text), and *proclivi lectioni praestat ardua*, the harder reading is to be preferred (on the assumed propensity of scribes to attempt to simplify the text when confronted with a supposed difficulty).

On the basis of such considerations, Hort declared the "Syrian" text to be characterized by "lucidity and completeness," "apparent simplicity," "harmonistic assimilation," and as being "conspicuously a full text."[26] He said further:

> In themselves Syrian readings hardly ever offend at first. With rare exceptions they run smoothly and easily in form, and yield at once to even a careless reader a passable sense, free from surprises and seemingly transparent. But when distinctively Syrian readings are minutely compared one after the other with the rival variants, their claim to be regarded as the original readings is found gradually to diminish, and at last to disappear.[27]

Hort's characterization of the "Syrian" text has been generally accepted by subsequent scholars.[28]

Even after demonstrating, as he thought, the "Syrian" text to be eclectic and late, Hort had a major obstacle to hurdle. He had to explain how this "text" came into being, and above all how it came to dominate the field from the fifth century on. An organized revision of the text, executed and imposed upon the churches by ecclesiastical authority, was his solution to the problem.

The "Lucianic Recension" and the Peshitta

"The Syrian text," Hort said, "must in fact be the result of a 'recension' in the proper sense of the word, a work of attempted criticism, performed deliberately by editors and not merely by scribes."[29]

> An authoritative Revision at Antioch . . . was itself subjected to a second authoritative Revision carrying out more completely the purposes of the first. At what date between A.D. 250 and 350 the first process took place, it is impossible to say with confidence. The final process was apparently completed by A.D. 350 or thereabouts.[30]

Hort tentatively suggested Lucian (who died in 311) as

perhaps the leader in the movement and some scholars subsequently became dogmatic on the subject.

The matter of the Syriac Peshitta version is often treated in connection with the "Lucianic recension" of the Greek because of a supposed connection between them. Because the Peshitta does witness to the "Byzantine" text Hort had to get it out of the second and third centuries. Accordingly, he posited a late recension to account for it. F.C. Burkitt went further than Hort and specified Rabbula, Bishop of Edessa from A.D. 411–435, as the author of the revision.[31]

Both ideas have had a wide acceptance. H. C. Thiessen's statement is typical, both in content and dogmatism.

> This [Peshitta] was formerly regarded as the oldest of the Syrian versions; but Burkitt has shown that it is in reality a revision of the Old Syriac made by Rabbula, Bishop of Edessa, about the year 425. This view is now held by nearly all Syriac scholars. . . . The text of the Peshitta is now identified as the Byzantine text, which almost certainly goes back to the revision made by Lucian of Antioch about A.D. 300.[32]

Summary and Consequences

And there you have the essence of the W-H critical theory. I have read every word of Hort's "Introduction," all 324 difficult pages of it, and I believe the description offered above is a reasonable one. Suffice it to say that Hort achieved his purpose, even if it took him twenty-eight years. Although such men as Tischendorf, Tregelles, and Alford had done much to undermine the position of the TR (*Textus Receptus*), Westcott and Hort are generally credited with having furnished the death blow, beginning a new era. Many scholars have written to this effect,[33] but Colwell expresses it as well as anyone.

> The dead hand of Fenton John Anthony Hort lies heavy upon us. In the early years of this century Kirsopp Lake described Hort's work as a failure, though a glorious one. But Hort did *not* fail to reach his major goal. He dethroned the Textus

Receptus. After Hort, the late medieval Greek Vulgate was not used by serious students, and the text supported by earlier witnesses became the standard text. This was a sensational achievement, an impressive success. Hort's success in this task and the cogency of his tightly reasoned theory shaped—and still shapes—the thinking of those who approach the textual criticism of the NT through the English language.[34]

And that explains the nature and extent of the common divergence of the modern versions from the AV (King James Version)—they are all based essentially on the W-H theory and text whereas the AV is essentially based on the *Textus Receptus*.

But the question remains: Has the apparent potential for improving the text (arising from increased materials and "wisdom") been realized? Did the translators of the RSV, for instance, make better use of the manuscripts and employ superior principles of textual criticism than did the translators of the AV? Well, the principles they used led them to adopt the W-H text with very little variation, and that text is based essentially on just two manuscripts, Codices B and Aleph.[35]

Hort declared: "It is our belief (1) that the readings of א B should be accepted as the true readings until strong internal evidence is found to the contrary, and (2) that no readings of א B can safely be rejected absolutely. . . ."[36]

Again, Hort said of B and Aleph, "The fullest comparison does but increase the conviction that their preeminent relative purity is likewise approximately absolute, a true approximate reproduction of the text of the autographs."[37] One wonders whether the W-H theory and text would ever have seen the light of day had Codex B not been extant. Hort gave himself away while discussing genealogy.

In the Apocalypse the difficulty of recognizing the ancient texts is still greater, owing to the great relative paucity of documents, and especially the absence or loss of this book from the Vatican MS (B) which is available for nearly all the rest of the New Testament; and thus the power of using a directly genealogical method is much limited.[38]

The practical effect of the W-H theory was a complete rejection of the "Syrian" text and an almost exclusive preference for the "Neutral" text (equals B and Aleph). Subsequent scholarship has generally rejected the notion of a "Neutral" text but sustained the rejection of the "Syrian" text.

Curiously, there seems to be a determination not to reconsider the status of the "Syrian" text even though each of the arguments Hort used in relegating it to oblivion has been challenged. Thus J.N. Birdsall, after referring to the work of Lake, Lagrange, Colwell and Streeter, as well as his own, declares: "It is evident that all presuppositions concerning the Byzantine text—or texts—except its inferiority to other types, must be doubted and investigated *de novo*."[39] (But doesn't the supposed inferiority depend on those presuppositions?)

Recalling what has already been said above in the discussion of eclecticism, it seems evident that Clark is quite right when he says that "textual theory appears to have reached an impasse in our time."[40]

Since Hort's purpose was to get rid of the "Syrian" text and that is the one point of his theory that subsequent scholars have generally not questioned, perhaps it is time to ask whether that circumstance may not have something to do with the present confusion and impasse, and to wonder whether Hort was really right. I proceed to work through Hort's theory again, point by point, to inquire to what extent it corresponds to the evidence.

4

AN EVALUATION OF THE
W-H THEORY

The Basic Approach

Should the New Testament be treated just like any other book? Will the procedures used on the works of Homer or Aristotle suffice? If both God and Satan had an intense interest in the fate of the New Testament text, presumably not. But how can we test the fact or extent of supernatural intervention? Happily we have eyewitness accounts to provide at least a partial answer. Hort said that "there are no signs of deliberate falsification of the text for dogmatic purposes," but the early Church Fathers disagree. Metzger states:

Irenaeus, Clement of Alexandria, Tertullian, Eusebius, and many other Church Fathers accused the heretics of corrupting the Scriptures in order to have support for their special views. In the mid-second century, Marcion expunged his copies of the Gospel according to Luke of all references to the Jewish background of Jesus. Tatian's Harmony of the Gospels contains several textual alterations which lent support to ascetic or encratite views.[1]

Gaius, an orthodox Father who wrote between A.D. 175 and

200, names Asclepiades, Theodotus, Hermophilus, and Apollonides as heretics who prepared corrupted copies of the Scriptures and who had disciples who multiplied copies of their fabrications.[2]

Surely Hort knew the words of Origen.

> Nowadays, as is evident, there is a great diversity between the various manuscripts, either through the negligence of certain copyists, or the perverse audacity shown by some in correcting the text, or through the fault of those, who, playing the part of correctors, lengthen or shorten it as they please (*In Matth. tom.* XV, 14; *P. G.* XIII, 1293).[3]

Even the orthodox were capable of changing a reading for dogmatic reasons. Epiphanius states (ii.36) that the orthodox deleted "he wept" from Luke 19:41 out of jealousy for the Lord's divinity.[4]

Subsequent scholarship has tended to recognize Hort's mistake. Colwell has done an instructive about-face.

> The majority of the variant readings in the New Testament were created for theological or dogmatic reasons.
>
> Most of the manuals and handbooks now in print (including mine!) will tell you that these variations were the fruit of careless treatment which was possible because the books of the New Testament had not yet attained a strong position as "Bible." The reverse is the case. It was because they were the religious treasure of the church that they were changed.[5]

> The New Testament copies differ widely in nature of errors from copies of the classics. The percentage of variations due to error in copies of the classics is large. In the manuscripts of the New Testament most variations, I believe, were made deliberately.[6]

Matthew Black says flatly:

> The difference between sacred writings in constant popular and ecclesiastical use and the work of a classical author has

never been sufficiently emphasized in the textual criticism of the New Testament. Principles valid for the textual restoration of Plato or Aristotle cannot be applied to sacred texts such as the Gospels (or the Pauline Epistles). We cannot assume that it is possible by a sifting of 'scribal errors' to arrive at the prototype or autograph text of the Biblical writer.[7]

H.H. Oliver gives a good summary of the shift of recent scholarship away from Hort's position in this matter.[8]

The fact of deliberate, and apparently numerous, alterations in the early years of textual history is a considerable inconvenience to Hort's theory for two reasons: it introduces an unpredictable variable which the canons of internal evidence cannot handle, and it puts the recovery of the Original beyond reach of the genealogical method.[9]

To illustrate the second point, Hort's view of early textual history may be represented by figure A whereas the view suggested by the Church Fathers may be represented by figure B. The dotted lines in figure B represent the fabrications introduced by different heretics (as the early Fathers called them).

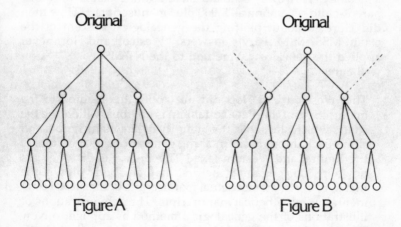

Genealogy cannot arbitrate the conflicting claims posed by

the first line of descendants in Figure B.[10] Further, in Colwell's words, this method (genealogy)

> rested on identity in *error* as the clue to common ancestry. These errors were unintentional changes which can be identified objectively as error. Agreement in readings of this kind seldom occurs by chance or coincidence. The New Testament copies differ widely from copies of the classics at this point. The percentage of variations due to error in copies of the classics is large. In the manuscripts of the New Testament, on the other hand, scholars now believe that most variations were made deliberately.[11]

The reconstruction of family trees is seriously complicated by the presence of deliberate alterations. And those are not the only difficulties under which genealogy labors.

Genealogy

We have already noted Hort's definition and supposed use of genealogy. However, scholars have so far isolated only one parent-child set among all 5,000 plus manuscripts.[12] How then did Hort go about plotting the genealogical descent of the extant MSS? M.M. Parvis answers: "Westcott and Hort never applied the genealogical method to the NT MSS, . . ."[13] Colwell agrees.

> That Westcott and Hort did not apply this method to the manuscripts of the New Testament is obvious. Where are the charts which start with the majority of late manuscripts and climb back through diminishing generations of ancestors to the Neutral and Western texts? The answer is that they are nowhere. Look again at the first diagram, and you will see that a, b, c, etc. are not actual manuscripts of the New Testament, but hypothetical manuscripts. The demonstrations or illustrations of the genealogical method as applied to New Testament manuscripts by the followers of Hort, the "Horticuli" as Lake called them, likewise use hypothetical manu-

scripts, not actual codices. Note, for example, the diagrams and discussions in Kenyon's most popular work on textual criticism, including the most recent edition. All the manuscripts referred to are imaginary manuscripts, and the later of these charts was printed sixty years after Hort.[14]

How then could Hort speak of only "occasional ambiguities in the evidence for the genealogical relations,"[15] or say—

So far as genealogical relations are discovered with perfect certainty, the textual results which follow from them are perfectly certain, too, being directly involved in historical facts; and any apparent presumptions against them suggested by other methods are mere guesses against knowledge[16]—

when he had not demonstrated the existence of *any* such relations, much less with "perfect certainty"?

Another challenge to genealogy is "mixture."

The second limitation upon the application of the genealogical method to the manuscripts of the New Testament springs from the almost universal presence of mixture in these manuscripts. . . .

The genealogical diagram printed above (p. 110) from Westcott and Hort shows what happens *when there is no mixture*. When there *is* mixture, and Westcott and Hort state that it is common, in fact almost universal in some degree, then the genealogical method *as applied to manuscripts* is useless.

Without mixture a family tree is an ordinary tree-trunk with its branches—standing on the branches with the single trunk—the original text—at the top. The higher up—or the further back—you go from the mass of late manuscripts, the fewer ancestors you have!

With mixture you reverse this in any series of generations. The number of possible combinations defies computation, let alone the drawing of diagrams.[17]

Other scholars have agreed that the genealogical method has never been applied to the New Testament, and they state further that it *cannot* be applied. Thus, Zuntz says it is "inapplicable,"[18] Vaganay that it is "useless,"[19] and Aland that it "cannot be applied to the NT."[20] Colwell also declares emphatically "that it *cannot be* so applied."[21] In the light of all this, what are we to think of Hort when he asserts:

> For skepticism as to the possibility of obtaining a trustworthy genealogical interpretation of documentary phenomena in the New Testament there is, we are persuaded, no justification either in antecedent probability or in experience. . . . Whatever may be the ambiguity of the whole evidence in particular passages, the general course of future criticism must be shaped by the happy circumstance that the fourth century has bequeathed to us two MSS of which even the less incorrupt must have been of exceptional purity among its own contemporaries.[22]

After demolishing the genealogical method, Colwell concludes his article by saying, "yet Westcott and Hort's genealogical method slew the Textus Receptus. The *a priori* demonstration is logically irrefutable."[23] However, the *a priori* demonstration cannot stand in the face of an *a posteriori* demonstration to the contrary. Colwell himself, some twelve years prior to this statement, recognized that the "*a priori* demonstration" to which he here refers has been refuted.

> The universal and ruthless dominance of the middle ages by one texttype is now recognized as a myth. . . .
> The complexities and perplexities of the medieval text have been brought forcibly to our attention by the work of two great scholars: Hermann von Soden and Kirsopp Lake. . . .
> This invaluable pioneer work of von Soden greatly weakened the dogma of the dominance of a homogenous Syrian text. But the fallacy received its death blow at the hands of Professor Lake. In an excursus published with his study of the Caesarean text of Mark, he annihilated the theory that the middle ages were ruled by a single recension which attained a high degree of uniformity.[24]

Actually, Hort produced no "demonstration" at all—just assumptions. Since the genealogical method has not been applied to the MSS of the New Testament it may not be used as an integral part of a theory of NT textual criticism. If it was Hort's genealogical method that "slew the Textus Receptus" then the TR must still be alive and well—the weapon was never used. But Hort claimed to have used it, and the weapon was so fearsome, and he spoke of the "results" with such confidence, that he won the day.

Since Westcott and Hort, the genealogical method has been the canonical method of restoring the original text of the books of the New Testament. It dominates the handbooks. Sir Frederic Kenyon, C.R. Gregory, Alexander Souter, and A.T. Robertson are a few of the many who declare its excellence.[25]

The situation is essentially the same today, and the warning Colwell gave ten years ago is still valid.

Many years ago I joined others in pointing out the limitations in Hort's use of genealogy, and the inapplicability of genealogical method—strictly defined—to the textual criticism of the NT. Since then many others have assented to this criticism, and the building of family trees is only rarely attempted. Therefore we might assume that the influence of Hort's emphasis upon genealogical method is no longer a threat. But this assumption is false.

Hort's brilliant work still captivates our minds. So when confronted by a reading whose support is minimal and widely divorced in time and place, we think first and only of genealogical relationships. Hort has put genealogical blinders on our eyes. . . .[26]

Present-day scholars, exegetes, and translators continue to act as though the genealogical method not only can be, but has been, applied to the NT MSS, and to base their work on the supposed results. But what about those "results"?

Text-types and Recensions

Although Hort claimed absolute certainty for the results of genealogical evidence as described by him, it is clear that the "results" were a fabrication. How could there be results if the method was never applied to the MSS? A contemporary of W-H protested that such claims would only be allowable if the textual critic had first indexed every principal Church Father and reduced MSS to families by a laborious process of induction.[27]

Still, Hort's "results" became accepted as fact by many—George Salmon spoke of "the servility with which his [Hort] history of the text has been accepted, and even his nomenclature adopted, as if now the last word had been said on the subject of New Testament criticism. . . ."[28]

Subsequent scholarship

Subsequent scholars have been obliged to reconsider the matter by the discovery of the Papyri and closer looks at MSS previously extant. Parvis complains:

> We have reconstructed text-types and families and sub-families and in so doing have created things that never before existed on earth or in heaven. We have assumed that manuscripts reproduced themselves according to the Mendelian law. But when we have found that a particular manuscript would not fit into any of our nicely constructed schemes, we have thrown up our hands and said that it contained a mixed text.[29]

Allen Wikgren shows that sweeping generalizations about text-types in general and the "Byzantine" text and lectionaries in particular, should not be made.[30] Colwell affirms:

> The major mistake is made in thinking of the "old text-types" as frozen blocks, even after admitting that no one manuscript is a perfect witness to any text-type. If no one MS is a perfect witness to any type, then all witnesses are mixed in ancestry (or individually corrupted, and thus parents of mixture).[31]

After careful study of P[46], Zuntz makes certain observations and concludes:

> One would like to think that observations like these must put an end to time-honoured doctrines such as that the text of B is the 'Neutral' text or that the 'Western' text is 'the' text of the second century. If the factors of each of these equations are meant to be anything but synonyms, they are wrong; if they are synonyms, they mean nothing.[32]

Klijn doubts "whether any grouping of manuscripts gives satisfactory results,"[33] and goes on to say:

> It is still customary to divide manuscripts into the four well-known families: the Alexandrian, the Caesarean, the Western and the Byzantine.
> This classical division can no longer be maintained. . . .
> If any progress is to be expected in textual criticism we have to get rid of the division into local texts. New manuscripts must not be allotted to a geographically limited area but to their place in the history of the text.[34]

After a long discussion of the "Caesarean" text, Metzger says by way of summary that "it must be acknowledged that at present the Caesarean text is disintegrating."[35] Two pages later, referring to the impact of P[45], he asks, "Was there a fundamental flaw in the previous investigation which tolerated so erroneous a grouping?" Evidently there was. Could it be the mentality that insists upon thinking in terms of text-types and recensions as recognized and recognizable entities?[36] Those few men who have done extensive collations of manuscripts, or paid attention to those done by others, as a rule have not accepted such erroneous groupings.[37]

H. C. Hoskier, whose collations of NT MSS are unsurpassed in quality and perhaps in quantity, commented as follows after collating Codex 604 (today's 700) and comparing it with other MSS:

> I defy anyone, after having carefully perused the foregoing

lists, and after having noted the almost incomprehensible combinations and permutations of both the uncial and cursive manuscripts, to go back to the teaching of Dr. Hort with any degree of confidence. How useless and superfluous to talk of Evan. 604 having a large "Western element," or of its siding in many places with the "neutral text." The whole question of families and recensions is thus brought prominently before the eye, and with space one could largely comment upon the deeply interesting combinations which thus present themselves to the critic. But *do* let us realize that we are in the infancy of this part of the science, and not imagine that we have successfully laid certain immutable foundation stones, and can safely continue to build thereon. It is not so, and much, if not all, of these foundations must be demolished.[38]

The "text-types" themselves

To take the "text-types" one by one, Kenyon says of the "Western" text:

What we have called the δ-text, indeed, is not so much a text as a congeries of various readings, not descending from any one archetype, but possessing an infinitely complicated and intricate parentage. No one manuscript can be taken as even approximately representing the δ-text, if by "text" we mean a form of the Gospel which once existed in a single manuscript.[39]

Colwell observes that the Nestle text (25th edition) denies the existence of the "Western" text as an identifiable group, saying it is "a denial with which I agree."[40] Speaking of von Soden's classification of the "Western" text, Metzger says, "so diverse are the textual phenomena that von Soden was compelled to posit seventeen sub-groups of witnesses which are more or less closely related to this text."[41] And Klijn, speaking of "a 'pure' or 'original' Western Text" affirms that "such a text did not exist."[42]

As for today's "Alexandrian" text, which seems essentially to include Hort's "Neutral" and "Alexandrian," Colwell offers the results of an interesting experiment.

After a careful study of all alleged Beta Text-type witnesses in the first chapter of Mark, six Greek manuscripts emerged as primary witnesses: ℵ B L 33 892 2427. Therefore, the weaker Beta manuscripts C Δ 157 517 579 1241 and 1342 were set aside. Then on the basis of the six primary witnesses an 'average' or mean text was reconstructed including all the readings supported by the majority of the primary witnesses. Even on this restricted basis the amount of variation recorded in the apparatus was dismaying. In this first chapter, each of the six witnesses differed from the 'average' Beta Text-type as follows: L, nineteen times (Westcott and Hort, twenty-one times); Aleph, twenty-six times; 2427, thirty-two times; 33, thirty-three times; B, thirty-four times; and 892, forty-one times. These results show convincingly that any attempt to reconstruct an archetype of the Beta Text-type on a quantitative basis is doomed to failure. The text thus reconstructed is not reconstructed but constructed; it is an artificial entity that never existed.[43]

Hoskier, after filling 450 pages with a detailed and careful discussion of the errors in Codex B and another 400 on the idiosyncrasies of Codex ℵ, affirms that *in the Gospels alone* these two MSS differ well over 3,000 times, which number does not include minor errors such as spelling, nor variants between certain synonyms which might be due to "provincial exchange."[44]

Of the "Byzantine" text, Zuntz says that "the great bulk of Byzantine manuscripts defies all attempts to group them."[45] Clark says much the same.

The main conclusion regarding the Byzantine text is that it was extremely fluid. Any single manuscript may be expected to show a score of shifting affinities. Yet within the variety and confusion, a few textual types have been distinguished. . . . These types are not closely grouped like the families, but are like the broad Milky Way including many members within a general affinity.[46]

Colwell's emphatic statement to the same effect has been given above. The work of Lake referred to by Colwell was a collation of Mark, chapter eleven, in all the MSS of Mt. Sinai, Patmos, and the Patriarchal Library and collection of St. Saba at Jerusalem. Lake, with R.P. Blake and Silva New, found that the "Byzantine" text was not homogeneous, that there was an absence of close relationship between MSS, but that there was less variation "within the family" than would be found in a similar treatment of "Neutral" or "Caesarean" texts. In their own words:

> This collation covers three of the great ancient collections of MSS; and these are not modern conglomerations, brought together from all directions. Many of the MSS, now at Sinai, Patmos, and Jerusalem must be copies written in the scriptoria of these monasteries. We expected to find that a collation covering all the MSS in each library would show many cases of direct copying. But there are practically no such cases. . . . Moreover, the amount of direct genealogy which has been detected in extant codices is almost negligible. Nor are many known MSS sister codices. The Ferrar group and family 1 are the only reported cases of the repeated copying of a single archetype, and even for the Ferrar group there were probably two archetypes rather than one. . . .
>
> There are cognate groups—families of distant cousins— but the manuscripts which we have are almost all orphan children without brothers or sisters.
>
> Taking this fact into consideration along with the negative result of our collation of MSS at Sinai, Patmos, and Jerusalem, it is hard to resist the conclusion that the scribes usually destroyed their exemplars when they had copied the sacred books.[47]

J.W. Burgon,[48] because he had himself collated numerous minuscule MSS, had remarked the same thing years before Lake.

Now those many MSS were executed demonstrably at different times in different countries. They bear signs in their many hundreds of representing the entire area of the Church, except where versions were used instead of copies in the original Greek. . . . And yet, of multitudes of them that survive, hardly any have been copied from any of the rest. On the contrary, they are discovered to differ among themselves in countless unimportant particulars; and every here and there single copies exhibit idiosyncrasies which are altogether startling and extraordinary. There has therefore demonstrably been no collusion—no assimilation to an arbitrary standard—no wholesale fraud. It is certain that every one of them represents a MS, or a pedigree of MSS, older than itself; and it is but fair to suppose that it exercises such representation with tolerable accuracy.[49]

Kurt Aland[50] sums it up:

P[66] confirmed the observations already made in connection with the Chester Beatty papyri. With P[75] new ground has been opened to us. Earlier, we all shared the opinion, in agreement with our professors and in accord with NT scholarship, before and since Westcott and Hort, that, in various places, during the fourth century, recensions of the NT text had been made, from which the main text-types then developed. . . . We spoke of recensions and text-types, and if this was not enough, we referred to pre-Caesarean and other text-types, to mixed texts, and so on.

I, too, have spoken of mixed texts, in connection with the form of the NT text in the second and third centuries, but I have always done so with a guilty conscience. For, according to the rules of linguistic philology it is impossible to speak of mixed texts before recensions have been made (they only can follow them), whereas, the NT manuscripts of the second and third centuries which have a "mixed text" clearly existed before recensions were made. . . . The simple fact that all these papyri, with their various distinctive characteristics, did exist side by side, in the same ecclesiastical province, that is, in Egypt, where they were found, is the best argument against the existence of any text-types, including the Alexandrian and the Antiochian. We still live in the world of Westcott and Hort with our conception of different recensions and text-types, although this conception has lost its *raison d'être*, or, it needs at least to be newly and convincingly demonstrated. For, the increase of the documentary evidence and the entirely new areas of research which were opened to us on the discovery of the papyri, mean the end of Westcott and Hort's conception.[51]

(I have quoted men like Zuntz, Clark, and Colwell on the "Byzantine" text to show that modern scholars are prepared to reject the notion of a "Byzantine" recension, but the main lesson to be drawn from the variation among "Byzantine" MSS is the one noted by Lake and Burgon—they are orphans, independent witnesses, at least in their generation. The variation between two "Byzantine" MSS will be ·found to differ both in number and severity from that between two "Western" MSS or two "Alexandrian" MSS—the number and nature of the disagreements between two "Byzantine" MSS throughout the Gospels will seem trivial compared to the number (over 3,000) and nature (many serious) of the disagreements between Aleph and B, the chief "Alexandrian" MSS, in the same space.)

A recent return

Both Colwell[52] and Epp[53] take issue with Aland, claiming that the papyri fit right in with Hort's reconstruction of textual history. But the existence of an affinity between B and P[75] does not demonstrate the existence of a text-type or recension. We have just seen Colwell's demonstration and declaration that an "Alexandrian" archetype never existed. Epp himself, after going on to plot the early MSS on three trajectories ("Neutral," "Western," and "midway"), says:

Naturally, this rough sketch should not be understood to mean that the manuscripts mentioned under each of the three categories above necessarily had any *direct* connections one with another; rather, they stand as randomly surviving members of these three broad streams of textual tradition.[54]

The point is, although different manuscripts exhibit varying affinities, share certain peculiarities, they each differ substantially from all the others (especially the earlier ones) and therefore should not be lumped together. There is no such thing as the testimony of a "Western" or "Alexandrian" text-type (as an entity)—there is only the testimony of individual MSS, Fathers, Versions (or MSS of versions).

In disagreeing with Aland (see notes 51 and 53), Epp declared that our extant materials reveal "only two clear textual streams or trajectories" in the first four centuries of textual transmission, namely the "Neutral" and "Western" text-types.[55] He also suggested that P[75] may be considered as an early ancestor for Hort's "Neutral" text, P[66] for Hort's "Alexandrian" text, and P[45] for Hort's "Western" text.

But he himself had just finished furnishing counter evidence. Thus, with reference to 103 variation units in Mark 6–9 (where P[45] is extant), Epp records that P[45] shows a 38 percent agreement with Codex D, 40 percent with the *Textus Receptus*, 42 percent with B, 59 percent with f[13], and 68 percent with W.[56] How can Epp say that P[45] is a "Western" ancestor when it is closer to chief representatives of every other "text-type" than it is to D? In Mark 5-16, Epp records that Codex W shows a 34 percent agreement with B, 36 percent with D, 38 percent with the *Textus Receptus*, and 40 percent with ℵ.[57] To which "textual stream" should W be assigned?

Both P[66] and P[75] have been generally affirmed to belong to the "Alexandrian text-type."[58] Klijn offers the results of a comparison of Aleph, B, P[45], P[66] and P[75] in the passages where they are all extant (John 10:7-25, 10:32-11:10, 11:19-33 and 11:43-56). He considered only those places where Aleph and B disagree *and* where at least one of the papyri joins either Aleph or B. He found eight such places *plus* 43 where all three of the papyri line up with Aleph or B. He stated the result for the 43 places as follows (to which I have added figures for the *Textus Receptus*, BFBS 1946):

P[45] agrees with Aleph 19 times, with B 24 times, with TR 32 times

P[66] agrees with Aleph 14 times, with B 29 times, with TR 33 times

P[75] agrees with Aleph 9 times, with B 33 times, with TR 29 times

P[45,66,75] agree with Aleph 4 times, with B 18 times, with TR 20 times

P[45,66] agree with Aleph 7 times, with B 3 times, with TR 8 times

P[45,75] agree with Aleph 1 time, with B 2 times, with TR 2 times

P[66,75] agree with Aleph 0 times, with B 8 times, with TR 5 times.[59]

As for the eight other places,

P[45] agrees with Aleph 2 times, with B 1 time, with TR 1 time

P[66] agrees with Aleph 2 times, with B 3 times, with TR 5 times

P[75] agrees with Aleph 2 times, with B 3 times, with TR 4 times.[60] (Each of the three papyri has other readings as well.)

Is the summary assignment of P[66] and P[75] to the "Alexandrian text-type" altogether reasonable?

G.D. Fee goes to considerable lengths to interpret the evidence in such a way as to support his conclusion that "P[66] is basically a member of the Neutral tradition,"[61] but the evidence itself as he records it, for John 1-14, is as follows: P[66] agrees with the TR 315 times out of 663 (47.5%), with P[75] 280 out of 547 (51.2%), with B 334 out of 663 (50.4%), with Aleph 295 out of 662 (44.6%), with A 245 out of 537 (45.6%), with C 150 out of 309 (48.5%), with D 235 out of 604 (38.9%), with W 298 out of 662 (45.0%).[62]

Does this evidence really suggest "two clear textual streams"?

In these third-century manuscripts, whose evidence takes us back into the mid-second century at least, we find no pristine purity, no unsullied ancestors of Vaticanus, but marred and fallen representatives of the original text. Features of all the main texts isolated by Hort or von Soden are here found— very differently 'mingled' in P[66] and P[45].[63]

The classifying of MSS

A serious part of the problem is the manner in which MSS

have been assigned to one "text-type" or another. For example, the editors of P[1] (Oxyrh. 2), Grenfell and Hunt, stated that "the papyrus clearly belongs to the same class as the Sinaitic and Vatican codices, and has no Western or Syrian proclivities." The papyrus contains only Matt. 1:1-9a, 12b-20 (not all of it legible) but C.H. Turner declared that it agrees closely with the text of B and "may be fairly held to carry back the whole B text of the Gospels into the third century."[64] To this day P[1] is assigned to the "Alexandrian text-type."[65] It evidently agrees with B seven times, against the TR, but four of those variants have some "Western" support; however it *dis*agrees with B ten times, albeit supporting the TR in only two of those.[66] Is it really reasonable to lump P[1] and B together?

For a clear demonstration of the folly of characterizing a manuscript on the basis of just one chapter (or even less!) the reader is referred to the study of P[66] by Fee. He plots the percentage of agreement between P[66] and the T.R., P[75], B, Aleph, A, C, D, and W respectively, chapter by chapter, throughout the first 14 chapters of John.[67] For each of the documents the graph bounces up and down from chapter to chapter in an erratic fashion. All of them show a range of variation in excess of 30%—e.g. Codex B goes from 71.1% agreement with P[66] in chapter 5 to 32.3% agreement in chapter 7.

It has already been noted that B and Aleph disagree well over 3,000 times just in the Gospels. (Their agreements are fewer.)[68] Should they be lumped together? It is not enough to notice only the shared peculiarities between two MSS; the extent of disagreement is equally germane to any effort at classification.[69]

Rather than lining up in "clear streams" or "text-types" (as objectively defined entities) the earliest manuscripts are dotted helter-skelter over a wide spectrum of variation. Although varying degrees of affinity exist between and among them, they should be treated as individuals in the practice of textual criticism. Until such time as the relationships among the later manuscripts are empirically plotted, they also should be treated as individuals. To dump them into a "Byzantine" basket is untenable.

Since genealogy has not been (and cannot be?) applied to the MSS, the witnesses must be counted, after all—including many of the later minuscules, which evidently had independent lines of transmission (cf. quotes 47 and 49). It will immediately be protested that "witnesses are to be weighed, not counted." Because of the importance of this question I will discuss it in some detail, in its turn.[70] But first, we must continue our evaluation of the W-H theory and for that purpose I will still speak of "text-types" in Hort's terms.

Conflation

Hort's whole case against the *Textus Receptus*, under this heading, was based upon just *eight* examples, taken from two Gospels (Mark and Luke). To characterize a whole text for the whole New Testament on the basis of eight examples is foolish. Colwell states the problem well.

No text or document is homogeneous enough to justify judgment on the basis of *part* of its readings for the rest of its readings. This was Hort's Achilles' heel. He is saying here that since these eight conflate readings occur in the Syrian text that text as a whole is a mixed text; if a manuscript or text lacks these readings, it is in its other readings a witness to a text antecedent to mixture. . . .

Westcott and Hort state this fallacy very clearly in their argument for the importance of the evidence of a document as over against readings:

"Where then one of the documents is found habitually to contain these morally certain or at least strongly preferred readings, and the other habitually to contain their rejected rivals, we can have no doubt, first, that the text of the first has been transmitted in comparative purity, and that the text of the second has suffered comparatively large corruption; and, next, that the *superiority of the first must be as great in the variations in which Internal Evidence of Readings has furnished no decisive criterion as in those which have enabled us to form a comparative appreciation of the two texts.*"

This would be true if we knew that there was no mixture involved and that manuscripts and texts were rigorously homogeneous. Everything we have learned since Hort confirms the opposite position. [71]

It has been generally supposed and stated that there are many other examples. Thus Harrison says, "Another objection was the paucity of examples of conflation. Hort cited only eight, but he could have given others." [72] Kenyon and Lake made the same claim, [73] but where are the "other" examples? Why does not Harrison, or Kenyon, or Lake produce them? Because there are very few that have the required phenomena. Kenyon does refer in passing to *An Atlas of Textual Criticism* by E. A. Hutton (London: Cambridge University Press, 1911) which he says contains added examples of conflation.

Upon inspection, the central feature of the 125-page work proves to be a purportedly complete list of triple variant readings in the New Testament where the "Alexandrian," "Western," and "Byzantine" texts are pitted against each other. Hutton adduces 821 instances exhibiting the required phenomena. Out of all that, a few cases of possible "Syrian conflation," aside from Hort's eight, may be culled—such as in Matt. 27:41, John 18:40, Acts 20:28 or Rom. 6:12. Twenty years ago a Hortian might have insisted that John 10:31 also has a "Syrian conflation," but now that P[66] moves the "Syrian" reading back to 200 A.D. a different interpretation is demanded.

Hutton's list may well be open to considerable question, but if we may take it at face value for the moment it appears that the ratio of "Alexandrian-Western-Byzantine" triple variants to possible "Syrian conflations" is about 100:1. In other words, for every instance where the "Syrian" text is possibly built on the "Neutral" and "Western" texts there are a hundred where it is *not*.

That raises another problem. If the "Syrian" text is eclectic, where did it get the material that is its private property? As Burgon observed at the time,

It is impossible to 'conflate' in places where B ℵ and their associates furnish no materials for the supposed conflation.

Bricks cannot be made without clay. The materials actually existing are those of the Traditional Text itself.[74]

But there is another consideration which is fatal to Hort's purpose. He claimed that inversions do not exist; but they do. He himself cited one of each kind; D conflates in John 5:37 and B conflates in Col. 1:12 and 2 Thess. 3:4.[75] Further, there are a number of other conflations, not only on the part of D, B, and Aleph, but also the "Western" and "Alexandrian" text-types. Please see Appendix D for examples and evidence. Not listed there is Revelation 17:4 where Aleph has a conflation of the two main cursive bodies for that book. Marcion (2nd century) conflates the "Byzantine" and "Neutral-Western" readings in 1 Corinthians 14:19!

Bodmer II shows some "Syrian" readings to be *anterior* to corresponding "Neutral" readings around 200 A.D.

The Bodmer John (P[66]) is also a witness to the early existence of many of the readings found in the Alpha text-type (Hort's "Syrian"). Strangely enough to our previous ideas, the contemporary corrections in that papyrus frequently change an Alpha-type reading to a Beta-type reading (Hort's "Neutral"). This indicates that at this early period readings of both kinds were known, and the Beta-type were supplanting the Alpha-type—at least as far as this witness is concerned.[76]

Hoskier, after his thorough (450 pages) study of Codex B, offered this verdict: "the maligned Textus Receptus served in large measure as the base which B tampered with and changed."[77]

It is clear that Hort's characterization of the "Syrian" text as eclectic and secondary, as posterior to and building upon the "Western" and "Neutral" texts, does not square with the evidence. But while we are on the subject, what of Hort's eight examples; do they lend themselves to his interpretation? We must ask whether they really qualify as possible conflations and then consider the reverse explanation, namely that the shorter forms are independent simplifications of the original long form.

Burgon examined the eight at length and observed that most of them simply do not exhibit the required phenomena.[78] The reader may see for himself by consulting any reasonably complete *apparatus criticus*. Whatever explanation may be given of the origin of the "Byzantine" readings in Mark 8:26, Luke 11:54, and Luke 12:18, they are not "conflations" of the "Neutral" and "Western" readings. The same thing may be said, though not so emphatically, about Mark 6:33 and Luke 9:10.

In almost every case the witnesses within the "Neutral" and "Western" camps are divided among themselves, so that a somewhat arbitrary choice has to be made in order to give *the* "Neutral" or "Western" reading. Hort approached his discussion of the eight examples of conflation he adduced "premising that we do not attempt to notice every petty variant in the passages cited, for fear of confusing the substantial evidence."[79]

But in a question of this sort the confusion must be accounted for. If the "Neutral" witnesses disagree among themselves, what credence can we give to the "Neutral" testimony as a whole?

Given an instance, such as Luke 24:53, where the required phenomena for a conflation are present, it must be demonstrated that the two shorter readings did not arise through independent omissions of different parts of the longer reading before it can be asserted that conflation took place. Apart from such demonstration it is not fair to assume a conflation and then build a theory upon it. Hort's total demonstration relative to Luke 24:53 is, "This simple instance needs no explanation."[80]

Burgon (who personally collated D) observed that in the last chapter of Luke the Received Text has 837 words—of these D omits 121, or one word in seven.[81] To someone using Nestle's Text (24th) D omits 66 out of 782, or one in twelve (Nestle has omitted thirty-eight words from the Greek text of Luke 24 on the sole Greek authority of D, and another five on D and ℵ alone).

In the face of such an inveterate propensity for omission, it is not unreasonable to suspect that in verse 53 D has omitted "and blessing" from the original "praising and blessing" rather than that the reading of all but six of the extant Greek MSS is a conflation. Furthermore, the reading of D may easily have arisen from the "Byzantine" by homoioteleuton (ΟΥΝΤΕΣ-ΟΥΝΤΕΣ). Kilpatrick is among the most recent of a number of scholars who have argued that at least some of Hort's "Syrian conflations" are the original reading.[82]

K. Lake spoke of the problem of deciding which interpretation to take.

> The keystone of their [W-H] theory is in the passages where we get this triple variation, and the point of the argument lies in the assumption that the longer reading is made by uniting the two shorter ones—not the two shorter by different dealings with the longer. This point can be tested only by an appeal to Patristic evidence and general probability.
>
> The latter argument is precarious because subjective, so that the ultimate and decisive criterion is Patristic evidence.[83]

It appears, according to Lake, that patristic evidence is to decide the issue. But neither Lake nor anyone else has produced any Patristic citations of these passages in the first three centuries. The few citations available after that time all support the Byzantine readings.[84]

Actually, the whole matter of "conflation" is a pseudo-issue, a tempest in a teapot. There simply are not enough putative examples to support generalizations. Such evidence as there is, however, is certainly not unfavorable to the "Syrian" text. As Zuntz says, the idea that the late text was derived from the two earlier "recensions" combined is erroneous.[85]

"Syrian" Readings Before Chrysostom

Hort's statements concerning the nature of the ante-Nicene patristic testimony are still widely believed. Thus, Chrysostom is widely affirmed to have used the "Byzantine" text.[86] But, Lake has stated:

> Writers on the text of the New Testament usually copy from

one another the statement that Chrysostom used the Byzantine, or Antiochian, text. But directly any investigation is made it appears evident, even from the printed text of his works, that there are many important variations in the text he quotes, which was evidently not identical with that found in the MSS of the Byzantine text.[87]

Metzger calls attention to the work of Geerlings and New.

It has often been stated by textual scholars that Chrysostom was one of the first Fathers to use the Antiochian text. This opinion was examined by Jacob Geerlings and Silva New in a study based on evidence which, in default of a critical edition, was taken from Migne's edition of Chrysostom's *opera*. Their conclusions are that "Chrysostom's text of Mark is not that of any group of manuscripts so far discovered and classified. . . . His text of Mark, or rather the text which can faintly be perceived through his quotations, is a 'mixed text,' combining some of the elements of each of the types which had flourished before the end of the fourth century."[88]

They say further: "No known manuscript of Mark has the text found in Chrysostom's homilies, or anything approaching it. And probably no text which existed in the fourth century came much nearer to it."[89] They did a collation of Chrysostom's text and observe concerning it:

The number of variants from the Textus Receptus is not appreciably smaller than the number of variants from Westcott and Hort's text. This proves that it is no more a typical representative of the late text (von Soden's K) than it is of the Neutral text.[90]

What about Origen; does he really represent the "Neutral" text?

It is impossible to reproduce or restore the text of Origen. Origen had no settled text. A reference to the innumerable places where he is upon *both* sides of the question, as set forth in detail herein, will show this clearly. Add the places where he is in direct opposition to ℵ and B, and we must reconsider the whole position.[91]

Zuntz agrees.

The insuperable difficulties opposing the establishment of 'the' New Testament text of Origen and Eusebius are well known to all who have attempted it. . . . Leaving aside the common difficulties imposed by the uncertainties of the transmission, the incompleteness of the material, and the frequent freedom of quotation, there is the incontestable fact that these two Fathers are frequently at variance; that each of them quotes the same passage differently in different writings; and that sometimes they do so even within the compass of one and the same work. . . . Wherever one and the same passage is extant in more than one quotation by Origen or Eusebius, variation between them is the rule rather than the exception.[92]

Metzger affirms: "Origen knows of the existence of variant readings which represent each of the main families of manuscripts that modern scholars have isolated."[93] (That includes the "Byzantine.") Edward Miller, in his exhaustive study of the Fathers, found that Origen sided with the Traditional Text 460 times while siding with the "Neologian" text 491 times.[94] (The "Neologian"[95] text, as Miller used the term, includes both "Neutral" and "Western" readings, while "Traditional Text" is his term for Hort's "Syrian" text.) How then could Hort say of Origen, "On the other hand his quotations to the best of our belief exhibit no clear and tangible traces of the Syrian text"?[96]

What about Irenaeus; does he really represent the "Western" text? Miller found that Irenaeus sided with the Traditional Text 63 times and with the "Neologian" text 41 times.[97] He said further:

Hilary of Poictiers is far from being against the Traditional Text, as has been frequently said: though in his commentaries he did not use so Traditional a text as in his De Trinitate and his other works. The texts of Hippolytus, Methodius, Irenaeus, and even of Justin, are not of that exclusively Western character which Dr. Hort ascribes to them. Traditional readings occur almost equally with others in Justin's works, and predominate in the works of the other three.[98]

Hoskier adds a word concerning Hippolytus.

Let us take another most interesting witness, viz. *Hippolytus*, who, like *Lucifer*, frequently quotes at such length from both Old and New Testaments that it is absolutely beyond question that he was *copying* from his exemplar of the Scriptures.
Hippolytus cites 1 Thess. iv. 13-17, 2 Thess. ii. 1-12, in full.
In the face of these quotations it is seen how loosely Turner argues when he says "Hort was the last and perhaps the ablest of a long line of editors of the Greek Testament, commencing in the eighteenth century, who very tentatively at first, but quite ruthlessly in the end, *threw over the* LATER *in favour of the* EARLIER *Greek* MSS, and that issue will never have to be tried again."
But permit me to ask what Mr. Turner means by this lighthearted sentence. What does he mean by earlier and later Manuscripts? He cannot mean that Hippolytus' manuscript was later than that of B? Yet, allow me to state that in these long passages, comprising twelve consecutive verses from one epistle and four from the other, Hippolytus' early third-century MS is found generally on the side of what Turner would call the "later" MSS.[99]

According to Miller's study, the advantage of the Traditional Text over the "Neologian" before Origen was actually 2:1, setting aside Justin Martyr, Heracleon, Clement of Alexandria and Tertullian. If these four are included, the advantage of the Traditional Text drops to 1.33:1 since the confusion which is most obvious in Origen is already observable in these men. From Origen to Macarius Magnus the advantage of the Traditional Text drops to 1.24:1 while from Macarius to 400 A.D. it is back up to 2:1.[100]

Miller vs. Kenyon

Because of the importance of Miller's study, already cited, I will now consider it more in detail along with Kenyon's answer. Miller saw clearly the crucial nature of Hort's proposition.

It is evident that the turning point of the controversy between ourselves and the Neologian school must lie in the centuries before St. Chrysostom. If, as Dr. Hort maintains, the Traditional Text not only gained supremacy at that era but did not exist in the early ages, then our contention is vain. . . . On the other hand if it is proved to reach back in unbroken line to the time of the Evangelists, or to a period as near to them as surviving testimony can prove, then Dr. Hort's theory of a 'Syrian' text formed by recension or otherwise just as evidently falls to the ground.[101]

Miller, posthumous editor to Burgon, probed the question of ante-Nicene testimony exhaustively, making full use of Burgon's massive index of patristic citations (86,489 of them) from the New Testament. He deserves to be heard, in detail.

As to the alleged absence of readings of the Traditional Text from the writings of the Ante-Nicene Fathers, Dr. Hort draws largely upon his imagination and his wishes. The persecution of Diocletian is here also the parent of much want of information. But is there really such a dearth of these readings in the works of the Early Fathers as is supposed?[102]

I made a toilsome examination for myself of the quotations occurring in the writings of the Fathers before St. Chrysostom, or as I defined them in order to draw a self-acting line, of those who died before 400 A.D., with the result that the Traditional Text is found to stand in the general proportion of 3:2 against other variations, and in a much higher proportion upon thirty test passages. Afterwards, not being satisfied with resting the basis of my argument upon one scrutiny, I went again through the writings of the seventy-six Fathers concerned (with limitations explained in this book), besides others who yielded no evidence, and I found that although several more instances were consequently entered in my note-book, the general results remained almost the same. I do not flatter myself that even now I have recorded all the instances that could be adduced:—any one who is really acquainted with this work will know that such a feat is absolutely impossible, because such perfection cannot be obtained except after many repeated efforts. But I claim, not only that my attempts have been honest and fair even to self-abnegation, but that the general results which are much more than is required by my argument, as is explained in the body of this work, abundantly establish the antiquity of the Traditional Text, by proving the superior acceptance of it during the period at stake to that of any other.[103]

Kenyon acknowledged Miller's work and stated the results correctly.

Here is a plain issue. If it can be shown that the readings which Hort calls "Syrian" existed before the end of the fourth century, the keystone would be knocked out of the fabric of his theory; and since he produced no statistics in proof of his assertion [!], his opponents were perfectly at liberty to challenge it. It must be admitted that Mr. Miller did not shirk the test. A considerable part of his work as editor of Dean Burgon's papers took the form of a classification of patristic quotations, based upon the great indices which the Dean left behind him, according as they testify for or against the Traditional Text of the Gospels.

The results of his examination are stated by him as follows. Taking the Greek and Latin (not the Syriac) Fathers who died before A.D. 400, their quotations are found to support the Traditional Text in 2,630 instances, the "neologian" in 1753. Nor is this majority due solely to the writers who belong to the end of this period. On the contrary, if only the earliest writers be taken, from Clement of Rome to Irenaeus and Hippolytus, the majority in favour of the Traditional Text is proportionately even greater, 151 to 84. Only in the Western and Alexandrian writers do we find approximate equality of votes on either side. Further, if a select list of thirty important passages be taken for detailed examination, the preponderance of early patristic evidence in favour of the Traditional Text is seen to be no less than 530 to 170, a quite overwhelming majority.

Now it is clear that if these figures were trustworthy, there would be an end to Hort's theory, for its premises would be shown to be thoroughly unsound.[104]

Before proceeding to Kenyon's rebuttal it will be well to pause and review the implications of this exchange. Hort, and the many like Kenyon who have repeated his words after him, have asserted that not a single "strictly Byzantine" reading is to be found in the extant works of any Church Father who dates before Chrysostom (d. 407). To disprove Hort's assertion, it is only necessary to find *some* "strictly Byzantine" readings before the specified time, since the question immediately in focus is the existence of the "Byzantine" readings, not necessarily their dominance. Miller affirms that the Byzantine text not only is to be found in the writings of the early Fathers, but that in fact it *predominates*.

As far as the Fathers who died before 400 A.D. are concerned, the question may now be put and answered. Do they witness to the Traditional Text as existing from the first, or do they not? The results of the evidence, both as regards the quantity and the quality of the testimony, enable us to reply, not only that the Traditional Text was in existence, but that it was predominant, during the period under review. Let any one who disputes this conclusion make out for the Western Text, or the Alexandrian, or for the Text of B and ℵ, a case from the evidence of the Fathers which can equal or surpass that which has been now placed before the reader.[105]

No one has ever taken up Miller's challenge.

As quoted above, Kenyon recognized that if Miller's figures are right then Hort's theory is at an end. But Kenyon continued:

An examination of them however, shows that they cannot be accepted as representing in any way the true state of the case. In the first place, it is fairly certain that critical editions of the several Fathers, if such existed, would show that in many cases the quotations have been assimilated in later MSS to the Traditional Text, whereas in the earlier they agree rather with the "Neutral" or "Western" witnesses. For this defect, however, Mr. Miller cannot be held responsible. The critical editions of the Greek and Latin Fathers, now in course of production by the Academies of Berlin and Vienna, had covered very little of the ground at the time when his materials were compiled, and meanwhile he might legitimately use the materials accessible to him; and the errors arising from this source would hardly affect the general result to any very serious extent.[106]

After raising the quibble about critical editions he admitted that "the errors arising from this source would hardly affect the general result." However, Kenyon's suggestion that "in many cases the quotations have been assimilated in later MSS to the Traditional Text" gives the essence of a contention widely used today to parry the thrusts of the mounting evidence in favor of an early "Byzantine" text. To this we must presently return. Kenyon proceeded:

The real fallacy in his statistics is different, and is revealed in the detailed examination of the thirty select passages. From these it is clear that he wholly misunderstood Hort's contention. The thirty "traditional" readings, which he shows to be so overwhelmingly vindicated by the Fathers, are not what Hort would call pure "Syrian" readings at all. In nearly every case they have Western or Neutral attestation in addition to that of the later authorities.[107]

He then referred briefly to specific instances in Matt. 17:21, Matt. 18:11, Matt. 19:16, Matt. 23:38, Mark 16:9-20, Luke 24:40, and John 21:25 and continued:

In short, Mr. Miller evidently reckoned on his side every reading which occurs in the Traditional Text, regardless of whether, on Hort's principles, they are old readings which kept their place in the Syrian revision, or secondary readings which were then introduced for the first time. According to Hort, the Traditional Text is the result of a revision in which old elements were incorporated; and Mr. Miller merely points to some of these old elements, and argues therefrom that the whole is old. It is clear that by such argumentation Hort's theory is untouched.[108]

It is hard to believe that Kenyon was precisely fair here. He had obviously read Miller's work with care. Why did he not say anything about "to repentance" in Matt. 9:13 and Mark 2:17,[109] or "vinegar" in Matt. 27:34,[110] or "from the door" in Matt. 28:2,[111] or "the prophets" in Mark 1:2,[112] or "good will" in Luke 2:14,[113] or the Lord's prayer for His murderers in Luke 23:34,[114] or "an honeycomb" in Luke 24:42,[115] or "whom" in John 17:24?[116]

These instances are also among "the thirty." They would appear to be "strictly Syrian" readings, if there really is such a thing. Why did Kenyon ignore them? The cases Kenyon cited fell within the scope of Miller's inquiry because they are Traditional readings, whatever other attestation they may also have, and because the English Revisers of 1881 rejected them. Kenyon asserted that Miller's figures "cannot be accepted as representing in any way the true state of the case," but he has not shown us why. Kenyon said nothing about the alleged "secondary readings" that have early Patristic support.

Miller's figures represent precisely what he claimed that they represent—"the true state of the case" is that the Traditional Text ("Byzantine") receives *more support* from the early Church Fathers than does the critical text (essentially W-H) used by the English Revisers. It should be noted that there are doubtless numerous so-called "Western" and "Alexandrian" readings[117] to be found in the early Fathers which are not included in Miller's figures because the Revisers rejected them. If they were all tabulated the "Byzantine" readings would perhaps lose the absolute majority of early patristic attestation but they would still be present and attested, from the very first, and that is the question just now in focus.

Pure "Syrian" readings

Kenyon's statement contains another problem. He referred

to "pure 'Syrian' readings" and in effect denied to the "Syrian" text any reading that chances to have any "Western" or "Alexandrian" attestation (which attestation has been arbitrarily pigeon-holed according to the presuppositions of the theory). But just which are those late or "pure Syrian" elements?

E. F. Hills evidently conducted a search for them. He observes:

> The second accusation commonly urged against the Byzantine text is that it contains so many late readings. A text with all these late readings, it is said, must be a late text. But it is remarkable how few actually were the Byzantine readings which Westcott and Hort designated as late. In his *Notes on Select Readings* Hort discussed about 240 instances of variation among the manuscripts of the Gospels, and in only about twenty of these instances was he willing to characterize the Byzantine reading as a late reading. Thus it would seem that even on Hort's own admission only about ten percent of the readings of the Byzantine text are late readings, and since Hort's day the number of these allegedly late Byzantine readings has been gradually dwindling.[118]

(And yet Hort wrote off the whole "Syrian" witness as late.)

It seems clear the "Byzantine" text cannot win in a court presided over by a judge of Kenyon's bent. Whenever an early witness surfaces it is declared to be "Alexandrian" or "Western" or "Caesarean" and thereupon those "Syrian" readings which it contains cease to be "pure Syrian" and are no longer allowed as evidence. Such a procedure is evidently useful to defenders of Hort's theory, but is it right?

It is commonplace among the many who are determined to despise the "Byzantine" text to dodge the issue, as Kenyon did above. The postulates of Hort's theory are assumed to be true and the evidence is interpreted on the basis of these presuppositions. Apart from the imaginary nature of the "Alexandrian" and "Western" texts, as strictly definable entities, their priority to the "Byzantine" text is the very point to be proved and may not be assumed.

Kirsopp Lake's statement is representative. Taking Origen, Irenaeus, and Chrysostom as representatives of the "Neutral," "Western," and "Byzantine" texts respectively, he asserted:

> Though Chrysostom and Origen often unite in differing from Irenaeus, and Chrysostom and Irenaeus in differing from Origen, yet Chrysostom does not differ from them both at once. And this is almost demonstrative proof that his text, characteristically representative of the later Fathers, versions and MSS, is an eclectic one.[119]

Even if Lake's description of the phenomena were true, there is another perfectly adequate interpretation of such phenomena. In Hill's words,

> There is surely a much more reasonable way of explaining why each non-Byzantine text (including Papyrus Bodmer II) contains Byzantine readings not found in other non-Byzantine texts. If we regard the Byzantine text as the original text, then it is perfectly natural that each non-Byzantine text should agree with the Byzantine text in places in which the other non-Byzantine texts have departed from it.[120]

Also, given the priority of the "Byzantine" text, the places where all the divergent texts happened to abandon the "Byzantine" at the same time would be few. To arbitrarily assign Fathers and manuscripts and versions to the "Alexandrian" and "Western" families and then to deny to the "Byzantine" text readings which one or more of these arbitrarily assigned witnesses happen also to support seems neither honest nor scholarly.

A biased expedient

Before closing this section, it remains to take up the expedient, alluded to earlier, whereby many seek to evade the ante-Nicene patristic evidence for the "Byzantine" text. Vincent Taylor states the expedient as baldly as anyone.

In judging between two alternative readings [of a given

Father in a given place] the principle to be adopted is that the one which *diverges* from the later ecclesiastical text (the TR) is more likely to be original.[121]

This expedient is extended even to cases where there is no alternative. The allegation is that copyists altered the Fathers' wording to conform to the "Byzantine," which the copyists regarded as "correct."[122] It is obvious that the effect of such a proceeding is to place the "Byzantine" text at a disadvantage. An investigation based on this principle is "rigged" against the TR.[123]

Even if there appear to be certain instances where this has demonstrably happened, such instances do not justify a wide-spread generalization. The generalization is based on the presupposition that the "Byzantine" text is late—but this is the very point to be proved and may not be assumed.

If the "Byzantine" text is early there is no reason to suppose that a "Byzantine" reading in an early Father is due to a later copyist unless a clear demonstration to that effect is possible. Miller shows clearly that he was fully aware of this problem and alert to exclude any suspicious instances from his tabulation.

An objection may perhaps be made, that the texts of the books of the Fathers are sure to have been altered in order to coincide more accurately with the Received Text. This is true of the Ethica, or Moralia, of Basil, and of the Regulae brevius Tractatae, which seem to have been read constantly at meals, or were otherwise in continual use in Religious Houses. The monks of a later age would not be content to hear every day familiar passages of Holy Scripture couched in other terms than those to which they were accustomed and which they regarded as correct. This fact was perfectly evident upon examination, because these treatises were found to give evidence for the Textus Receptus in the proportion of about 6:1, whereas the other books of St. Basil yielded according to a ratio of about 8:3.

For the same reason I have not included Marcion's edition of St. Luke's Gospel, or Tatian's Diatessaron, in the list of books and authors, because such representations of the Gospels having been in public use were sure to have been revised from time to time, in order to accord with the judgment of those who read or heard them. Our readers will observe that these were self-denying ordinances, because by the inclusion of the works mentioned the list on the Traditional side would have been greatly increased. Yet our foundations have been strengthened, and really the position of the Traditional Text rests so firmly upon what is undoubted, that it can afford to dispense with services which may be open to some suspicion. (Yet Marcion and Tatian may fairly be adduced as witnesses upon individual readings.) And the natural inference remains, that the difference between the witness of the Ethica and Regulae brevius Tractatae on the one hand, and that of the other works of Basil on the other, suggests that too much variation, and too much which is evidently characteristic variation, of readings meets us in the works of the several Fathers, for the existence of any doubt that in most cases we have the words, though perhaps not the spelling, as they issued originally from the author's pen. Variant readings of quotations occurring in different editions of the Fathers are found, according to my experience, much less frequently than might have been supposed. Where I saw a difference between MSS noted in the Benedictine or other editions or in copies from the Benedictine or other prints, of course I regarded the passage as doubtful and did not enter it. Acquaintance with this kind of testimony cannot but render its general trustworthiness the more evident.[124]

After this careful screening Miller still came up with 2,630 citations, from 76 Fathers or sources, ranging over a span of 300 years (100-400 A.D.), supporting readings of the "Byzantine" text as opposed to those of the critical text of the English Revisers (which received 1,753 citations). Will anyone seriously propose that all or most of those citations had been altered? What objective grounds are there for doing so?

Hills discusses the case of Origen as follows:

In the first fourteen chapters of the Gospel of John (that is, in the area covered by Papyrus Bodmer II) out of 52 instances in which the Byzantine text stands alone Origen agrees with the Byzantine text 20 times and disagrees with it 32 times. Thus the assertion of the critics that Origen knew nothing of the Byzantine text becomes difficult indeed to maintain. On the contrary, these statistics suggest that Origen was familiar with the Byzantine text and frequently adopted its readings in preference to those of the Western and Alexandrian texts.

Naturalistic critics, it is true, have made a determined effort to explain away the "distinctively" Byzantine readings which appear in the New Testament quotations of Origen (and other ante-Nicene Fathers). It is argued that these Byzantine readings are not really Origen's but represent alterations made by scribes who copied Origen's works. These scribes, it is maintained, revised the original quotations of Origen and made them conform to the Byzantine text. The evidence of Papyrus Bodmer II, however, indicates that this is not an adequate explanation of the facts. Certainly it seems a very unsatisfactory way to account for the phenomena which appear in the first fourteen chapters of John. In these chapters, 5 out of the 20 "distinctively" Byzantine readings which occur in Origen occur also in Papyrus Bodmer II. These 5 readings at least must have been Origen's readings, not those of scribes who copied Origen's works, and what is true of these 5 readings is probably true of the other 15, or at least of most of them. [125]

This demonstration makes it clear that the expedient deprecated above is in fact untenable.

The testimony of the early Fathers

To recapitulate, "Byzantine" readings are recognized (most notably) by the *Didache*, Diognetus, and Justin Martyr in the first half of the second century; by the Gospel of Peter Athenagorus, Hegesippus, and Irenaeus (heavily) in the second half; by Clement of Alexandria, Tertullian, Clementines, Hippolytus, and Origen (all heavily) in the first half of the third century; by Gregory of Thaumaturgus, Novatian, Cyprian (heavily), Dionysius of Alexandria, and Archelaus in the second half; by Eusebius, Athanasius, Macarius Magnus, Hilary, Didymus, Basil, Titus of Bostra, Cyril of Jerusalem, Gregory of Nyssa, Apostolic Canons and Constitutions, Epiphanius, and Ambrose (all heavily) in the fourth century. To which may be added the testimony of the early Papyri.

The testimony of the early Papyri

In Hort's day and even in Miller's the early Papyri were not extant—had they been the W-H theory could scarcely have appeared in the form that it did. Each of the early Papyri (300 A.D. or earlier) vindicates some "Byzantine" readings. G. Zuntz did a thorough study of P[46] and concluded:

> To sum up. A number of Byzantine readings, most of them genuine, which previously were discarded as 'late', are anticipated by P[46]. . . . How then—so one is tempted to go on asking—where no Chester Beatty papyrus happens to vouch for the early existence of a Byzantine reading? Are all Byzantine readings ancient? In the cognate case of the Homeric tradition G. Pasquali answers the same question in the affirmative.[126]

Colwell takes note of Zuntz's statement and concurs.[127] He had said of the "Byzantine New Testament" some years previous, "Most of its readings existed in the second century."[128]

Hills claims that the Beatty papyri vindicate 26 "Byzantine" readings in the Gospels, 8 in Acts and 31 in Paul's epistles.[129] He says concerning P[66]:

> To be precise, Papyrus Bodmer II contains thirteen percent of all the alleged late readings of the Byzantine text in the area which it covers (18 out of 138). Thirteen percent of the Byzantine readings which most critics have regarded as late have now been proved by Papyrus Bodmer II to be early readings.[130]

Colwell's statement on P[66] has already been given.

Many other studies are available, but that of H. A. Sturz sums it up.[131] He surveyed "all the available papyri" to discover how many papyrus-supported "Byzantine" readings exist. In trying to decide which were "distinctively Byzantine" readings he made a conscious effort to "err on the conservative side" so that the list is shorter than it might be (p. 106).

He found, and lists the evidence for, more than 150 "distinctively Byzantine" readings that have early (before 300 A.D.) papyrus support (pp. 108-26). He found 170 "Byzantine-Western" readings with early papyrus support (pp. 128-46). He found 170 "Byzantine-Alexandrian" readings with early papyrus support (pp. 149-64). He gives evidence for 175 further "Byzantine" readings but which have scattered "Western" or "Alexandrian" support, with early papyrus support.[132] He refers to still another 195 readings where the "Byzantine" reading has papyrus support, but he doesn't bother to list them (apparently he considers these variants to be of lesser consequence).[133]

The magnitude of this vindication can be more fully appreciated by recalling that only about 30 percent of the New Testament has early papyrus attestation, and much of that 30 percent has only one papyrus. Where more than one covers a stretch of text, each new MS discovered vindicates added Byzantine readings. Extrapolating from the behavior of those in hand, if we had at least 3 papyri covering all parts of the New Testament, almost all the 5000+ Byzantine readings rejected by the critical (eclectic) texts would be vindicated by an early papyrus.

It appears that Hort's statement or treatment of external evidence has no basis in fact. What about his statement of internal evidence?

Internal Evidence of Readings

We have already noted something of the use Hort made of internal evidence, but he himself recognized its weaknesses. He said: "In dealing with this kind of evidence [Intrinsic Evidence of Readings] equally competent critics often arrive at contradictory conclusions as to the same variations."[134]

And again, four pages later:

Not only are mental impulses unsatisfactory subjects for estimates of comparative force; but a plurality of impulses recognized by ourselves as possible in any given case by no means implies a plurality of impulses as having been actually in operation.[135]

Exactly! No twentieth century man confronting a set of variant readings can know or prove what actually took place to produce the variants.

Again Hort's preaching is better than his practice:

The summary decisions inspired by an unhesitating instinct as to what an author must needs have written, or dictated by the supposed authority of "canons of criticism" as to what transcribers must needs have introduced, are in reality in a large proportion of cases attempts to dispense with the solution of problems that depend on genealogical data.[136]

If we but change the words "genealogical data" to "external evidence" we may agree with him. Unfortunately, the fine sentiments quoted above were but a smoke screen. As Fee says:

The internal evidence of readings was also the predominant factor in the choice of his "Neutral" text over the "Western" and "Alexandrian" texts . . . and his choice of B. . . .

The point is that Hort did not come to his conclusions about the Byzantines and B by the genealogical method, . . .[137]

The precarious and unsatisfactory nature of internal evidence has already received some attention in the discussion of eclecticism. Colwell says specifically of the use of intrinsic and transcriptional probability,

Unfortunately these two criteria frequently clash in a head-on collision, because ancient scribes as well as modern editors often preferred the reading which best fits the context.[138]

If we choose the reading that best explains the origin of the other reading, we are usually choosing the reading that does not fit the context. The two criteria cancel each other out.[139]

And that leaves the scholar "free to choose in terms of his own prejudgments."[140]

Burgon said of internal considerations:

Often they are the product of personal bias, or limited observation: and where one scholar approves, another dogmatically condemns. Circumstantial evidence is deservedly rated low in the courts of justice: and lawyers always produce witnesses when they can.[141]

We venture to declare that inasmuch as one expert's notions of what is 'transcriptionally probable' prove to be the diametrical reverse of another expert's notions, the supposed evidence to be derived from this source may, with advantage, be neglected altogether. Let the study of *Documentary Evidence* be allowed to take its place. Notions of 'Probability' are the very pest of those departments of Science which admit of an appeal to *Fact*.[142]

He also called attention to a danger involved in the use of a system of strict canons. "People are ordinarily so constituted, that when they have once constructed a system of Canons they place no limits to their operation, and become slaves to them."[143] (Gordon Fee's use of *ardua lectio potior* seems to me to be a case in point.)[144]

The shorter reading

Perhaps the canon most widely used against the "Byzantine" text is *brevior lectio potior*—the shorter reading is to be preferred. As Hort stated the alleged basis for the canon, "In the New Testament, as in almost all prose writings which have been much copied, corruptions by interpolation are many times more numerous than corruptions by omission."[145] Accordingly it has been customary since Hort to tax the Received

Text as being full and interpolated and to regard B and Aleph as prime examples of non-interpolated texts.[146]

But is it really true that interpolations are "many times more numerous" than omissions in the transmission of the New Testament? B. H. Streeter thought not.

> Hort speaks of "the almost universal tendency of transcribers to make their text as full as possible, and to eschew omissions"; and infers that copyists would tend to prefer an interpolated to an uninterpolated text. This may be true of some of the local texts of the second century; it is the very opposite of the truth where scribes or editors trained in the tradition of Alexandrian textual criticism are concerned. The Alexandrian editors of Homer were as eagle-eyed to detect and obelise "interpolations" in Homer as a modern critic. . . .
>
> That Christian scholars and scribes were capable of the same critical attitude we have irrefragable evidence. . . . The notion is completely refuted that the regular tendency of scribes was to choose the longer reading, and that therefore the modern editor is quite safe so long as he steadily rejects. . . .
>
> Now, whoever was responsible for it, the B text has been edited on the Alexandrian principle.[147]

> The whole question of interpolations in ancient MSS has been set in an entirely new light by the researches of Mr. A. C. Clark, Corpus Professor of Latin at Oxford. . . . In *The Descent of Manuscripts*, an investigation of the manuscript tradition of the Greek and Latin Classics, he proves conclusively that the error to which scribes were most prone was not interpolation but accidental omission. . . . Hitherto the maxim *brevior lectio potior* . . . has been assumed as a postulate of scientific criticism. Clark has shown that, so far as classical texts are concerned, the facts point entirely the other way.[148]

Burgon had objected long before.

How indeed can it possibly be more true to the infirmities of copyists, to the verdict of evidence on the several passages, and to the origin of the New Testament in the infancy of the Church and amidst associations which were not literary, to suppose that a terse production was first produced and afterwards was amplified in a later age with a view to 'lucidity and completeness,' rather than that words and clauses and sentences were omitted upon definitely understood principles in a small class of documents by careless or ignorant or prejudiced scribes?[149]

Leo Vaganay also had reservations concerning this canon.

As a rule the copyist, especially when at the work of revision, is inclined to amplify the text. . . . But the rule suffers many exceptions. . . . Distraction of the copyist, . . . intentional corrections. . . . And finally, . . . the fundamental tendency of some recension, of which a good example is the Egyptian recension. . . . And also we must not forget that the writers of the New Testament were Orientals, who are more given to length than to brevity.[150]

Kilpatrick actually suggests that a substitute canon, "the longer reading is preferable," would be no worse. He concludes:

On reflection we do not seem able to find any reason for thinking that the maxim *lectio brevior potior* really holds good. We can only hope that a fuller acquaintance with the problems concerned will enable us increasingly to discern reasons in each instance why the longer or the shorter reading seems more probable.[151]

Colwell has published a most significant study of scribal habits as illustrated by the three early papyri P[45], P[66], and P[75]. It demonstrates that broad generalizations about scribal habits should never have been made and it follows that ideas about variant readings and text-types based on such generalizations should be reconsidered. It will be well to quote Colwell at some length.

The characterization of these singular readings can go on further until the individual scribes have been characterized. Their peculiar readings are due to their peculiarities. This has been well said by Dain. He reminds us that although all scribes make mistakes and mistakes of the same kind, yet each scribe has a personal coefficient of the frequency of his mistakes. Each has his own pattern of errors. One scribe is liable to dittography, another to the omission of lines of text; one reads well, another remembers poorly; one is a good speller; etc., etc. In these differences must be included the seriousness of intention of the scribe and the peculiarities of his own basic method of copying.[152]

In general, P[75] copies letters one by one; P[66] copies syllables, usually two letters in length. P[45] copies phrases and clauses.

The accuracy of these assertions can be demonstrated. That P[75] copied letters one by one is shown in the pattern of the errors. He has more than sixty readings that involve a single letter, *and* not more than ten careless readings that involve a syllable. But P[66] drops sixty-one syllables (twenty-three of them in "leaps") and omits as well a dozen articles and thirty short words. In P[45] there is not one omission of a syllable in a "leap" nor is there any list of "careless" omissions of syllables. P[45] omits words and phrases.[153]

As an editor the scribe of P[45] wielded a sharp axe. The most striking aspect of his style is its conciseness. The dispensable word is dispensed with. He omits adverbs, adjectives, nouns, participles, verbs, personal pronouns—without any compensating habit of addition. He frequently omits phrases and clauses. He prefers the simple to the compound word. In short, he favors brevity. He shortens the text in at least fifty places in *singular readings alone*. But he does *not* drop syllables or letters. His shortened text is readable.[154]

Enough of these have been cited to make the point that P[66] editorializes as he does everything else—in a sloppy fashion. He is not guided in his changes by some clearly defined goal which is always kept in view. If he has an inclination toward omission, it is not "according to knowledge," but is whimsical and careless, often leading to nothing but nonsense.[155]

P[66] has 54 leaps forward, and 22 backward; 18 of the forward leaps are haplography.
P[75] has 27 leaps forward, and 10 backward.
P[45] has 16 leaps forward, and 2 backward.
From this it is clear that the scribe looking for his lost place looked ahead three times as often as he looked back. In other words, the loss of position usually resulted in a loss of text, an omission.[156]

The tables have been turned. Here is a clear statistical demonstration that interpolations are *not* "many times more numerous" than omissions. Omission is more common as an unintentional error than addition, and P[45] shows that with some scribes omissions were *deliberate* and extensive. Is it mere coincidence that Aleph and B were probably made in the same area as P[45] and exhibit similar characteristics? In any case, the "fullness" of the Traditional Text, rather than a proof of inferiority, emerges as a point in its favor.

The harder reading

Another canon used against the "Byzantine" text is *proclivi lectioni praestat ardua*—the harder reading is to be preferred. The basis for this is an alleged propensity of scribes or copyists to simplify or change the text when they found a supposed difficulty or something they didn't understand. But where is the statistical demonstration that warrants such a generalization? Probably, as in the case of the canon just discussed, when such a demonstration is forthcoming it will prove the opposite.
Vaganay said of this canon:

But the more difficult reading is not always the more probably authentic. The rule does not apply, for instance, in the case of some accidental errors. . . . But, what is worse, we sometimes find difficult or intricate readings that are the outcome of intentional corrections. A copyist, through misunderstanding some passage, or through not taking the context into account, may in all sincerity make something obscure that he means to make plain.[157]

Have we not all heard preachers do this very thing?
Metzger notes Jerome's complaint:

> Jerome complained of the copyists who "write down not what they find but what they think is the meaning; and while they attempt to rectify the errors of others, they merely expose their own."[158]

(Just so, producing what would appear to us to be "harder readings" but which readings are spurious.)
After recounting an incident at an assembly of Cypriot bishops in 350 A.D. Metzger concludes:

> Despite the vigilance of ecclesiastics of Bishop Spyridon's temperament, it is apparent from even a casual examination of a critical apparatus that scribes, offended by real or imagined errors of spelling, grammar, and historical fact, deliberately introduced changes into what they were transcribing.[159]

Would not many of these changes appear to us to be "harder readings"?
In any case, the amply documented fact that numerous people in the second century made deliberate changes in the text, whether for doctrinal or other reasons, introduces an unpredictable variable which invalidates this canon. Once a person arrogates to himself the authority to alter the text there is nothing in principle to keep individual caprice from intruding or taking over—we have no way of knowing what factors influenced the originator of a variant (whoever he was) or whether the result would appear to us to be "harder" or "easier." This canon is simply inapplicable.[160]
Another problem with this canon is its vulnerability to the manipulation of a skillful and determined imagination. With sufficient ingenuity, virtually any reading can be made to look

"convincing." Hort is a prime example of this sort of imagination and ingenuity. Zuntz has stated:

> Dr. Hort's dealing with this and the other patristic evidence for this passage [I Cor. 13:3] requires a word of comment. No one could feel greater respect, nay reverence, for him than the present writer; but his treatment of this variant, in making every piece of the evidence say the opposite of its true meaning, shows to what distortions even a great scholar may be driven by the urge to square the facts with an erroneous, or at least imperfect theory. Souter, Plummer, and many others show the aftereffect of Dr. Hort's tenacity.[161]

Salmon has noted the same thing:

> That which gained Hort so many adherents had some adverse influence with myself—I mean his extreme cleverness as an advocate; for I have felt as if there were no reading so improbable that he could not give good reasons for thinking it to be the only genuine.[162]

Samuel Hemphill wrote of Hort's role in the New Testament Committee that produced the Revised Version of 1881:

> Nor is it difficult to understand that many of their less resolute and decided colleagues must often have been completely carried off their feet by the persuasiveness and resourcefulness, and zeal of Hort, . . . In fact, it can hardly be doubted that Hort's was the strongest will of the whole Company, and his adroitness in debate was only equaled by his pertinacity.[163]

(It would appear that the composition of the Greek text used by the English Revisers—and consequently for the RSV, NASB, etc.—was determined in large measure by Hort's cleverness and pertinacity, inspired by his devotion to a single Greek manuscript.)

Hort's performance shows the reasonableness of Colwell's warning against "the distortion of judgment which so easily manipulates the criteria of internal evidence."[164]

Harmonization[165]

It is widely asserted that the "Byzantine" text is characterized by harmonizations, e.g. Metzger: "The framers of this text sought . . . to harmonize divergent parallel passages."[166] By the choice of this terminology it is assumed that the diverse readings found in the minority of MSS are original and that copyists felt impelled to make parallel accounts agree. Perhaps it is time to ask whether it ever has been or can be proved that such an interpretation is correct. Jakob Van Bruggen says of Metzger's statement, "this judgment has not been proven, and can not be proven."[167]

1) Van Bruggen
Because Van Bruggen's valuable work may not be available to many readers, I will quote from his treatment of the subject in hand at some length. His reaction to Metzger's statement continues:

> Often illustrative examples are given to support this negative characterization of the Byzantine text. But it would not be difficult to "prove", with the aid of specially chosen examples from other text-types, that those types are also guilty of harmonizing, conflating readings and smoothing the diction.[168]

Kilpatrick, using strictly internal evidence, concludes that,

> though the Syrian text has its share of harmonizations, other texts including the Egyptian have suffered in this way. We cannot condemn the Syrian text for harmonization. If we do, we must condemn the other texts too on the same grounds.[169]

Van Bruggen continues:

> Here illustrations do not prove anything. After all, one could without much difficulty give a large number of examples from the Byzantine text to support the proposition that this text does *not* harmonize and does *not* smooth away. In

commentaries the exegete is often satisfied with the incidental example without comparing it to the textual data as a whole. Yet a proposition about the Byzantine *type* should not be based on illustrations, but on arguments from the text *as a whole*. Whoever wishes to find such arguments will meet a number of methodical problems and obstacles, which obstruct the way to the proof. Here we can mention the following points:

1. Methodically we must first ask how a "type" is determined. This can not be done on the basis of selected readings, because then the selection will soon be determined by what one is trying to prove. You can only speak of a text-type if the characteristics which must distinguish the type are not incidental but are found all along, and if they do not appear in other types from which the type must be distinguished. The criteria must be distinctive and general. As far as this is concerned, suspicion is roused when Hort remarks that the harmonizing and assimilating interpolations in the Byzantine text are "fortunately capricious and incomplete" (*Introduction*, p. 135). Did Hort then indeed generalize and make characteristics of some readings into characteristics of the text-type? This suspicion becomes certainty when Metzger in his *Textual Commentary* has to observe more than once that non-Byzantine readings, for example, in the Codex Vaticanus, can be explained from the tendencies of scribes to assimilate and to simplify the text.[170]

In a footnote, Van Bruggen cites Metzger's discussion of Matthew 19:3 and 19:9, John 6:14, James 2:3, 4:14, 5:16, and 5:20, where harmonization and other smoothing efforts are ascribed to Codex B and its fellow-travellers. His discussion proceeds:

What is typical for the Byzantine text is apparently not so exclusive for this text-type! But if certain phenomena seem to appear in all types of text, then it is not right to condemn a type categorically and regard it as secondary on the ground of such phenomena.

2. Moreover, it is methodically difficult to speak of

harmonizing and assimilating deviations in a text, when the original is not known. Or is it an axiom that the original text in any case was so inharmonious, that every harmonious reading is directly suspect? Hort lets us sense that he personally does not prefer a New Testament "more fitted for cursory perusal or recitation than for repeated and diligent study" (*Introduction*, p. 153). Yet who, without the original at his disposal, can prove that this original had those characteristics which a philologist and a textual critic considers to be most recommendable?[171]

P. Walters comments upon Hort's sense of style as follows:

Hort's sense of style, his idea of what was correct and preferable in every alternative, was acquired from a close acquaintance with his "neutral" text. It did not occur to him that most of its formal aspects tallied with his standards just because these were taken from his model. So far his decisions are in the nature of a vicious circle. We today who live outside this magic circle, which kept a generation spellbound, are able to see through Hort's illusion.[172]

Van Bruggen continues:

4. If editors of the Byzantine text would have been out to harmonize the text and to fit parallel passages of the Gospels into each other, then we must observe that they let nearly all their opportunities go by. . . . In addition, what seems to be harmonization is in a different direction often no harmonization. A reading may seem adjusted to the parallel passage in an other Gospel, but then often deviates again from the reading in the third Gospel. A reading may seem borrowed from the parallel story, yet at the same time fall out of tune in the context of the Gospel itself. Here the examples are innumerable as long as one does not limit himself to a few texts and pays attention to the context and the Gospels as a whole.[173]

With reference to giving due attention to the context, Van Bruggen reports on a study wherein he compared the TR with

Nestle[25] in fourteen extended passages to see if either one could be characterized as harmonizing or assimilating.

> The comparison of the edition Stephanus (1550) with Nestle-Aland (25th edition) led to the result that the dilemma "harmonizing/not harmonizing" is unsuited to distinguish both of these text-editions. We examined Matthew 5:1–12; 6:9–13; 13:1–20; 19:1–12; Mark 2:18–3:6; Luke 9:52–62; 24:1–12; John 6:22–71; Acts 18:18–19:7; 22:6–21; 1 Corinthians 7; James 3:1–10; 5:10–20; Revelation 5. In the comparative examination not only the context, but also all the parallel passages were taken into account. Since the Stephanus-text is closely related to the Byzantine text and the edition Nestle-Aland is clearly non-Byzantine, the result of this investigation may also apply to the relation between the Byzantine text and other text-types: the dilemma "harmonizing/not harmonizing" or "assimilating/not assimilating" is unsound to distinguish *types* in the textual tradition of the New Testament.[174]

One is reminded of Burgon's observation that decisions based on internal considerations are often "the product of personal bias, or limited observation."[175] In this connection it will be well to consider some examples.

2) Examples

Mark 1:2—shall we read "in Isaiah the prophet" with the "Alexandrian-Western" texts or "in the prophets" with the "Byzantine" text? All critical editions follow the first reading and Fee affirms that it is "a clear example of 'the most difficult reading being preferred as the original.' "[176] I would say that Fee's superficial discussion is a "clear example" of personal bias (toward the "harder reading" canon) and of limited observation. The only other places that Isaiah 40:3 is quoted in the New Testament are Matthew 3:3, Luke 3:4, and John 1:23. The first two are in passages parallel to Mark 1:2 and join it in quoting the LXX verbatim. The quote in John differs from the LXX in one word and is also used in connection with John the Baptist. The crucial consideration, for our present purpose, is that Matthew, Luke, and John all identify the quote as being from Isaiah (without MSS variation). It seems clear that the "Alexandrian-Western" reading in Mark 1:2 is simply an assimilation to the other three Gospels. It should also be noted that the material from Malachi looks more like an allusion than a direct quote. Further, although Malachi is quoted (or alluded to) a number of times in the New Testament, he is never named. Mark's own habits may also be germane to this discussion. Mark quotes Isaiah in 4:12, 11:17, and 12:32 and alludes to him in about ten other places, all without naming his source. The one time he does use Isaiah's name is when quoting Jesus in 7:6.[177] It is the "Byzantine" text that has escaped harmonization and preserves the original reading.

Mark 10:47	— Ναζαρηνος	B L W Δ Θ Ψ 1 lat cop	
	Ναζορηνος	D	
	Ναζωραιος	Byz ℵ A C X Π 13 pl syr	
/ / Luke 18:37	— Ναζαρηνος	D 1 pc	
	Ναζωραιος	rell	
Mark 1:24	— Ναζαρηνε	all agree	
Mark 14:67	— Ναζαρηνου	all agree	
Mark 16:6	— Ναζαρηνου	all agree except that ℵ and	
		D omit.	

All critical editions follow the first reading in Mark 10:47 and interpret the "Byzantine" reading as an assimilation to Luke 18:37 (where they reject the reading of D). It should be observed, however, that everywhere else that Mark uses the word the -αρην- form occurs. Is it not just as possible that Codex B and company have assimilated to the prevailing Markan form?[178]

Mark 8:31	— μετα τρεις ἡμερας	all agree	
/ / Matt. 16:21	— μετα τρεις ἡμερας	D al	
	τη τριτη ἡμερα	rell	
/ / Luke 9:22	— μεϑ ἡμερας τρεις	D it	
	τη τριτη ἡμερα	rell	
Mark 9:31	— μετα τρεις ἡμερας	ℵ B C D L Δ	
	τη τριτη ἡμερα	Byz Θ pl	

// Matt. 17:23	— μετα τρεις ήμερας τη τριτη ήμερα	D it *rell*
Mark 10:34	— μετα τρεις ήμερας τη τριτη ήμερα	ℵ B C D L Δ Ψ it cop Byz Aᶜ K W X Θ Π 1 13 *pl* syr
// Matt. 20:19	— τη τριτη ήμερα	all agree
// Luke 18:33	— τη ήμερα τη τριτη	all agree

All critical editions follow the first reading in Mark 9:31 and 10:34 and interpret the "Byzantine" reading as an assimilation to Matthew, in both cases. But why did the "Byzantines" not also assimilate in Mark 8:31 where there was the pressure of both Matthew *and* Luke? Is it not more likely that the "Alexandrians" made Mark consistent (note that Matthew is consistent) by assimilating the latter two instances to the first one? Note that in this example and the preceding one it is Codex D that engages in the most flagrant assimilating activity.[179]

Mark 13:14—shall we read "spoken of through Daniel the prophet" with the "Byzantine" text or follow the "Alexandrian-Western" text wherein this phrase is missing? All critical editions take the second option and Fee assures us that the "Byzantine" text has assimilated to Matthew 24:15 where all witnesses have the phrase in question.[180] But let us consider the actual evidence:

Matt. 24:15	— το ρηθεν <u>δια</u> Δανιηλ του προφητου
Mark 13:14	— το ρηθεν <u>ύπο</u> Δανιηλ του προφητου

If the "Byzantines" were intent on copying from Matthew, why did they alter the wording? If their purpose was to harmonize, why did they *dis*harmonize, to use Fee's expression? Furthermore, if we compare the full pericope in both Gospels, Matthew 24:15-22 and Mark 13:14-20, using the "Byzantine" text, although the two accounts are of virtually equal length, fully one third of the words are different between them. The claim that the "Byzantines" were given to harmonizing becomes silly. Still further, there appear to be three clear assimilations to Mark on the part of the "Alexandrian-Western" witnesses, and one to Matthew—$\epsilon\pi\iota$ to $\epsilon\iota\varsigma$ in Matthew 24:15, $\kappa\alpha\tau\alpha\beta\alpha\iota\nu\epsilon\tau\omega$ to $\kappa\alpha\tau\alpha\beta\alpha\tau\omega$ in Matthew 24:17, $\tau\alpha$ $\iota\mu\alpha\tau\iota\alpha$ to τo $\iota\mu\alpha\tau\iota o\nu$ in Matthew 24:18, and the omission of $\omega\nu$ in Mark 13:16—plus three other "Western" assimilations— $\tau\alpha$ to $\tau\iota$ in Matthew 24:17, $\kappa\alpha\iota$ to $o\nu\delta$ in Mark 13:19, and $\delta\epsilon$ added to Matthew 24:17. But, returning to the first variant, why would the "Alexandrians" have omitted the phrase in question? A comparison of the LXX of Daniel with the immediate context suggests an answer. Mark's phrase, "where he ought not," is not to be found in Daniel. That some people felt Mark's integrity needed protecting is clear from the remedial actions attempted by a few Greek and version MSS. The "Alexandrian" omission may well be such an attempt.[181]

To conclude, it is demonstrable that all "text-types" have many possible harmonizations. It has not been demonstrated that the "Byzantine" text has more possible or actual harmonizations than the others. It follows that "harmonization" may not reasonably or responsibly be used to argue for an inferior "Byzantine" text type.

Inferiority

Hort did not offer a statistical demonstration in support of his characterization of the "Byzantine" text.[182] Metzger refers to von Soden as supplying adequate evidence for the characterization. Upon inspection of the designated pages,[183] we discover there is no listing of manuscript evidence and no discussion. His limited lists of references purportedly illustrating addition or omission or assimilation, etc., may be viewed differently by a different mind. In fact, Kilpatrick has argued for the originality of a considerable number of Byzantine readings of the sort von Soden listed.[184]

The length of the lists, in any case, is scarcely prepossessing. No one has done for the "Byzantine" text anything even remotely approximating what Hoskier did for Codex B, filling 450 pages with a careful discussion, one by one, of many of its errors and idiosyncracies.[185]

As we have already noted, Hort declared the *Textus Receptus* to be "villainous" and "vile" when he was only twenty-three years old—before he had studied the evidence, before he had worked through the text to evaluate variant readings one by one. Do you suppose he brought an open mind to that study and evaluation?

Elliott and Kilpatrick profess to do their evaluating with an open mind, with no predilections as to text-types, yet inescapably use the ambiguous canons of internal evidence. What do they conclude? Elliott decided the "Byzantine" text was right about as often as Aleph and D, the chief representatives of the "Alexandrian" and "Western" texts (in the Pastorals).[186] Kilpatrick affirms:

> Our principal conclusion is that the Syrian text is frequently right. It has avoided at many points mistakes and deliberate changes found in other witnesses. This means that at each variation we must look at the readings of the Byzantine manuscripts with the possibility in mind that they may be right. We cannot dismiss their characteristic variants as being in principle secondary.[187]

The basic deficiency, both fundamental and serious, of any characterization based upon subjective criteria is that the result is only opinion; it is not objectively verifiable. Is there no better way to determine the original wording of the New Testament? I believe there is, but first there is one more tenet of Hort's theory to scrutinize.

The "Lucianic Recension" and the Peshitta

Burgon gave the sufficient answer to this invention.

> Apart however from the gross intrinsic improbability of the supposed Recension,—the utter absence of one particle of evidence, traditional or otherwise, that it ever did take place, must be held to be fatal to the hypothesis that it *did*. It is simply incredible that an incident of such magnitude and interest would leave no trace of itself in history.[188]

It will not do for someone to say that the argument from silence proves nothing. In a matter of this "magnitude and interest" it is conclusive. Kenyon, also, found this part of Hort's theory to be gratuitous.

> The absence of evidence points the other way; for it would be very strange, if Lucian had really edited both Testaments, that only his work on the Old Testament should be mentioned in after times. The same argument tells against any theory of a deliberate revision at any definite moment. We know the names of several revisers of the Septuagint and the Vulgate, and it would be strange if historians and Church writers had all omitted to record or mention such an event as the deliberate revision of the New Testament in its original Greek.[189]

Colwell is blunt: "The Greek Vulgate—the Byzantine or Alpha text-type—had in its origin no such single focus as the Latin had in Jerome."[190] F. C. Grant is prepared to look into the second century for the origin of the "Byzantine" text-type.[191] Jacob Geerlings, who has done extensive work on certain branches of the "Byzantine" text-type, affirms concerning it: "Its origins as well as those of other so-called text-types probably go back to the autographs."[192]

In an effort to save Hort's conclusions, seemingly, Kenyon sought to attribute the "Byzantine" text to a "tendency."

> It seems probable, therefore, that the Syrian revision was rather the result of a tendency spread over a considerable period of time than of a definite and authoritative revision or revisions, such as produced our English Authorised and Revised Versions. We have only to suppose the principle to be established in Christian circles in and about Antioch, that in the case of divergent readings being found in the texts copied, it was better to combine both than to omit either, and that obscurities and roughnesses of diction should be smoothed away as much as possible.[193]

But what if we choose not "to suppose" anything, but rather to insist upon evidence? We have already seen from Hutton's *Atlas* that for every instance that the "Syrian" text possibly combines divergent readings there are a hundred where it does not. What sort of a "tendency" is that? To insist that a variety of scribes separated by time and space and working independently, but all feeling a responsibility to apply their critical faculties to the text, should produce a uniformity of text such as is exhibited within the "Byzantine" text seems to be asking a bit much, both of them and of us. Hodges agrees.

> It will be noted in this discussion that in place of the former idea of a specific revision as the source-point for the Majority text, some critics now wish to posit the idea of a "process" drawn out over a long period of time. It may be confidently predicted, however, that this explanation of the Majority text must likewise eventually collapse. The Majority text, it must be remembered, is relatively uniform in its general character with comparatively low amounts of variation between its major representatives. No one has yet explained how a long, slow process spread out over many centuries as well as over a wide geographical area, and involving a multitude of copyists, who often knew nothing of the state of the text outside of their own monasteries or scriptoria, could achieve this widespread uniformity out of the diversity presented by the earlier forms of text. Even an official edition of the New Testament—promoted with ecclesiastical sanction throughout the known world—would have had great difficulty achieving this result as the history of Jerome's Vulgate amply demonstrates. But an unguided process achieving relative stability and uniformity in the diversified textual, historical, and cultural circumstances in which the New Testament was copied, imposes impossible strains on our imagination.[194]

An ordinary process of textual transmission results in divergence, not convergence. Uniformity of text is usually greatest near the source and diminishes in transmission.

The accumulating evidence seems not to bother Metzger. He still affirmed in 1968 that the "Byzantine" text is based on a recension prepared by Lucian.[195] There is an added problem with that view.

Lucian was an Arian, a vocal one. Does Metzger seriously

invite us to believe that the victorious Athanasians embraced an Arian revision of the Greek New Testament?

As to the Syriac Peshitta, again Burgon protested the complete lack of evidence for Hort's assertions.[196] A. Vööbus says of Burkitt's effort:

> Burkitt has tried to picture the lifespan of Bishop Rabbula as a decisive period in the development of the New Testament text in the Syrian church.
> Regardless of the general acceptance of the axiom, established by him, that "the authority of Rabbula secured an instant success for the new revised version . . ." and that "copies of the Peshitta were rapidly multiplied, it soon became the only text in ecclesiastical use"—this kind of reconstruction of textual history is pure fiction without a shred of evidence to support it.[197]

Vööbus finds that Rabbula himself used the Old Syriac type of text. His researches show clearly that the Peshitta goes back at least to the mid-fourth century and that it was not the result of an authoritative revision.[198]

Here again there is an added historical difficulty.

> The Peshitta is regarded as authoritative Scripture by both the Nestorians and the Monophysites. It is hard to see how this could have come to pass on the hypothesis that Rabbula was the author and chief promoter of the Peshitta. For Rabbula was a decided Monophysite and a determined opponent of the Nestorians. It is almost contrary to reason, therefore, to suppose that the Nestorian Christians would adopt so quickly and so unanimously the handiwork of their greatest adversary.[199]

It is hard to understand how men like F. F. Bruce, E. C. Colwell, F. G. Kenyon, etc. could allow themselves to state dogmatically that Rabbula produced the Peshitta.

Conclusion

And that completes our review of the W-H critical theory. It is evidently erroneous at every point. Our conclusions concerning the theory of necessity apply also to any Greek text constructed on the basis of it, as well as to those versions based upon such texts (and to commentaries based upon them).

K. W. Clark says of the W-H text: "The textual history postulated for the *textus receptus* which we now trust has been exploded."[200]

Epp confesses that "we simply do not have a theory of the text."[201] The point is that "the establishment of the NT text can be achieved only by a reconstruction of the history of that early text. . . ."[202]

Colwell agrees: "Without a knowledge of the history of the text, the original reading cannot be established."[203]

In Aland's words, "Now as in the past, textual criticism without a history of the text is not possible."[204]

Or as Hort himself put it, "ALL TRUSTWORTHY RESTORATION OF CORRUPTED TEXTS IS FOUNDED ON THE STUDY OF THEIR HISTORY."[205]

As already noted, one of the fundamental deficiencies of the eclectic method is that it ignores the history of the text. Hort did not ignore it, but what are we to say of his "clear and firm view"[206] of it? What Clark says is:

The textual history that the Westcott-Hort text represents is no longer tenable in the light of newer discoveries and fuller textual analysis. In the effort to construct a congruent history, our failure suggests that we have lost the way, that we have reached a dead end, and that only a new and different insight will enable us to break through.[207]

(The evidence before us indicates that Hort's history never was tenable.)

The crucial question remains—*what sort of a history does the evidence reflect?* The identity of the New Testament text, our recognition of it, hinges upon our answer!

5

THE HISTORY OF THE TEXT

The logical place to start is with the possibility that the process of transmission of the text was normal.

Under normal circumstances the older a text is than its rivals, the greater are its chances to survive in a plurality or a majority of the texts extant at any subsequent period. But the *oldest* text of all is the autograph. Thus it ought to be taken for granted that, barring some radical dislocation in the history of transmission, a majority of texts will be far more likely to represent correctly the character of the original than a small minority of texts. This is especially true when the ratio is an overwhelming 8:2. Under any reasonably normal transmissional conditions, it would be . . . quite impossible for a later text-form to secure so one-sided a preponderance of extant witnesses.[1]

But were the transmissional conditions reasonably normal?

Were the N.T. Writings Recognized?

Naturalistic critics like to assume that the New Testament writings were not recognized as Scripture when they first appeared and thus through the consequent carelessness in transcription the text was confused and the original wording "lost" (in the sense that no one knew for sure what it was) at the very start. Thus Colwell says:

> Most of the manuals and handbooks now in print (including mine!) will tell you that these variations were the fruit of careless treatment which was possible because the books of the New Testament had not yet attained a strong position as "Bible."[2]

And Hort had said:

> Textual purity, as far as can be judged from the extant literature, attracted hardly any interest. There is no evidence to show that care was generally taken to choose out for transcription the exemplars having the highest claims to be regarded as authentic, if indeed the requisite knowledge and skill were forthcoming.[3]

Rather than take Hort's word for it, prudence calls for a review of the premises. The place to start is at the beginning, when the apostles were still penning the Autographs.

The apostolic period

It is clear that the apostle Paul, at least, considered his writings to be authoritative—see 1 Cor. 14:37, 2 Cor. 10:1-16, Gal. 1:6-12 and 2 Thess. 3:6-14. And it is reasonable to infer from Col. 4:16 that he expected his writings to have a wider audience than just the particular church addressed.

Peter, also, puts the commandments of the apostles (himself included) in the same class with "the holy prophets" (2 Pet. 3:2). In 1 Tim. 5:18 Paul puts the Gospel of Luke (10:7) on the same level as Deuteronomy (25:4), calling them both "Scripture."

Taking the traditional and conservative point of view, 1 Timothy is generally thought to have been written within five years after Luke.[4] Luke was recognized and declared by apostolic authority to be Scripture as soon as it came off the press, so to speak.

In 2 Pet. 3:15-16, Peter puts the Epistles of Paul on the same level as "the other Scriptures." Although some had been out for perhaps fifteen years, the ink was scarcely dry on others, and perhaps 2 Timothy had not yet been penned when Peter wrote. Paul's writings were recognized and declared by apostolic authority to be Scripture as soon as they appeared.

Clement of Rome, whose first letter to the Corinthians is usually dated about 96 A.D., made liberal use of Scripture, appealing to its authority, and used New Testament material right alongside Old Testament material. Clement quoted Ps. 118:18 and Heb. 12:6 side by side as "the holy word" (56:3-4).[5] He ascribes 1 Corinthians to "the blessed Paul the apostle" and says of it, "with true inspiration he wrote to you" (47:1-3). He clearly quotes from Hebrews, 1 Corinthians and Romans and possibly from Matthew, Acts, Titus, James, and 1 Peter. Here is the bishop of Rome, before the close of the first century, writing an official letter to the church at Corinth wherein a selection of New Testament books are recognized and declared by episcopal authority to be Scripture, including Hebrews.

The Epistle of Barnabas, variously dated from A.D. 70 to 135, says in 4:14, "let us be careful lest, as it is written, it should be found with us that 'many are called but few chosen.' " The reference seems to be to Matt. 22:14 (or 20:16) and the phrase "as it is written" may fairly be taken as a technical expression referring to Scripture. In 5:9 there is a quote from Matt. 9:13 (or Mark 2:17 or Luke 5:32). In 13:7 there is a loose quote from Rom. 4:11-12, which words are put in God's mouth. Similarly, in 15:4 we find:

> Note, children, what "he ended in six days" means. It means this: that the Lord will make an end of everything in six thousand years, for a day with Him means a thousand years. And He Himself is my witness, saying: "Behold, the day of the Lord shall be as a thousand years."[6]

The author, whoever he was, is clearly claiming divine authorship for this quote which appears to be from 2 Pet. 3:8.[7] In other words, 2 Peter is here regarded to be Scripture, as well as Matthew and Romans. Barnabas also has possible allusions to

1 and 2 Corinthians, Ephesians, Colossians, 1 and 2 Timothy, Titus, Hebrews, and 1 Peter.

The second century

The seven letters of Ignatius (c. 110 A.D.) contain probable allusions to Matthew, John, Romans, 1 Corinthians and Ephesians (in his own letter to the Ephesians Ignatius says they are mentioned in "all the epistles of Paul"—a bit of hyperbole, but he was clearly aware of a Pauline corpus), and possible allusions to Luke, Acts, Galatians, Philippians, Colossians, 1 Thessalonians, 1 and 2 Timothy, and Titus, but very few are clear quotations and even they are not identified as such.

Polycarp, writing to the Philippian church (c. 115 A.D.?), weaves an almost continuous string of clear quotations and allusions to New Testament writings. His heavy use of Scripture is reminiscent of Clement of Rome; however, Clement used mostly the Old Testament while Polycarp usually used the New. There are perhaps fifty clear quotations taken from Matthew, Luke, Acts, Romans, 1 and 2 Corinthians, Galatians, Ephesians, Philippians, Colossians, 1 and 2 Thessalonians, 1 and 2 Timothy, 1 and 2 Peter, and 1 John, and many allusions including to Mark, Hebrews, James, and 2 and 3 John.

His attitude toward the New Testament writings is clear from 12:1:

I am sure that you are well trained in the sacred Scriptures, . . . Now, as it is said in these Scriptures: 'Be angry and sin not,' and 'Let not the sun go down upon your wrath.' Blessed is he who remembers this.[8]

Both parts of the quotation could come from Eph. 4:26 but since Polycarp split it up he may have been referring to Ps. 4:5 (LXX) in the first half. In either case he is declaring Ephesians to be "sacred Scripture." A further insight into his attitude is found in 3:1-2.

Brethren, I write you this concerning righteousness, not on my own initiative, but because you first invited me. For neither I, nor anyone like me, is able to rival the wisdom of the blessed and glorious Paul, who, when living among you, carefully and steadfastly taught the word of truth face to face with his contemporaries and, when he was absent, wrote you letters. By the careful perusal of his letters you will be able to strengthen yourselves in the faith given to you, "which is the mother of us all," . . .[9]

(This from one who was perhaps the most respected bishop in Asia Minor, in his day. He was martyred in 156 A.D.)

The so-called second letter of Clement of Rome is usually dated before 150 A.D. and seems clearly to quote from Matthew, Mark, Luke, Acts, 1 Corinthians, Ephesians, 1 Timothy, Hebrews, James, and 1 Peter, with possible allusions to 2 Peter, Jude, and Revelation. After quoting and discussing a passage from the Old Testament, the author goes on to say in 2:4, "Another Scripture says: 'I came not to call the just, but sinners' " (Matt. 9:13; Mark 2:17; Luke 5:32). Here is another author who recognized the New Testament writings to be Scripture.

Two other early works, the *Didache* and the letter to Diognetus, employ New Testament writings as being authoritative but without expressly calling them Scripture.

The *Didache* apparently quotes from Matthew, Luke, 1 Corinthians, Hebrews, and 1 Peter and has possible allusions to Acts, Romans, Ephesians, 1 and 2 Thessalonians, and Revelation.

The letter to Diognetus quotes from Acts, 1 and 2 Corinthians while alluding to Mark, John, Romans, Ephesians, Philippians, 1 Timothy, Titus, 1 Peter, and 1 John.

Another early work—the Shepherd of Hermas—widely used in the second and third centuries, has fairly clear allusions to Matthew, Mark, 1 Corinthians, Ephesians, Hebrews, and especially James.

From around the middle of the second century fairly extensive works by Justin Martyr (martyred in 165) have come down to us. His "Dialogue with Trypho" shows a masterful knowledge of the Old Testament to which he assigns the highest possible authority, evidently holding to a dictation view of inspiration—in *Trypho* 34 he says, "to persuade you that you have not understood anything of the Scriptures, I will remind you of another psalm, dictated to David by the Holy Spirit.[10] The whole point of *Trypho* is to prove that Jesus is Christ and God and therefore what He said and commanded was of highest authority.

In *Apol.* i.66 Justin says, "For the apostles in the memoirs composed by them, which are called Gospels, thus handed down what was commanded them. . . ."[11] And in *Trypho* 119 he says that just as Abraham believed the voice of God, "in like manner we, having believed God's voice spoken by the apostles of Christ . . ."

It also seems clear from *Trypho* 120 that Justin considered New Testament writings to be Scripture. Of considerable interest is an unequivocal reference to the book of Revelation in *Trypho* 81. "And further, there was a certain man with us, whose name was John, one of the apostles of Christ, who prophesied, by a revelation that was made to him, that those who believe in our Christ would dwell a thousand years in Jerusalem."[12]

Justin goes right on to say, "Just as our Lord also said," and quotes Luke 20:35, so evidently he considered Revelation to be authoritative. (While on the subject of Revelation, in 165 Melito, Bishop of Sardis, wrote a commentary on the book.)

A most instructive passage occurs in *Apol.* i.67.

> And on the day called Sunday there is a meeting in one place of those who live in cities or the country, and the memoirs of the apostles or the writings of the prophets are read as long as time permits. When the reader has finished, the president in a discourse urges and invites us to the imitation of these noble things.[13]

Whether or not the order suggests that the Gospels were preferred to the Prophets, it is clear that they both were considered to be authoritative and equally enjoined upon the hearers. Notice further that each assembly must have had its own copy of the apostles' writings to read from and that such reading took place every week.

Athenagorus, in his "Plea," written in early 177, quotes

Matt. 5:28 as Scripture: ". . . we are not even allowed to indulge in a lustful glance. For, says the Scripture, 'He who looks at a woman lustfully, has already committed adultery in his heart' " (32).[14] He similarly treats Matt. 19:9, or Mark 10:11, in 33.

Theophilus, Bishop of Antioch, in his treatise to Autolycus, quotes 1 Tim. 2:1 and Rom. 13:7 as "the Divine Word" (iii.14), quotes from the fourth Gospel, saying that John was "inspired by the Spirit" (ii.22), Isaiah and "the Gospel" are mentioned in one paragraph as Scripture (iii.14), and he insists in several passages that the writers never contradicted each other: "The statements of the Prophets and of the Gospels are found to be consistent, because all were inspired by the one Spirit of God" (ii.9; ii.35; iii.17).[15]

The surviving writings of Irenaeus (died in 202), his major work *Against Heretics* being written about 185, are about equal in volume to those of all the preceding Fathers put together.

His testimony to the authority and inspiration of Holy Scripture is clear and unequivocal. It pervades the whole of his writings; and this testimony is more than ordinarily valuable because it must be regarded as directly representing three churches at least, those of Lyons, Asia Minor, and Rome. The authoritative use of both Testaments is clearly laid down.[16]

Irenaeus stated that the apostles taught that God is the Author of both Testaments (*Against Heretics* IV. 32.2) and evidently considered the New Testament writings to form a second Canon. He quoted from every chapter of Matthew, 1 Corinthians, Galatians, Ephesians, Colossians, and Philippians, from all but one or two chapters of Luke, John, Romans, 2 Thessalonians, 1 and 2 Timothy, and Titus, from most chapters of Mark (including the last twelve verses), Acts, 2 Corinthians, and Revelation, and from every other book except Philemon and 3 John. These two books are so short that Irenaeus may not have had occasion to refer to them in his extant works—it does not necessarily follow that he was ignorant of them or rejected them. Evidently the dimensions of the New Testament Canon recognized by Irenaeus are very close to what we hold today.

From the time of Irenaeus on there can be no doubt concerning the attitude of the Church toward the New Testament writings—they are Scripture. Tertullian (in 208) said of the church at Rome, "the law and the prophets she unites in one volume with the writings of evangelists and apostles" (*Prescription against Heretics*, 36).

Were Early Christians Careful?

It has been widely affirmed that the early Christians were either unconcerned or unable to watch over the purity of the text. (Recall Hort's words given above.) Again a review of the premises is called for. Many of the first believers had been devout Jews who had an ingrained reverence and care for the Old Testament Scriptures which extended to the very jots and tittles. This reverence and care would naturally be extended to the New Testament Scriptures.

Why should modern critics assume that the early Christians, in particular the spiritual leaders among them, were inferior in integrity or intelligence? A Father's quoting from memory or tailoring a passage to suit his purpose in sermon or letter by no means implies that he would take similar liberties when transcribing a book or corpus. Ordinary honesty would require him to produce a faithful copy. Are we to assume that everyone who made copies of New Testament books in those early years was a knave or a fool? Paul was certainly as intelligent a man as any of us. If Hebrews was written by someone else, here was another man of high spiritual insight and intellectual power. There was Barnabas and Apollos and Clement and Polycarp, etc., etc. The Church has had men of reason and intelligence all down through the years. Starting out with what they *knew* to be the pure text, the earliest Fathers did not need to be textual critics. They had only to be reasonably honest and careful. But is there not good reason to believe they would be *especially* watchful and careful?

The apostles

Not only did the apostles themselves declare the New Testament writings to be Scripture, which would elicit reverence and care in their treatment, they expressly warned the believers to be on their guard against false teachers—see Acts 20:27-32, Gal. 1:6-12, 2 Tim. 3:1—4:4, 2 Pet. 2:1-2, 1 John. 2:18-19, 2 John. 7-11, Jude 3-4, 16-19. Peter's statement concerning the "twisting" Paul's words were receiving (2 Pet. 3:16) suggests there was awareness and concern as to the text and the way it was being handled. The clearest possible expression of this concern is given in Rev. 22:18-19. Faced with such a sanction, would any true believer dare to tamper with the text, or transcribe it carelessly?

The early Fathers

The early Fathers furnish a few helpful clues as to the state of affairs. The letters of Ignatius contain several references to a considerable traffic between the churches (of Asia Minor, Greece, Rome) by way of messengers (often official), which seems to indicate a deep sense of solidarity binding them together, and a wide circulation of news and attitudes—a problem with a heretic in one place would soon be known all over, etc. That there was strong feeling about the integrity of the Scriptures is made clear by Polycarp (7:1), "Whoever perverts the sayings of the Lord . . . that one is the firstborn of Satan."

Similarly, Justin Martyr says (*Apol.* i.58), "the wicked demons have also put forward Marcion of Pontus." And in *Trypho* xxxv he says of heretics teaching doctrines of the spirits of error, that fact "causes us who are disciples of the true and pure doctrine of Jesus Christ to be more faithful and stedfast in the hope announced by Him."

It seems obvious that heretical activity would have precisely the effect of putting the faithful on their guard and forcing them to define in their own minds what they were going to defend. Thus Marcion's truncated canon evidently stirred the faithful to define the true canon. But Marcion also altered the wording of Luke and Paul's Epistles, and by their bitter complaints it is clear that the faithful were both aware and concerned.

Dionysius, Bishop of Corinth (168-176), complained that his own letters had been tampered with, and worse yet the Holy Scriptures also.

And they insisted that they had received a pure tradition. Thus Irenaeus said that the doctrine of the apostles had been handed down by the succession of bishops, being guarded and preserved, without any forging of the Scriptures, allowing neither addition nor curtailment, involving public reading without falsification (*Against Heretics* IV. 32:8).

Tertullian, also, says of his right to the New Testament Scriptures, "I hold sure title-deeds from the original owners themselves . . . I am the heir of the apostles. Just as they carefully prepared their will and testament, and committed it to a trust . . . even so I hold it."[17]

Irenaeus

In order to ensure accuracy in transcription, authors would sometimes add at the close of their literary works an adjuration directed to future copyists. So, for example, Irenaeus attached to the close of his treatise *On the Ogdoad* the following note: "I adjure you who shall copy out this book, by our Lord Jesus Christ and by his glorious advent when he comes to judge the living and the dead, that you compare what you transcribe, and correct it carefully against this manuscript from which you copy; and also that you transcribe this adjuration and insert it in the copy.[18]

If Irenaeus took such extreme precautions for the accurate transmission of his own work, how much more would he be concerned for the accurate copying of the Word of God? In fact, he demonstrates his concern for the accuracy of the text by defending the traditional reading of a *single letter*. The question is whether John the Apostle wrote χξϛ' (666) or χιϛ' (616) in Rev. 13:18. Irenaeus asserts that 666 is found "in all the most approved and ancient copies" and that "those men who saw John face to face" bear witness to it. And he warns those who made the change (of a single letter) that "there shall be no light punishment upon him who either adds or subtracts anything from the Scripture" (xxx.1).

Considering Polycarp's intimacy with John, his personal copy of Revelation would most probably have been taken from the Autograph. And considering Irenaeus' veneration for Polycarp his personal copy of Revelation was probably taken from Polycarp's. Although Irenaeus evidently was no longer able to refer to the Autograph (not ninety years after it was written!) he was clearly in a position to identify a faithful copy and to declare with certainty the original reading—this in 186 A.D. Which brings us to Tertullian.

Tertullian

Around the year 208 he urged the heretics to

run over the apostolic churches, in which the very thrones of the apostles are still pre-eminent in their places, in which their own authentic writings (*authenticæ*) are read, uttering the voice and representing the face of each of them severally. Achaia is very near you, (in which) you find Corinth. Since you are not far from Macedonia, you have Philippi; (and there too) you have the Thessalonians. Since you are able to cross to Asia, you get Ephesus. Since, moreover, you are close upon Italy, you have Rome, from which there comes even into our own hands the very authority (of the apostles themselves).[19]

It seems that Tertullian is claiming that Paul's Autographs were still being read in his day (208), but at the very least he must mean they were using faithful copies. Was anything else to be expected? For example, when the Ephesian Christians saw the Autograph of Paul's letter to them getting tatters, would they not carefully execute an identical copy for their continued use? Would they let the Autograph perish without making such a copy? I believe we are obliged to conclude that in the year 200 the Ephesian Church was still in a position to identify the original wording of her letter (and so for the others)—but this is coeval with P[46], P[66] and P[75]!

Both Justin Martyr and Irenaeus claimed that the Church was spread throughout the whole earth, in their day—remember that Irenaeus, in 177, became bishop of Lyons, in *Gaul*, and he was not the first bishop in that area. Coupling this information with Justin's statement that the memoirs of the apostles were read each Sunday in the assemblies, it becomes clear that there must have been hundreds of copies of the New Testament writings in use by 200 A.D. Each assembly would need a copy to read from, and there must have been private copies among those who could afford them. And now we are ready to answer the question, "Was the transmission normal?" and to attempt to trace the history of the text.

Was the Transmission Normal?

Was the transmission normal? Yes and no. Assuming the faithful were persons of at least average integrity and intelligence they would produce reasonable copies of the manuscripts they had received from the previous generation, persons whom they trusted, being assured that they were transmitting the true text. There would be accidental copying mistakes in their work, but no deliberate changes. But there were others who expressed an interest in the New Testament writings, persons lacking in integrity, who made their own copies with malicious intent. There would be accidental mistakes in their work too, but also deliberate alteration of the text. I will trace first the normal transmission.

The normal transmission

We have seen that the faithful recognized the authority of the New Testament writings from the start—had they not they would have been rejecting the authority of the apostles, and hence not been among the faithful. To a basic honesty would be added reverence in their handling of the text, from the start. And to these would be added vigilance, since the apostles had repeatedly and emphatically warned them against false teachers.

But were all the faithful equally situated for transmitting the true text? Evidently not. The possessors of the Autographs would obviously be in the best position. Who were they?

1) The possessors of the Autographs

Speaking in terms of regions, Asia Minor may be safely said to have had twelve (John, Galatians, Ephesians, Colossians, 1 and 2 Timothy, Philemon, 1 Peter, 1 and 2 and 3 John, and Revelation), Greece may be safely said to have had six (1 and 2 Corinthians, Philippians, 1 and 2 Thessalonians, and Titus in Crete), Rome may be safely said to have had two (Mark and Romans)—as to the rest, Luke, Acts, and 2 Peter were probably held by either Asia Minor or Rome; Matthew and James by either Asia Minor or Palestine; Hebrews by Rome or Palestine; while it is hard to state even a probability for Jude it was quite possibly held by Asia Minor. Taking Asia Minor and Greece together, the Aegean area held the Autographs of at least eighteen (two-thirds of total) and possibly as many as twenty-four of the twenty-seven New Testament books; Rome held at least two and possibly up to seven; Palestine may have held up to three; Alexandria (Egypt) held *none*. The Aegean region clearly had the best start, and Alexandria the worst. On the face of it, we may reasonably assume that in the earliest period of the transmission of the N.T. text the most reliable copies of the Autographs would be circulating in the region that held the Autographs.

2) The spread of good copies

The making of copies would have begun at once. The authors clearly intended their writings to be circulated, and the quality of the writings was so obvious that the word would get around and each assembly would want a copy. That Clement and Barnabas quote and allude to a variety of N.T. books by the turn of the century makes clear that copies were in circulation. A Pauline corpus was known to Peter before 70 A.D. Polycarp (XIII), in answer to a request from the Philippian church, sent a collection of Ignatius' letters to them, possibly within five years after Ignatius wrote them. Evidently it was normal procedure to make copies and collections (of worthy writings) so each assembly could have a set. Ignatius referred to the free travel and exchange between the churches and Justin to the weekly practice of reading the Scriptures in the assemblies. Already by the year 100 there must have been many copies of the various books (some more than others) while it was certainly still possible to check a copy against the original, should a question arise.

The point is that there was a swelling stream of faithfully executed copies emanating from the holders of the Autographs to the rest of the Christian world. In those early years the producers of copies would know that the true wording could be verified, which would discourage them from taking liberties with the text. As already indicated in the discussion of Irenaeus and Tertullian above, I see no reason to suppose the situation was much different by the year 200. Ephesus would still have the Autograph of John's Gospel, or an identical copy if the Autograph had perished, and the surrounding regions would be blanketed with faithful copies.[20]

3) The emerging majority text form[21]

With an ever-increasing demand and consequent proliferation of copies throughout the Graeco-Roman world and with the potential for verifying copies by having recourse to the centers still possessing the Autographs, the early textual situation was presumably highly favorable to the wide dissemination of MSS in close agreement with the original text. By the early years of the second century the dissemination of such copies can reasonably be expected to have been very widespread, with the logical consequence that the form of text they embodied would early become entrenched throughout the area of their influence.

The considerations just cited are crucial to an adequate understanding of the history of the transmission of the text because they indicate that a basic trend was established at the very beginning—a trend that would continue inexorably until the advent of a printed N.T. text. I say "inexorably" because, given a normal process of transmission, the science of statistical probability demonstrates that a text form in such circumstances could scarcely be dislodged from its dominant position—the probabilities against a competing text form ever achieving a majority attestation would be prohibitive no matter how many generations of MSS there might be. (The demonstration vindicating my assertion is in Appendix C.) It would take an extraordinary upheaval in the transmissional history to give currency to an aberrant text form. We know of no place in history that will accommodate such an upheaval.

The argument from probability would apply to secular writings as well as the New Testament and does not take into account any unusual concern for purity of text. I have argued, however, that the early Christians did have a special concern for their Scriptures and that this concern accompanied the spread of Christianity. Thus Irenaeus clearly took his concern for textual purity (which extended to a single letter) to Gaul and undoubtedly influenced the Christians in that area. The point is that the text form of the N.T. Autographs had a big advantage over that of any secular literature, so that its commanding position would become even greater than the argument from probability would suggest. The rapid multiplication and spread of good copies would raise to absolutely prohibitive levels the chances against an opportunity for aberrant text forms to gain any kind of widespread acceptance or use.[22]

It follows that within a relatively few years after the writing of the N.T. books there came rapidly into existence a "Majority" text whose form was essentially that of the Autographs themselves. This text form would, in the natural course of things, continue to multiply itself and in each succeeding generation of copying would continue to be exhibited in the mass of extant manuscripts. In short, it would have a "normal" transmission.

So then, I claim that the N.T. text had a normal transmission, namely the fully predictable spread and reproduction of reliable copies of the Autographs from the earliest period down through the history of transmission until the availability of printed texts brought copying by hand to an end.

The abnormal transmission

Turning now to the abnormal transmission, it no doubt commenced right along with the normal. The apostolic writings themselves contain strong complaints and warning against heretical and malicious activity. Large sections of the extant writings of the early Fathers are precisely and exclusively concerned with combating the heretics. It is clear that during the second century, and possibly already in the first, such persons produced many copies of N.T. writings incorporating their alterations.[23] Some apparently were quite widely circulated, for a time. The result was a welter of variant readings, to confuse the uninformed and mislead the unwary.

1) Most damage done by 200 A.D.

It is generally agreed that most significant variants existed by the end of the second century. "The overwhelming majority of readings were created before the year 200," affirms Colwell.[24] "It is no less true to fact than paradoxical in sound that the worst corruptions to which the New Testament has ever been subjected, originated within a hundred years after it was composed," said Scrivener decades before.[25] Kilpatrick comments on the evidence of the earliest Papyri.

> Let us take our two manuscripts of about this date [A.D. 200] which contain parts of John, the Chester Beatty Papyrus and the Bodmer Papyrus. They are together extant for about seventy verses. Over these seventy verses they differ some seventy-three times apart from mistakes.
>
> Further in the Bodmer Papyrus the original scribe has frequently corrected what he first wrote. At some places he is correcting his own mistakes but at others he substitutes one form of phrasing for another. At about seventy-five of these substitutions both alternatives are known from other manuscripts independently. The scribe is in fact replacing one variant reading by another at some seventy places so that we may conclude that already in his day there was variation at these points.[26]

Zuntz also recognized all of this. "Modern criticism stops before the barrier of the second century; the age, so it seems, of unbounded liberties with the text."[27]

Kilpatrick goes on to argue that the creation of new variants ceased by about 200 A.D. because it became impossible to "sell" them. He discusses some of Origen's attempts at introducing a change into the text, and proceeds:

> Origen's treatment of Matt. 19:19 is significant in two other

ways. First he was probably the most influential commentator of the Ancient Church and yet his conjecture at this point seems to have influenced only one manuscript of a local version of the New Testament. The Greek tradition is apparently quite unaffected by it. From the third century onward even an Origen could not effectively alter the text.

This brings us to the second significant point—his date. From the early third century onward the freedom to alter the text which had obtained earlier can no longer be practised. Tatian is the last author to make deliberate changes in the text of whom we have explicit information. Between Tatian and Origen Christian opinion had so changed that it was no longer possible to make changes in the text whether they were harmless or not.[28]

He feels this attitude was a reaction against the rehandling of the text by the second-century heretics. Certainly there had been a great hue and cry, and whatever the reason it does appear that little further damage was done after 200 A.D.

2) The aberrant text forms

The extent of the textual difficulties of the 2nd century can easily be exaggerated. Nevertheless, the evidence cited does prove that aberrant forms of the N.T. text were produced. Naturally, some of those text forms may have acquired a local and temporary currency, but they could scarcely become more than eddies along the edge of the "majority" river. Recall that the possibility of checking against the Autographs must have served to inhibit the spread of such text forms.

For example, Gaius, an orthodox Father who wrote near the end of the second century, named four heretics who not only altered the text but had disciples who multiplied copies of their efforts. Of special interest here is his charge that they could not deny their guilt because they could not produce the originals from which they made their copies.[29] This would be a hollow accusation from Gaius if he could not produce the Originals either. I have already argued that the churches in Asia Minor, for instance, did still have either the Autographs or exact copies that they themselves had made—thus they *knew*, absolutely, what the true wording was and could repel the aberrant forms with confidence. A man like Polycarp would still be able to affirm in 150 A.D., letter by letter if need be, the original wording of the text for most of the New Testament books. And presumably his MSS were not burned when he was.

Not only would there have been pressure from the Autographs, but also the pressure exerted by the already-established momentum of transmission enjoyed by the majority text form. As already discussed, the statistical probabilities militating against any aberrant text forms would be overwhelming. In short, although a bewildering array of variants came into existence, judging from extant witnesses, and they were indeed a perturbing influence in the stream of transmission, they would not succeed in thwarting the progress of the normal transmission.

The Stream of Transmission

Now then, what sort of a picture may we expect to find in the surviving witnesses on the assumption that the history of the transmission of the New Testament Text was normal? We may expect a broad spectrum of copies, showing minor differences due to copying mistakes but all reflecting one common tradition. The simultaneous existence of abnormal transmission in the earliest centuries would result in a sprinkling of copies, helter-skelter, outside of that main stream. The picture would look something like Figure C.

And what do we find upon consulting the witnesses? Just such a picture. We have the Majority Text (Aland), or the Traditional Text (Burgon), dominating the stream of transmission with a few individual witnesses going their idiosyncratic ways. We have already seen that the notion of "text-types" and recensions, as defined and used by Hort and his followers, is gratuitous. Epp's notion of "streams" fares no better. There is just one stream, with a number of small eddies along the edges.[30] When I say the Majority Text dominates the stream, I mean it is represented in from 80 to 90% of the MSS.[31]

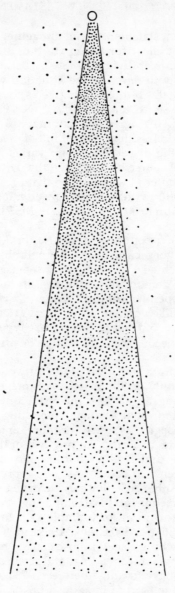

Figure C

Actually, such a statement is not altogether satisfactory because it does not allow for the mixture or shifting affinities encountered within individual MSS. A better, though more cumbersome, way to describe the situation would be something like this: 100% of the MSS agree as to, say, 80% of the Text; 99% agree as to another 10%; over 95% agree as to another 4%; over 90% agree as to another 3%; only for 3% (or less) of the Text do less than 90% of the MSS agree.[32] And the membership of the dissenting group varies from reading to reading. (I will of course be reminded that witnesses are to be weighed, not counted; I will come to that presently, so please bear with me.) Still, with the above reservation, one may reasonably speak of up to 90% of the extant MSS belonging to the Majority text-type.

I see no way of accounting for a 90% (or 80%) domination unless that text goes back to the Autographs. Hort saw the problem and invented a revision. Sturz seems not to have seen the problem. He demonstrates that the "Byzantine text-type" is early and independent of the "Western" and "Alexandrian text-types," and like von Soden, wishes to treat them as three equal witnesses.[33] But if the three "text-types" were equal, how ever could the so-called "Byzantine" gain an 80-90% preponderance?

The argument from statistical probability enters here with a vengeance. Not only do the extant MSS present us with one text form enjoying an 80-90% majority, but the remaining 10-20% do not represent a single competing text form. The minority MSS disagree as much (or more) among themselves as they do with the majority. For any two of them to agree so closely as do P[75] and B is an oddity. We are not judging, therefore, between two text forms, one representing 80% of the MSS and the other 20%. Rather, we have to judge between 80-90% and a fraction of 1% (comparing the Majority Text with the P[75], B text form for example). Or to take a specific case, in 1 Tim. 3:16 over 300 Greek MSS read "God" while only eleven read something else. Of those eleven, two have private readings, two have a third reading, and seven agree in reading "who."[34] So we have to judge between 97% and 2%, "God" versus "who." It is hard to imagine a possible set of circumstances in the transmissional history sufficient to produce the cataclysmic overthrow in statistical probability required by the claim that "who" is the original reading.

It really does seem that those scholars who reject the Majority Text are faced with a serious problem. How is it to be explained if it does not reflect the Original? Hort's notion of a Lucianic revision has now been abandoned by all scholars (as far as I know). The eclecticists are not even trying. The "process" view has not been articulated in sufficient detail to permit refutation, but on the face of it that view is flatly contradicted by the argument from statistical probability.[35] How could any amount of "process" bridge the gap between B or Aleph and the TR?

But there is a more basic problem with the process view. Hort saw clearly, and correctly, that the Majority Text must have a common archetype. Recall that Hort's genealogical method was based on community of *error*. On the hypothesis that the Majority Text is a late and inferior text form, the large mass of common readings which distinguish it from the so-called "Western" or "Alexandrian text-types" must be *errors* (which was precisely Hort's contention) and such an agreement in error would have to have a common source. The process view fails completely to account for such an agreement in error (on that hypothesis).

Hort saw the need for a common source and posited a Lucianic revision. Scholars now generally recognize that the "Byzantine text-type" must date back at least into the second century. But what chance would the original "Byzantine" document, the archetype, have of gaining currency when appeal to the Autographs was still possible?

Candidly, there is only one reasonable explanation for the Majority Text that has so far been advanced—it is the result of an essentially normal process of transmission and the common source for its consensus in the Autographs. Down through the centuries of copying, the original text has always been reflected with a high degree of accuracy in the manuscript tradition as a whole. The history of the text presented in this chapter not only accounts nicely for the Majority Text, it also accounts for the inconsistent minority of MSS. They are remnants of the abnormal transmission of the text, reflecting ancient aberrant forms. It is a dependence upon such aberrant forms that distinguishes contemporary critical editions of the New Testament.

6

SOME POSSIBLE OBJECTIONS

Are Not the Oldest MSS the Best?

Burgon recognized the "antecedent probability" with these words:

> The more ancient testimony is probably the better testimony. That it is not by any means always so is a familiar fact. . . . But it remains true, notwithstanding, that until evidence has been produced to the contrary in any particular instance, the more ancient of two witnesses may reasonably be presumed to be the better informed witness.[1]

This *a priori* expectation seems to have been elevated to a virtual certainty in the minds of many textual critics of the past century. The basic ingredient in the work of men like Tregelles, Tischendorf and Hort was a deference to the oldest MSS, and in this they followed Lachmann.

> The 'best' attestation, so Lachmann maintained, is given by the oldest witnesses. Taking his stand rigorously with the oldest, and disregarding the whole of the recent evidence, he drew the consequences of Bengel's observations. The material which Lachmann used could with advantage have been increased; but the principle that the text of the New

Testament, like that of every other critical edition, must throughout be based upon the best available evidence, was once and for all established by him.[2]

Note that Zuntz here clearly equates "oldest" with "best." He evidently exemplifies what Oliver has called "the growing belief that the oldest manuscripts contain the most nearly original text." Oliver proceeds:

Some recent critics have returned to the earlier pattern of Tischendorf and Westcott and Hort: to seek for the original text in the oldest MSS. Critics earlier in the 20th century were highly critical of this 19th century practice. The return has been motivated largely by the discovery of papyri which are separated from the autographs by less than two centuries.[3]

But, the "contrary evidence" is in hand. We have already seen that most significant variants had come into being by the year 200, before the time of the earliest extant MSS, therefore. The *a priori* presumption in favor of age is nullified by the known existence of a variety of deliberately altered texts in the second century. Each witness must be evaluated on its own. As Colwell has so well put it, "the crucial question for early as for late witnesses is still, 'WHERE DO THEY FIT INTO A PLAUSIBLE RECONSTRUCTION OF THE HISTORY OF THE MANUSCRIPT TRADITION?' "[4]

It is generally agreed that all the earliest MSS, the ones upon which our critical texts are based, come from Egypt.

When the textual critic looks more closely at his oldest manuscript materials, the paucity of his resources is more fully realized. All the earliest witnesses, papyrus or parchment, come from Egypt alone. Manuscripts produced in Egypt, ranging between the third and fifth centuries, provide only a half-dozen extensive witnesses (the Beatty Papyri, and the well-known uncials, Vaticanus, Sinaiticus, Alexandrinus, Ephraem Syrus, and Freer Washington).[5] [To these the Bodmer Papyri must now be added.]

But what are Egypt's claims upon our confidence? And how wise is it to follow the witness of only one locale? Anyone who finds the history of the text presented herein to be convincing will place little confidence in the earliest MSS.

Their quality judged by themselves

Quite apart from the history of the transmission of the text, the earliest MSS bear their own condemnation on their faces. P66 is widely considered to be the earliest extensive manuscript. What of its quality? Again I borrow from Colwell's study of P45, P66, and P75. Speaking of "the seriousness of intention of the scribe and the peculiarities of his own basic method of copying," he continues:

> On these last and most important matters, our three scribes are widely divided. P75 and P45 seriously intend to produce a good copy, but it is hard to believe that this was the intention of P66. The nearly 200 nonsense readings and 400 itacistic spellings in P66 are evidence of something less than disciplined attention to the basic task. To this evidence of carelessness must be added those singular readings whose origin baffles speculation, readings that can be given no more exact label than carelessness leading to assorted variant readings. A hurried count shows P45 with 20, P75 with 57, and P66 with 216 purely careless readings. As we have seen, P66 has, in addition, more than twice as many "leaps" from the same to the same as either of the others.[6]

Colwell's study took into account only singular readings—readings with no other MS support. He found P66 to have 400 itacisms plus 482 other singular readings, 40 percent of which are nonsensical.[7] "P66 editorializes as he does everything else—in a sloppy fashion."[8] In short, P66 is a very poor copy—and yet it is one of the earliest!

P75 is placed close to P66 in date. Though not as bad as P66, it is scarcely a good copy. Colwell found P75 to have about 145 itacisms plus 257 other singular readings, 25 percent of which are nonsensical.[9] Although Colwell gives the scribe of P75 credit for having tried to produce a good copy, P75 looks good only by comparison with P66. (If you were asked to write out the Gospel of John by hand, would you make over 400 mistakes?[10] Try it and see!) It should be kept in mind that the figures offered by Colwell deal only with errors which are the exclusive property of the respective MSS. They doubtless contain many other errors which happen to be found in some other witness(es) as well. In other words, they are actually worse even than Colwell's figures indicate.

P[45], though a little later in date, will be considered next because it is the third member in Colwell's study. He found P[45] to have approximately 90 itacisms plus 275 other singular readings, 10 percent of which are nonsensical.[11] However P[45] is shorter than P[66] (P[75] is longer) and so is not comparatively so much better as the figures might suggest at first glance. Colwell comments upon P[45] as follows:

> Another way of saying this is that when the scribe of P[45] creates a singular reading, it almost always makes sense; when the scribes of P[66] and P[75] create singular readings, they frequently do not make sense and are obvious errors. Thus P[45] must be given credit for a much greater density of intentional changes than the other two.[12]

> As an editor the scribe of P[45] wielded a sharp axe. The most striking aspect of his style is its conciseness. The dispensable word is dispensed with. He omits adverbs, adjectives, nouns, participles, verbs, personal pronouns—without any compensating habit of addition. He frequently omits phrases and clauses. He prefers the simple to the compound word. In short, he favors brevity. He shortens the text in at least fifty places in *singular readings alone*. But he does *not* drop syllables or letters. His shortened text is readable.[13]

Of special significance is the possibility of affirming with certainty that the scribe of P[45] deliberately and extensively shortened the text. Colwell credits him with having tried to produce a good copy. If by "good" he means "readable," fine, but if by "good" we mean a faithful reproduction of the original, then P[45] is bad. Since P[45] contains many *deliberate alterations* it can only be called a "copy" with certain reservations.

P[46] is thought by some to be as early as P[66]. Zuntz's study of this manuscript is well-known.

> In spite of its neat appearance (it was written by a professional scribe and corrected—but very imperfectly—by an expert), P[46] is by no means a good manuscript. The scribe committed very many blunders . . . My impression is that he was liable to fits of exhaustion.[14]

It should be remarked in passing that Codex B is noted for its "neat appearance" also, but it should not be assumed that therefore it must be a good copy.

Zuntz says further: "P[46] abounds with scribal blunders, omissions, and also additions."[15]

> . . . the scribe who wrote the papyrus did his work very badly. Of his innumerable faults, only a fraction (less than one in ten) have been corrected and even that fraction—as often happens in manuscripts—grows smaller and smaller towards the end of the book. Whole pages have been left without any correction, however greatly they were in need of it.[16]

Hoskier, also, has discussed the "large number of omissions" which disfigure P[46].[17]

Again Zuntz says:

> We have observed that, for example, the scribe of P[46] was careless and dull and produced a poor representation of an excellent tradition. Nor can we ascribe the basic excellence of this tradition to the manuscript from which P[46] was copied (we shall see that it, too, was faulty).[18]

It is interesting to note that Zuntz feels able to declare the *parent* of P[46] to be faulty also. But, that P[46] represents an "excellent tradition" is a gratuitous assertion, based on Hort's theory. What is incontrovertible is that P[46] as it stands is a very poor copy—as Zuntz himself has emphatically stated.

Aland says concerning P[47]: "We need not mention the fact

that the oldest manuscript does not necessarily have the best text. P[47] is, for example, by far the oldest of the manuscripts containing the full or almost full text of the Apocalypse, but it is certainly not the best."[19]

Their quality judged between themselves

As to B and Aleph, we have already noted Hoskier's statement that these two MSS disagree over 3,000 times in the space of the four Gospels. Simple arithmetic imposes the conclusion that one or the other must be wrong 3,000 times—that is, they have 3,000 mistakes between them. (If you were to write out the four Gospels by hand do you suppose you could manage to make 3,000 mistakes, or 1,500?) Aleph and B disagree, on the average, in almost every verse of the Gospels. Such a showing seriously undermines their credibility.

Burgon personally collated what in his day were "the five old uncials" (Aleph, A, B, C, D). Throughout his works he repeatedly calls attention to the *concordia discors,* the prevailing confusion and disagreement, which the early uncials display between themselves. Luke 11:2-4 offers one example.

"The five Old Uncials" ($\aleph$ ABCD) falsify the Lord's Prayer as given by St. Luke in no less than forty-five words. But so little do they agree among themselves, that they throw themselves into six different combinations in their departures from the Traditional Text; and yet they are never able to agree among themselves as to one single various reading: while only once are more than two of them observed to stand together, and their grand point of union is no less than an omission of the article. Such is their eccentric tendency, that in respect of thirty-two out of the whole forty-five words they bear in turn solitary evidence.[20]

Mark 2:1-12 offers another example.

In the course of those 12 verses . . . there will be found to be 60 variations of reading. . . . Now, in the present instance, the 'five old uncials' *cannot be* the depositories of a tradition—whether Western or Eastern—because they render inconsistent testimony *in every verse*. It must further be admitted, (for this is really not a question of opinion, but a plain matter of fact,) that it is unreasonable to place confidence in such documents. What would be thought in a Court of Law of five witnesses, called up 47 times for examination, who should be observed to bear contradictory testimony *every time*?[21]

Hort, also, had occasion to notice an instance of this *concordia discors*. Commenting on the four places in Mark's Gospel (14:30, 68, 72a,b) where the cock's crowing is mentioned he said: "The confusion of attestation introduced by these several cross currents of change is so great that of the seven principal MSS ℵ A B C D L Δ no two have the same text in all four places."[22] He might also have said that in these four places the seven uncials present themselves in *twelve* different combinations (and only A and Δ agree together three times out of the four). If we add W and Θ the confusion remains the same except that now there are thirteen combinations. Are such witnesses worthy of credence?

Recalling Colwell's effort to reconstruct an "Alexandrian" archetype for chapter one of Mark, either Codex B is wrong 34 times in that one chapter or else a majority of the remaining primary "Alexandrian" witnesses is wrong, and so for Aleph and L, etc. Further, Kenyon admitted B is "disfigured by many blunders in transcription."[23] Scrivener said of B:

One marked feature, characteristic of this copy, is the great number of its omissions. . . . That no small portion of these are mere oversights of the scribe seems evident from the circumstance that this same scribe has repeatedly written words and clauses *twice over*, a class of mistakes which Mai and the collators have seldom thought fit to notice, . . . but which by no means enhances our estimate of the care employed in copying this venerable record of primitive Christianity.[24]

Even Hort conceded that the scribe of B "reached by no

means a high standard of accuracy."[25] Aleph is acknowledged on every side to be worse than B in every way.

Codex D is in a class by itself. Said Scrivener:

> The internal character of the Codex Bezae is a most difficult and indeed an almost inexhaustible theme. No known manuscript contains so many bold and extensive interpolations (six hundred, it is said, in the Acts alone). . . . Mr. Harris from curious internal evidence, such as the existence in the text of a vitiated rendering of a verse of Homer which bears signs of having been retranslated from a Latin translation, infers that the Greek has been made up from the Latin.[26]

Hort spoke of "the prodigious amount of error which D contains."[27] Burgon concluded that D resembles a Targum more than a transcription.[28]

Conclusion

If these are our best MSS we may as well agree with those who insist the recovery of the original wording is impossible, and turn our minds to other pursuits. But the evidence indicates that the earliest MSS are the worst. It is clear that the Church in general did not propagate the sort of text found in the earliest MSS, which demonstrates that they were not held in high esteem in their day.

Zuntz says of the scribe of P[46]:

> Of his innumerable faults, only a fraction (less than one in ten) have been corrected and even that fraction—as often happens in manuscripts—grows smaller and smaller towards the end of the book. Whole pages have been left without any correction, however greatly they were in need of it.[29]

A similar thing happens in P[66]. Why? Probably because the corrector lost heart, gave up. Perhaps he saw the transcription was so hopelessly bad that no one would want to use it, even if he could patch it up. It should also be noted that although many collations and discussions of MSS ignore errors of spelling, to a person in the year 250 wishing to *use* a copy, for devotional study or whatever, errors in spelling would be just as annoying and distracting as more serious ones. A copy like P[66], with roughly two mistakes per verse, would be set aside in disgust.

Further, how could the early MSS survive for 1,500 years if they had been used? (I have worn out several Bibles in my short life.) Considering the relative difficulty of acquiring copies in those days (expensive, done by hand) any worthy copy would have been used until it wore out. Which brings us to the next possible objection.

Why Are There No Early "Byzantine" MSS?

Why would or should there be? To demand that a MS survive for 1,500 years is in effect to require both that it have remained unused and that it have been stored in Egypt (or Qumran). Even an unused MS would require an arid climate to last so long.

But is either requirement reasonable? Unless there were persons so rich as to be able to proliferate copies of the Scriptures for their health or amusement, copies would be made on demand, in order to be *used.* As the use of Greek died out in Egypt the demand for Greek Scriptures would die out too, so we should not expect to find many Greek MSS in Egypt.

It should not be assumed, however, that the "Byzantine" text was not used in Egypt. Although none of the early Papyri can reasonably be called "Byzantine," they each contain "Byzantine" readings. Further, Codices A and W, both of the fifth century, are partly "Byzantine."

The study and conclusions of Lake, Blake, and New, already discussed in a prior section, are of special interest here. They looked for evidence of direct genealogy and found virtually none. I repeat their conclusion.

> . . . the manuscripts which we have are almost all orphan children without brothers or sisters.
>
> Taking this fact into consideration along with the negative result of our collation of MSS at Sinai, Patmos, and Jerusalem, it is hard to resist the conclusion that the scribes usually destroyed their exemplars when they had copied the sacred books.[30]

Is it unreasonable to suppose that once an old MS became tattered and almost illegible in spots the faithful would make an exact copy of it and then destroy it, rather than allowing it to suffer the indignity of literally rotting away? What would such a practice do to our chances of finding an early "Byzantine" MS? Anyone who objects to this conclusion must still account for the fact that in three ancient monastic libraries, equipped with scriptoria (rooms designed to facilitate the faithful copying of MSS), there are only "orphan children." Why are there no parents?!

Van Bruggen addresses the problem from a slightly different direction. He says of the "Byzantine" text:

> The fact that this text-form is known to us via later manuscripts is as such no proof for a late text-type, but it does seem to become a proof when at the same time a different text is found in all older manuscripts. The combination of these two things seems to offer decisive proof for the late origin of the traditional text.[31]

He answers the "seeming proof" in the following way:

> Let us make ourselves aware of *what* we have presupposed with this seemingly convincing argumentation. What conditions must be satisfied if we wish to award the prize to the older majuscules? While asking this question we assumed wittingly or unwittingly that we were capable of making a fair comparison between manuscripts in an earlier period and those in a later period. After all, we can only arrive at positive statements if that is the case. Imagine that someone said: in the Middle Ages mainly cathedrals were built, but in modern times many small and plainer churches are being built. This statement seems completely true when we today look around in the cities and villages. Yet we are mistaken. An understandable mistake: many small churches of the Middle Ages have disappeared, and usually only the cathedrals were restored. Thus, a great historical falsification of perspective with regard to the history of church-building arises. We are not able to make a general assertion about church-building in the Middle Ages on the basis of the sur-

viving materials. If we would still dare to make such an assertion, then we wrongly assumed that the surviving materials enabled us to make a fair comparison. But how is the situation in the field of New Testament manuscripts? Do we have a *representative* number of manuscripts from the first centuries? Only if that is the case, do we have the right to make conclusions and positive statements. Yet it is just at this point that difficulties arise. The situation is even such that we know with certainty that we *do not* possess a representative number of manuscripts from the first centuries.[32]

The conclusion of Lake, Blake, and New reflects another consideration. The age of a manuscript must not be confused with the age of the text it exhibits. Any copy, by definition, contains a text that is older than it is. In Burgon's words, it "represents a MS, or a pedigree of MSS, older than itself; and it is but fair to suppose that it exercises such representation with tolerable accuracy."[33]

Further, a late MS may more faithfully reflect the common ancestor than its earlier cousin, as illustrated by Codices II and A; II is from the ninth century, A from the fifth. Silva Lake did a study of these, and related MSS, and concluded that they had a common ancestor, perhaps in the fourth century, and that the text of II was closer to the ancestor's than was the text of A.[34] In effect, therefore, II contains a fourth century text, even though the parchment is ninth century, and it might fairly be declared to be an "early Byzantine MS."

Van Bruggen discusses yet another relevant consideration.

In the codicology the great value of the transliteration-process in the 9th century and thereafter is recognized. At that time the most important New Testament manuscripts written in majuscule script were carefully transcribed into minuscule script. It is assumed that after this transliteration-process the majuscule was taken out of circulation. . . . The import of this datum has not been taken into account enough in the present New Testament textual criticism. For it implies, that just the oldest, best and most customary manuscripts come to us in the new uniform of the minuscule script, does it not? This is even more cogent, since it appears that various archetypes can be detected in this transliteration-process for the New Testament. Therefore we do not receive one mother-manuscript through the flood-gates of the transliteration, but several. The originals have, however, disappeared! This throws a totally different light on the situation that we are confronted with regarding the manuscripts. Why do the surviving ancient manuscripts show another text-type? Because they are the only survivors of their generation, and because their survival is due to the fact that they were of a different kind. Even though one continues to maintain that the copyists at the time of the transliteration handed down the wrong text-type to the Middle Ages, one can still never prove this codicologically with the remark that older majuscules have a different text. This would be circular reasoning. There certainly were majuscules just as venerable and ancient as the surviving Vaticanus or Sinaiticus, which, like a section of the Alexandrinus, presented a Byzantine text. But they have been renewed into minuscule script and their majuscule-appearance has vanished. Historically it *seems* as though the most ancient majuscule manuscripts exclusively contain a non-Byzantine text, but the prespective [sic] is falsified here just like it is regarding church-building in the Middle Ages and at present.[35]

There is yet another relevant consideration.

It is historically certain that the text of the New Testament endured a very hard time in the first centuries. Many good and official editions of the text were confiscated and destroyed by the authorities during the time of the persecutions.[36]

Roberts refers to "the regular requisition and destruction of books by the authorities at times of persecution, so often recorded in the martyr acts."[37] Such official activity seems to have come to a climax in Diocletian's campaign to destroy the New Testament manuscripts around A.D. 300.

If there was any trauma in the history of the normal transmission of the text, this was it; the more so since the campaign evidently centered upon the Aegean area. Many MSS were found, or betrayed, and burned, but others must have escaped. That many Christians would have spared no effort to hide and preserve their copies of the Scriptures is demonstrated by their attitude towards those who gave up their MSS—the Donatist schism that immediately followed Diocletian's campaign partly hinged on the question of punishment for those who had given up MSS. The Christians whose entire devotion to the Scriptures was thus demonstrated would also be just the ones that would be the most careful about the pedigree of their own MSS; just as they took pains to protect their MSS they presumably would have taken pains to ensure that their MSS preserved the true wording.

In fact, the campaign of Diocletian may even have had a purifying effect upon the transmission of the text. If the laxity of attitude toward the text reflected in the willingness of some to give up their MSS also extended to the quality of text they were prepared to use, then it may have been the more contaminated MSS that were destroyed, in the main, leaving the purer MSS to replenish the earth.[38] But these surviving pure MSS would have been in unusually heavy demand for copying (to replace those that had been destroyed) and been worn out faster than normal.

In short, if the history of transmission presented herein is valid we should not necessarily expect to find any early "Byzantine" MSS. They would have been used and worn out. (But the text they contained would be preserved by their descendants.) An analogy is furnished by the fate of the *Biblia Pauperum* in the fifteenth century.

Of all the *Xylographic* works, that is, such as are printed from wooden blocks, the BIBLIA PAUPERUM is perhaps the rarest, as well as the most ancient; it is a manual, or kind of catechism of the Bible, for the use of young persons, and of the common people, whence it derives its name,—*Biblia Pauperum,—the Bible of the Poor;* who were thus enabled to acquire, at a comparatively low price, an imperfect knowledge of some of the events recorded in the Scriptures. Being much in use, the few copies of it which are at present to be found in the libraries of the curious are for the most part either mutilated or in bad condition. The extreme rarity of this book, and the circumstances under which it was produced, concur to impart a high degree of interest to it.[39]

Although it went through five editions, presumably totalling thousands of copies, it was so popular that the copies were worn out by use.

Adding to all this the discussion of the quality of the earliest MSS, in the prior section, early age in a MS might well arouse our suspicions—why did it survive? And that brings us to a third possible objection.

Should Not Witnesses Be Weighed, Rather Than Counted?

The form of the question, which reflects that of the assertion usually made, is tendentious. It infers that weighing and counting are mutually exclusive. But why? In any investigation, legal or otherwise, witnesses should be *both* weighed and counted. First they should be weighed, to be sure, but then they must be counted—or else why bother weighing them, or why bother with witnesses at all? I will discuss the two activities in order, beginning with the weighing.

Weighing first

Just how are MSS to be weighed? And who might be competent to do the weighing? As the reader is by now well aware, Hort and most subsequent scholars have done their "weighing" on the basis of so-called "internal evidence"—the two standard criteria are, "choose the reading which fits the context" and "choose the reading which explains the origin of the other reading."

One problem with this has been well stated by Colwell. "As a matter of fact these two standard criteria for the appraisal of the internal evidence of readings can easily cancel each other out and leave the scholar free to choose in terms of his own prejudgments."[40] Further, "the more lore the scholar knows, the easier it is for him to produce a reasonable defense of both readings. . . ."[41]

The whole process is so subjective that it makes a mockery of the word "weigh." The basic meaning of the term involves an evaluation made by an objective instrument. If we wish our weighing of MSS to have objective validity we must find an objective procedure.

How do we evaluate the credibility of a witness in real life? We watch how he acts, listen to what he says and how he says it, and listen to the opinion of his neighbors and associates. If we can demonstrate that a witness is a habitual liar or that his critical faculties are impaired then we receive his testimony with scepticism. It is quite possible to evaluate MSS in a similar way, to a considerable extent, and it is hard to understand why scholars have generally neglected to do so.

Please refer back to the evidence given in the discussion of the oldest MSS. Can we objectively "weigh" P[66] as a witness? Well, in the space of John's Gospel it has over 900 clear, indubitable errors—as a witness to the identity of the text of John it has misled us over 900 times. Is P[66] a credible witness? I would argue that neither of the scribes of P[66] and P[75] knew Greek; should we not say that as witnesses they were impaired?[42]

Recall from Colwell's study that the scribe of P[45] evidently made numerous *deliberate* changes in the text—should we not say that he was morally impaired? In any case, he has repeatedly misinformed us. Shall we still trust him?

Similarly, it has been shown by simple arithmetic that Aleph and B have over 3,000 mistakes between them, just in the Gospels. Aleph is clearly worse than B, but probably not twice as bad—at least 1,000 of those mistakes are B's. Do Aleph and B fit your notion of a good witness?

Even when it is not possible to affirm objectively that a particular witness is misinformed, his credibility suffers if he keeps dubious company. Several references have already been given to the phenomenon Burgon called *concordia discors*. I will add one more. Burgon invites us to turn to Luke 8:35-44 and collate the five old uncials Aleph, A, B, C, D throughout these verses. Comparing them to each other against the background of the majority of MSS—A stands alone 2 times; B, 6 times; Aleph, 8 times; C, 15 times; D, 93 times—A and B stand together by themselves once; B and Aleph, 4 times; B and C, once; B and D, once; Aleph and C, once; C and D, once—A, Aleph and C conspire once; B, Aleph and C, once; B, Aleph and D, once; A, B, Aleph and C, once; B, Aleph, C and D, once. Not once do all five agree against the majority. As Burgon observed, they "combine, and again stand apart, with singular impartiality," which led him to conclude:

> Will any one, after a candid survey of the premises, deem us unreasonable, if we avow that such a specimen of the *concordia discors* which everywhere prevails between the oldest uncials, but which especially characterizes ℵ B D, indisposes us greatly to suffer their unsupported authority to determine for us the Text of Scripture?[43]

Must we not agree with him?

We need also to check out the opinion of a witness' contemporaries. Do they testify to his good character, or are there reservations? To judge by the circumstance that Codices like Aleph and B were not copied, to speak of, that the Church by and large rejected their form of the text, it seems they were not respected in their day. What objective evidence do we have to lead us to reverse the judgment of their contemporaries?

Scholars like Zuntz will protest that a MS may represent an excellent tradition in spite of the poor job done by the scribe.[44] Perhaps so, but how can we know? I see only two ways of reaching the conclusion that a certain tradition is excellent— either through the testimony of witnesses that commend themselves as dependable, or through the preference and imagination of the critic. In neither case does the conclusion depend upon the poor copy itself—in the one case it rests upon the authority of independent, dependable witnesses, and in the other it rests upon the authority of the critic. The poor copy itself has no claims on our confidence.

Counting next

Having weighed the witnesses, we must then count them. In the counting, preference must be given to those copies that are not demonstrably poor, or bad. Just as before the law a person is considered innocent until proven guilty, so a witness must be assumed to be truthful until it can be proved a liar. But before counting, we must try to determine if there has been any collusion among the witnesses. Any that appear to be mutually dependent should be lumped together. Then, each witness that appears to be both independent and trustworthy must be allowed to vote; such witnesses must indeed be counted. If several hundred such witnesses agree against three or four inveterate prevaricators, can there be any reasonable doubt as to the identity of the true reading? I will return to this matter in the following chapter.

Should anyone still care to raise the objection that "Byzantine readings repeatedly prove to be inferior," I reply: "Prove it!" Since all such characterizations have been based upon the demonstrably fallacious canons of "internal evidence" they have no validity. I consider the allegation to be vacuous.

I have demonstrated that the W-H critical theory and history of the text are erroneous. I have outlined the history of the transmission of the text which I believe best accords with the available evidence. It remains to give a coherent statement of the procedure by which we may assure ourselves of the precise identity of the original wording of the New Testament text.

7

DETERMINING THE IDENTITY
OF THE TEXT

By way of a framework for the following discussion I shall use Burgon's seven "Notes of Truth." They are:
1. Antiquity, or Primitiveness;
2. Consent of Witnesses, or Number;
3. Variety of Evidence, or Catholicity;
4. Respectability of Witnesses, or Weight;
5. Continuity, or Unbroken Tradition;
6. Evidence of the Entire Passage, or Context;
7. Internal Considerations, or Reasonableness.[1]

Antiquity, or Primitiveness

A reading, to be a serious candidate for the original, should be old. If there is no attestation for a variant before the middle ages it is unlikely to be genuine. A word of caution is required here, however. Not only may age be demonstrated by a single early witness, but also by the agreement of a number of later independent witnesses—their common source would have to be a good deal older. Sturz has a good discussion of this point.[2] But any reading that has wide late attestation almost always has explicit early attestation as well.

To give a concrete definition to the idea of "antiquity" I will take the year 400 A.D. as an arbitrary cut-off point. Allowing only those witnesses who "spoke" before that date, "antiquity" would include over seventy Fathers, Codices Aleph and B and a number of fragmentary uncials, the early Papyri and the earliest Versions. By way of specific illustration, ever since 1881 the word "vinegar" in Matt. 27:34 has been despised as a "late, Byzantine" reading—but what is the verdict of "antiquity?" Against it are Codices Aleph and B, the Latin and Coptic versions, the Apocryphal Acts of the Apostles, the Gospel of Nicodemus, and Macarius Magnes—seven witnesses. In favor of it are the Gospel of Peter, *Acta Philippi*, Barnabas, Irenaeus, Tertullian, Celsus, Origen, pseudo-Tatian, Athanasius, Eusebius of Emesa, Theodore of Heraclea, Didymus, Gregory of Nyssa, Gregory of Nazianzus, Ephraem Syrus, Lactantius, Titus of Bostra and the Syriac version—eighteen witnesses.[3] The witnesses for "vinegar" are both older and more numerous than those for "wine."

Of course, age by itself is not enough. We have seen that most significant variants date to the second century. What we are after is the *oldest* reading, the original, and to judge between competing old readings we need other considerations.

Consent of Witnesses, or Number

A reading, to be a serious candidate for the original, should be attested by a majority of the *independent* witnesses. Please recall the discussion of weighing and counting given above. A reading attested by only a few witnesses is unlikely to be genuine—the fewer the witnesses the smaller the likelihood. Conversely, the greater the majority the more nearly certain is the originality of the reading so attested. Wherever the text has unanimous attestation the only reasonable conclusion is that it is certainly original.[4]

Even Hort acknowledged the presumption inherent in superior number. "A theoretical presumption indeed remains that a majority of extant documents is more likely to represent a majority of ancestral documents at each stage of transmission than *vice versa.*"[5] The work of those who have done extensive collating of MSS has tended to confirm this presumption. Thus Lake, Blake, and New found only orphan children among the MSS they collated, and declared further that there were almost no siblings—each MS is an "only child."[6] This means they are *independent witnesses*, at least in their own generation. In Burgon's words:

> . . . hardly any have been copied from any of the rest. On the contrary, they are discovered to differ among themselves in countless unimportant particulars; and every here and there single copies exhibit idiosyncrasies which are altogether startling and extraordinary. There has therefore demonstrably been no collusion—no assimilation to an arbitrary standard,—no wholesale fraud. It is certain that every one of them represents a MS., or a pedigree of MSS., older than itself; and it is but fair to suppose that it exercises such representation with tolerable accuracy.[7]

In accordance with good legal practice, it is unfair to arbitrarily declare that the ancestors were *not* independent; some sort of evidence must be produced. It has already been shown that Hort's "genealogical evidence," with reference to MSS, is fictitious. But it remains true that community of reading implies a common origin, unless it is the type of mistake that several scribes might have made independently. What is in view here is the common origin of individual readings, not of MSS, but where several MSS share a large number of readings peculiar to themselves their claim to independence is evidently compromised throughout. (The "Claremont Profile Method"[8] gives promise of being an effective instrument for plotting the relationship between MSS.)

However, there is one situation where community of reading does not compromise independence. If the common origin of a reading is the original, then the MSS that have it may not be disqualified; their claim to independence remains unsullied. Of course, we do not know, at this stage in the inquiry, which is the original reading, but some negative help is immediately available. If one or more of the competing variants is an obvious mistake, then those MSS which attest such variants are disqualified, at that one point (recall that genealogy was supposed to be based upon community in *error*).

For the rest, the history of transmission becomes an important factor, but to trace it with confidence we must take account of at least two further considerations. In the meantime, the independent status of MSS agreeing in readings that could be original must be held in abeyance—there is not sufficient evidence to disqualify them, yet.

Variety of Evidence, or Catholicity

A reading, to be a serious candidate for the original, should be attested by a wide variety of witnesses. By variety is meant, in the first place, many geographical areas, but also different kinds of witnesses—MSS, Fathers, Versions, and Lectionaries. The importance of "variety" is well stated by Burgon.

Variety distinguishing witnesses massed together must needs constitute a most powerful argument for believing such Evidence to be true. Witnesses of different kinds; from different countries; speaking different tongues:—witnesses who can never have met, and between whom it is incredible that there should exist collusion of any kind:—such witnesses deserve to be listened to most respectfully. Indeed, when witnesses of so varied a sort agree in large numbers, they must needs be accounted worthy of even implicit confidence. . . . Variety it is which imparts virtue to mere Number, prevents the witness-box from being filled with packed deponents, ensures genuine testimony. False witness is thus detected and condemned, because it agrees not with the rest. Variety is the consent of independent witnesses, . . .

It is precisely this consideration which constrains us to pay supreme attention to the combined testimony of the Uncials and of the whole body of the Cursive Copies. They are (a) doted over at least 1000 years: (b) they evidently belong to so many divers countries,—Greece, Constantinople, Asia Minor, Palestine, Syria, Alexandria, and other parts of Africa, not to say Sicily, Southern Italy, Gaul, England, and Ireland: (c) they exhibit so many strange characteristics and peculiar sympathies: (d) they so clearly represent countless families of MSS., being in no single instance absolutely identical in their text, and certainly not being copies of any other Codex in existence,—that their unanimous decision I hold to be an absolutely irrefragable evidence of the Truth.[9]

Variety helps us evaluate the independence of witnesses. If the witnesses which share a common reading come from only one area, say Egypt, then their independence must be doubted. It seems quite unreasonable to suppose that an original reading should survive in only one limited locale. If the history of the transmission of the text was largely normal, as I believe it was, then we must conclude that a reading found only in one limited area cannot be original. It follows that witnesses supporting such readings are disqualified, just like those supporting obvious mistakes—they are not independent, at that point. They are disqualified as independent witnesses, but their combined testimony still counts as one vote; their common ancestor is still an independent witness.

As Burgon points out, it is variety that lends validity to number, because variety implies independence. Conversely, lack of variety implies dependence, which is why a reading that lacks variety of attestation has little claim upon our confidence. It is an eloquent testimony to the soporific effects of the W-H theory (with its "genealogy") that subsequent scholarship has largely ignored the factor of variety in attestation. There has been an occasional murmur of disquiet,[10] but nothing approaching a recognition of the true place that "variety" should have in the practice of New Testament textual cricitism. Burgon stated the obvious when he said:

> Speaking generally, the consentient testimony of two, four, six, or more witnesses, coming to us from widely sundered regions is weightier by far than the same number of witnesses proceeding from one and the same locality, between whom there probably exists some sort of sympathy, and possibly some degree of collusion.[11]

Closely allied to variety is the factor of continuity.

Continuity, or Unbroken Tradition

A reading, to be a serious candidate for the original, should be attested throughout the ages of transmission, from beginning to end. If the history of the transmission of the text was at all normal, we would expect the original wording "to leave traces of its existence and of its use all down the ages."[12] If a reading or tradition died out in the fourth or fifth century we have the verdict of history against it. If a reading has no attestation before the twelfth century, it is certainly a late invention.[13]

Where there is variety there is almost always continuity as well, but they are not identical considerations. Continuity also helps us in evaluating the independence of witnesses. Readings which form little eddies in the late "Byzantine" stream convict their supporters of dependence at those points. Readings which enjoy both a wide variety and continuity of attestation vindicate the independence of their supporters. Apart from some objective demonstration to the contrary (such as Hort claimed for "genealogy") it is not fair to reject the independence of such witnesses. They must be allowed to vote. The punch line is this: The majority of the extant MSS emerge as independent witnesses, and they must be counted!

Hort, followed by Zuntz and others,[14] rejected this consideration absolutely. But the reader is now in some position to judge for himself. Since there was no authoritative revision of the text in 300 A.D., or any other time, and since the evidence indicates a reasonably normal history of transmission, how can the validity of "continuity" as a "note of truth" be reasonably denied? In my view, the factors of number, variety, and continuity form the backbone of a sound methodology in textual criticism. They form a three-strand rope, not easily broken. But there are several other considerations which are helpful, on occasion and in their way.

Respectability of Witnesses, or Weight

Whereas the previous four "notes" have centered on readings, this one centers on the witnesses. Whereas the "notes" of number, variety, and continuity help us to evaluate the independence of witnesses, this one is concerned with the credibility of a witness judged by its own performance.

> As to the Weight which belongs to separate Copies, that must be determined mainly by watching their evidence. If they go wrong continually, their character must be low. They are governed in this respect by the rules which hold good in life.[15]

The evidence offered above in the discussion of the oldest MSS and of weighing versus counting must suffice to illustrate both the importance and the applicability of this "note." The oldest MSS can be objectively, statistically shown to be habitually wrong, witnesses of very low character, therefore. Their respectability quotient hovers near zero. Their great age only renders their behavior the more reprehensible. (I am reminded of young King Henry's rebuke to Falstaff.[16]) In particular, I fail to see how anyone can read Hoskier's *Codex B and its Allies* with attention and still retain respect for B and Aleph as witnesses to the New Testament text—they have been weighed and found wanting.

Since the modern critical and eclectic texts are based precisely on B and Aleph and the other early MSS, blind guides all, it is clear that modern scholars have severely ignored the consideration of respectability, as an objective criterion. I submit that this "note of truth" must be taken seriously; the result will be the complete overthrow of the type of text currently in vogue.

Evidence of the Entire Passage, or Context

The "context" spoken of here is not what is usually understood by the word but is concerned with the behavior of a given witness in the immediate vicinity of the problem being considered. It is a specific and limited application of the previous "note."

> As regards the precise form of language employed, it will be found also a salutary safeguard against error in every

instance, to inspect with severe critical exactness the entire context of the passage in dispute. If in certain Codexes that context shall prove to be confessedly in a very corrupt state, then it becomes even self-evident that those Codexes can only be admitted as witnesses with considerable suspicion and reserve.[17]

An excellent illustration of the need for this criterion is furnished by Codex D in the last three chapters of Luke—the scene of Hort's famous "Western non-interpolations." After discussing sixteen cases of omission (where W-H deleted material from the TR) in these chapters, Burgon continues:

The *sole* authority for just half of the places above enumerated [Luke 22:19-20; 24:3, 6, 9, 12, 36, 40, 52] is *a single Greek codex*,—and that, the most depraved of all,—viz. Beza's D. It should further be stated that the only allies discoverable for D are a few copies of the old Latin. . . . When we reach down codex D from the shelf, we are reminded that, within the space of the three chapters of S. Luke's Gospel now under consideration, there are in all no less than 354 words omitted: *of which*, 250 *are omitted by* D *alone*. May we have it explained to us why, of those 354 words, only 25 are singled out by Drs. Westcott and Hort for permanent excision from the sacred Text? Within the same compass, no less than 173 words have been *added* by D to the commonly Received Text,—146, *substituted*,—243 *transposed*. May we ask how it comes to pass that of those 562 words *not one* has been promoted to their margin by the Revisionists?[18]

The focus here is upon Westcott and Hort. According to *their own judgment*, codex D has omitted 329 words from the genuine text of the last three chapters of Luke plus adding 173, substituting 146 and transposing 243. By their own admission the text of D here is in a fantastically chaotic state, yet in eight places they omitted material from the text on the *sole authority* of D! With the scribe on a wild omitting spree, to say nothing of his other iniquities, how can *any* value be given to the testimony of D in these chapters, much less prefer it above the united voice of every other witness?!?!

This Note of Truth has for its foundation the well-known law that mistakes have a tendency to repeat themselves in the same or in other shapes. The carelessness, or the vitiated atmosphere, that leads a copyist to misrepresent one word is sure to lead him into error about another. The ill-ordered assiduity which prompted one bad correction most probably did not rest there. And the errors committed by a witness just before or just after the testimony which is being sifted was given cannot but be held to be closely germane to the inquiry.[19]

Apart from the patent reasonableness of Burgon's assertion, the studies of Colwell in P[45], P[66], and P[75] have demonstrated it to be true. We have already seen how Colwell was able, on the basis of the pattern of their mistakes, to give a clear and different characterization to each of the three copyists.[20] Here again, this "note of truth" seems to be completely ignored by current scholars. Why? Is its validity not obvious?

Internal Considerations, or Reasonableness

This "note" has nothing to do with the "internal evidence" of which we have heard so much. It is only rarely applicable and concerns readings which are grammatically, logically, geographically, or scientifically impossible, such as in Luke 19:37, 23:45, 24:13, Mark 6:22 or 2 Cor. 3:3.

Conclusion

So then, how are we to identify the original wording? First we must gather the available evidence—this will include Greek MSS (including Lectionaries), Fathers, and Versions. Then we must evaluate the evidence to ascertain which form of the text enjoys the earliest, the fullest, the widest, the most respectable, the most varied attestation.[21] It must be emphasized that the strength of the "notes of truth" lies in their cooperation. They must all be considered and taken together because the very fact of competing variants means that some of the notes, at least, cannot be satisfied in full measure. But by applying all of them we will be able to form an intelligent judgment as to the independence and credibility of the several witnesses. The independent, credible witnesses must then be polled. I submit that due process requires us to receive as original that form of the text which is supported by the majority of those witnesses; to reject their testimony in favor of our own imagination as to what the reading ought to be is manifestly untenable.

8

CONCLUSION

As the reader now can see, the words from the preface of the RSV given on page 17 are highly misleading. The real potential which exists for improving upon the King James Version, and the *Textus Receptus,* has not been realized. The distressing realization is forced upon us that the "progress" of the past hundred years has been precisely in the wrong direction—our modern versions and critical texts are several times farther removed from the original than are the AV and TR![1] How could such a calamity have come upon us?![2]

Nor is that the full tale of our woe. Such has been the soporific effect of the W-H theory that the available evidence has not been evaluated, has not been assimilated. In Aland's words,

. . . the main problem of NT textual criticism lies in the fact that little more than their actual existence is known of most of the manuscripts so far identified, and that therefore we constantly have problems with many unknowns to solve. We proceed as if the few manuscripts, which have been fully, or almost fully, studied, contained all the problems in question. . . .[3]

Further, much of the work that *has* been done is flawed. Thus, in his status report on The International Greek New Testament Project given to the Society of Biblical Literature on December 29, 1967, Colwell stated:

The preparation of a comprehensive textual apparatus has required attention to previous editions of the Greek NT, viz., Tischendorf, Tregelles, von Soden, Legg. Careful study showed that the textual evidence in these editions cannot be used in the IGNT apparatus, since they fail to cite witnesses completely, consistently, and in some cases accurately.[4]

This means that not only are we presently unable to specify the precise wording of the original text, but it will require considerable time and effort before we can be in a position to do so. And the longer it takes us to mobilize and coordinate our efforts the longer it will be.[5]

The picture is not so dark as it might be, however. The Institut für neutestamentliche Textforschung in Münster, Germany has a collection of microfilms of some 4,500 of the extant Greek MSS (around 80 percent of them)[6] and scholars connected with the Institut are collating selected ones. Scholars connected with The International Greek New Testament Project are also doing some collating.

But it is the availability of sophisticated computers and programs that seems to me to hold the key. It is now feasible to collate the MSS in Münster and set up a computer program such that we can find out anything we want to know about the inter-relationships of the MSS. In this way it should be possible to identify and trace the pure stream of transmission of the text and to declare with confidence, based on objective criteria, the precise wording of the original text! It will take dedicated, competent men as well as money—plenty of both—but will it not be worth it? May God burden His servants!

In terms of closeness to the original, the King James Version and the *Textus Receptus* have been the best available up to now. Thomas Nelson Publishers is sponsoring a forthcoming critical edition of the Traditional Text (Majority, "Byzantine") under the editorship of Zane Hodges, Arthur Farstad, and others which while not definitive will prove to be very close to the final product, I believe. In it we have an excellent interim Greek Text to use until the full and final story can be told.[7] Although we might want to wait for the definitive text before proceeding to an authoritative revision of the AV, a careful job based on the interim Text would be an improvement over both the AV and all the modern versions.

In conclusion, I would like to borrow the words found at the close of one of Burgon's works.

And so I venture to hold, now that the question has been raised, both the learned and the well-informed will come gradually to see, that no other course respecting the Words of the New Testament is so strongly justified by the evidence, none so sound and large-minded, none so reasonable in every way, none so consonant with intelligent faith, none so productive of guidance and comfort and hope, as to maintain against all the assaults of corruption

THE TRADITIONAL TEXT.[8]

Appendix A

Inspiration and Preservation

I have deliberately avoided introducing any arguments based upon these doctrines in the preceding discussion in the hope that I will not be misrepresented by critics in the way that Burgon has been.[1] My procedure has been dictated by considerations of strategy based on a study of the history of the debate over the issue of the identity of the text. Please do not conclude that I lack conviction in these matters. I believe in the verbal plenary inspiration of the Autographs. I believe that God has providentially preserved the original wording of the text down to our day, and that it is possible for us to know precisely what it is (though due to our carelessness and laziness we do not, at this moment).

Although I believe passages such as Isa. 40:8, Matt. 5:18, Luke 16:17 and 21:33, John 10:35 and 16:12-13, and Luke 4:4 can reasonably be taken to imply a promise that the Scriptures (to the tittle) will be preserved for man's use (we are to live "by *every* word of God"), no intimation is given as to just how God proposes to do it.

My beliefs become presuppositions which I bring to my study of the evidence—any thoughtful person will realize that it is impossible to work without presuppositions—but a serious effort should be made to let the evidence tell its own story. It is not legitimate to declare *a priori* what the situation must be, on the basis of one's presuppositions. One's presuppositions do inescapably figure in his interpretation, so that different sets of presuppositions may result in differing conclusions, but the body of evidence should be the same for everybody. In the end, the reasonableness of the presuppositions themselves should be measured by the evidence.

So, how does my belief that God has preserved the N.T. text square with the evidence? I see in the Traditional Text ("Byzantine") both the result and the proof of that preservation. Please note that I am not imposing my presuppositions on the evidence—the Traditional Text does exist and so far as I can see represents the normal transmission of the original. I like Burgon's statement.

> There exists no reason for supposing that the Divine Agent, who in the first instance thus gave to mankind the Scriptures of Truth, straightway abdicated His office; took no further care of His work; abandoned those precious writings to their fate. That a perpetual miracle was wrought for their preservation—that copyists were protected against the risk of error, or evil men prevented from adulterating shamefully copies of the Deposit—no one, it is presumed, is so weak as to suppose. But it is quite a different thing to claim that all down the ages the sacred writings must needs have been God's peculiar care; that the Church under Him has watched over them with intelligence and skill; has recognized which copies exhibit a fabricated, which an honestly transcribed text; has generally sanctioned the one, and generally disallowed the other.[2]

We are still left with the necessity of carefully evaluating the evidence that has come down to us so as to be able to identify with confidence the exact original wording. Even when that is done, it will be necessary for us to candidly admit that we cannot *prove*, in any ultimate sense, that we have the original wording; we do not have the Autographs. In the end, my affirmation that God has preserved the original wording of the New Testament text is a statement of faith; an intelligent faith, a faith that accords with the available evidence, but faith nonetheless. It may be that God's purpose in creating the human race entailed not allowing the truth to be inescapable; if the evidence were absolute there would be no test.

> Without faith it is impossible to please him; for he that cometh to God must believe that he is, and that he is a rewarder of them that *diligently* seek him (Heb. 11:6).[3]

Appendix B

7Q5

The identification of papyrus fragment 5 from Qumran cave 7 with Mark 6:52-53 by Jesuit scholar Jose O'Callaghan in early 1972 produced a flurry of reaction.[1] The implications of such an identification are such that I suppose it was inevitable that much of the reaction should be partisan. But the lack of objectivity and restraint on the part of some scholars can only be construed as bad manners, at best.

O'Callaghan is an experienced papyrologist, a careful scholar, and is entitled to a respectful hearing.

To my mind, the lack of restraint and objectivity in M. Baillet's response borders on the reprehensible.[2] Unfortunately Baillet's article has been widely quoted and seems to have influenced many people, including K. Aland.[3] Having myself done a little work with papyri from the Ptolemaic period (third century B.C.) I should like to comment upon Baillet's response to O'Callaghan's transcription of 7Q5. The fragment contains five lines of text and I will discuss them in order.

Line 1: All that remains is a vestige of the bottom of one letter—that it is the bottom can be seen by measuring the average distance between the other lines. O'Callaghan reconstructs an *epsilon* and puts a dot under it to show that what is left of the ink itself is not sufficient to allow a certain identification of the letter. This is in strict accord with the norm universally followed by papyrologists. Baillet calls it a "gratuitous hypothesis" even though he himself gave *epsilon* as one of four possibilities in the *editio princeps*. In fact, the vestige looks precisely like the bottom extremity of either an *epsilon* or a *sigma*. It is important to note that the identification of the fragment is not based on this letter at all; it does not play a positive role. It could play a negative role if the vestige did not seem to fit the letter required by the reconstruction. But far from being an embarrassment to O'Callaghan's reconstruction, the vestige of ink agrees very nicely with it. Baillet's criticism is entirely unwarranted.

Line 2: Since there is some ink left on the papyrus, O'Callaghan is at perfect liberty to reconstruct an *epsilon* provided he puts a dot under it, as he has. Baillet grants that it is possible. Again, the identification of the fragment is not based on this letter; it is only necessary that the ink traces not be against the identification.

Everybody agrees that the *tau* and *omega* are certain. Following the *omega* O'Callaghan reconstructs a *nu,* which initiative Baillet dignifies with the epithets "absurd" and "impossible" while opining that an *iota* "appears certain." Baillet's rhetoric is disappointing and I begin to doubt his competence as a papyrologist. The most sharply preserved letter on the whole fragment is the *iota* in line 3, and the vertical stroke immediately following the *omega* in line 2 differs substantially from it. What it more nearly resembles is the left-hand vertical stroke of the *nu* or the *eta* in line 4. The horizontal extremity of the following vestige could easily be the bottom extremity of the diagonal stroke of a *nu* (but not the horizontal stroke of an *eta*). In short, O'Callaghan's reconstruction of a *nu* here, with a dot under it of course, is perfectly reasonable.

As for the *eta* that completes line 2 in O'Callaghan's reconstruction, although Baillet prefers an *alpha* he concedes that *eta* is possible, and the *editio princeps* (of which Baillet was co-editor) suggested *eta* as a possibility. O'Callaghan remarks that for him this is the most difficult piece in the puzzle—his response to Baillet's discussion of line 2 is a model of restraint and competence.[4]

A further consideration must be kept in mind. It is a rule of thumb among papyrologists that any proposed reconstruction of a text be accompanied by a translation (or an identification with a known piece of literature)—in other words, it must make sense. Frequently there are so many individual points that are uncertain, taken alone, that there is little point in offering a reconstruction unless a reasonable translation or identification can also be offered—it is the total picture that carries force. O'Callaghan has produced an identification, but Baillet has not. Until he does, his criticisms of O'Callaghan do not deserve to be taken seriously.

Line 3: It is generally agreed the line begins with an *eta* (with a dot under it) followed by a notable space, then the letters KAIT which are quite clear. After the *tau* O'Callaghan reconstructs an *iota,* which Baillet declares to be "impossible." I fail to see how any careful scholar could use the term "impossible" so freely. The letter in question is a close replica of the indubitable *iota* two spaces to the left, so much so that it could reasonably be written without a dot under it. But O'Callaghan does put a dot under it and is therefore above reproach.

Line 4: There is general agreement about this line. It begins with half a letter which is almost certainly a *nu*, followed by a clear *nu* and *eta*, followed by a dubious *sigma*. This is a very important line because of the unusual sequence of letters.

Line 5: There is general agreement that the first letter is a dubious *theta* and the second an indubitable *eta*. O'Callaghan calls the third letter a clear *sigma* while Baillet prefers to call it an *epsilon*. Just with the naked eye I would call it an obvious *sigma*, but O'Callaghan affirms that seen with a scope what appears to be a short crossbar is in reality two dots; how they got there or what they may signify is not known, but they evidently should not be used to interpret the letter as an *epsilon*. [5]

The last letter is given by O'Callaghan as a possible *alpha*; Baillet rises to new heights, "Mais jamais de la vie un *alpha*, . . ."[6] The papyrus is too lacerated at this point to tell much from a photograph, but after studying the original with a strong lens O'Callaghan affirms that the left half of an *alpha* is clearly visible, and he invites Baillet to go see for himself.[7]

In sum, I see no reason to take Baillet's criticisms seriously—on the contrary, wherever he says "impossible" we should understand "most likely." It seems to me that O'Callaghan's reconstruction is eminently reasonable, but there are several problems connected with identifying the fragment with Mark 6:52-53.

The fragment presents us with two variations from the wording found in all our printed texts. In line 3 the fragment has an indubitable *tau* where the text has a *delta*. More serious, the identification involves the omission of the words $\epsilon\pi\iota$ $\tau\eta\nu$ $\gamma\eta\nu$ between lines 3 and 4. Can anything be said in relief of these problems? Yes. Apparently the difference between a voiced and a voiceless alveolar stop (*delta* and *tau*) was not obvious to some users of Greek. At any rate, the substitution of one for the other is not infrequent in ancient Greek literature. O'Callaghan offers twenty examples from four biblical papyri of the very change in question.[8] What we have in 7Q5 could easily be just one more instance.

The omission of three words seems more awkward, until it is remembered that it is a characteristic of the earliest N.T. MSS that they are full of eccentricities. I have already discussed this at some length above. I will cite two specific examples.

P[66] is so full of errors that I suspect it would be nearly impossible to find any five consecutive lines such that if superimposed on a fragment the size of 7Q5 the reconstruction would not present us with singular variants. P[9] is similar to 7Q5 in that it also consists of only five lines, albeit with over three times as many letters. It has been identified with 1 John 4:11-12 by everyone. But it badly garbles a word in the first line, misspells a word in the second, omits a word and misspells another in the third and adds a nonsense word in the fourth (line 5 is all right). If only the first four or five letters of each line were preserved (instead of twelve or thirteen) I doubt that it would have been identified, or the suggestion of 1 John 4:11-12 accepted.[9]

The point is, our whole experience with early papyri should lead us to expect unique variants in any new one that is discovered—it would be far more surprising to discover one that had no variants. The identification of 7Q5 with Mark 6:52-53 should not be rejected on such grounds.

In spite of the problems, there is evidence in favor of the identification. In the first place, the total effect of the reconstruction is impressive—to match fifteen clear or reasonably clear letters spread over four lines with a stichometry of 23, 20, 21, 21 for the respective lines is all but conclusive. The felicitous way in which the unusual letter sequence NNHC fits into the reconstruction is a favorable argument. The sequence would presumably indicate a form related to the Greek word "generation" or a proper name like "Gennesaret."

Even more striking is the obvious space (two letters' worth—recall that words are run together in early MSS so there are usually no spaces) which occurs precisely at the boundary between verses 52 and 53. Since verse 53 begins a new paragraph the space is appropriate, so much so that to ascribe the occurrence of the space to mere chance seems scarcely credible. The combination of the space at a paragraph break and a felicitous match for NNHC I believe to be compelling. I see no reasonable way to reject O'Callaghan's identification. For further considerations and a discussion of some implications see the series of articles in the June, 1972 issue of *Eternity*.

Once 7Q5 is firmly identified with Mark 6:52-53 then the probability that 7Q4 is to be identified with 1 Tim. 3:16, 4:1,3 and 7Q8 with James 1:23-24 becomes very strong. The remaining fragments are so small that dogmatism is untenable—O'Callaghan's identifications are possible, but cannot be insisted upon. It seems to me that 7Q5, 4, and 8 may be viewed as relevant to the thesis of this book in the following sense. That someone should have such a collection of New Testament writings at such an early date may suggest their early recognition as Scripture and even imply an early notion of a New Testament canon.[10]

Appendix C

The Implications of Statistical Probability for the History of the Text[1]

by Zane C. Hodges and David M. Hodges

Today, the whole question of the derivation of "text-types" through definite, historical recensions is open to debate. Indeed, E. C. Colwell, one of the leading contemporary critics, affirms dogmatically that the so-called "Syrian" recension (as Hort would have conceived it) never took place.[2] Instead he insists that all text-types are the result of "process" rather than definitive editorial activity.[3] Not all scholars, perhaps, would agree with this position, but it is probably fair to say that few would be prepared to deny it categorically. At least Colwell's position, as far as it goes, would have greatly pleased Hort's great antagonist, Dean Burgon. Burgon, who defended the *Textus Receptus* with somewhat more vehemence than scholars generally like, had heaped scorn on the idea of the "Syrian" revision which was the keystone to Westcott and Hort's theory. For that matter, the idea was criticised by others as well, and so well-known a textual scholar as Sir Frederic Kenyon formally abandoned it.[4] But the dissent tended to die away, and the form in which it exists today is quite independent of the question of the value of the TR. In a word, the modern skepticism of the classical concept of recensions thrives in a new context (largely created by the papyri). But this context is by no means discouraging to those who feel that the *Textus Receptus* was too hastily abandoned.

The very existence of the modern-day discussion about the origin of text-types serves to set in bold relief what defenders of the Received Text have always maintained. Their contention was this: Westcott and Hort failed, by their theory of recensions, to adequately explain the actual state of the Greek manuscript tradition; and in particular, they failed to explain the relative uniformity of this tradition. This contention now finds support by reason of the questions which modern study has been forced to raise. The suspicion is well advanced that the Majority text (as Aland designates the so-called Byzantine family[5]) cannot be successfully traced to a single event in textual history. But, if not, how can we explain it?

Here lies the crucial question upon which all textual theory logically hinges. Studies undertaken at the Institut für neutestamentliche Textforschung in Münster (where already photos or microfilms of over 4,500 manuscripts have been collected) tend to support the general view that as high as 90 percent of the Greek cursive (minuscule) manuscripts extant exhibit substantially the same form of text.[6] If papyrus and uncial (majuscule) manuscripts are considered along with cursives, the percentage of extant texts reflecting the majority form can hardly be less than 80 percent. But this is a fantastically high figure and it absolutely demands explanation. In fact, apart from a rational explanation of a text form which pervades all but 20 percent of the tradition, no one ought to seriously claim to know how to handle our textual materials. If the claim is made that great progress toward the original is possible, while the origin of 80 percent of the Greek evidence is wrapped in obscurity, such a claim must be viewed as monstrously unscientific, if not dangerously obscurantist. No amount of appeal to subjective preferences for this reading or that reading, this text or that text, can conceal this fact. The Majority text must be explained *as a whole*, before its claims *as a whole* can be scientifically rejected.

It is the peculiar characteristic of New Testament textual criticism that, along with a constantly accumulating knowledge of our manuscript resources, there has been a corresponding diminution in the confidence with which the history of these sources is described. The carefully constructed scheme of Westcott and Hort is now regarded by all reputable scholars as quite inadequate. Hort's confident assertion that "it would be an illusion to anticipate important changes of text from any acquisition of new evidence" is rightly regarded today as extremely naive.[7]

The formation of the Institut für neutestamentliche Textforschung is virtually an effort to start all over again by doing the thing that should have been done in the first place—namely, collect the evidence! It is in this context of re-evaluation that it is entirely possible for the basic question of the origin of the Majority text to push itself to the fore. Indeed, it may be confidently anticipated that if modern criticism continues its trend toward more genuinely scientific procedures, this question will once again become a central consideration. For it still remains the most determinative issue, logically, in the whole field.

APPENDIX

Do the proponents of the *Textus Receptus* have an explanation to offer for the Majority text? The answer is yes. More than that, the position they maintain is so uncomplicated as to be free from difficulties encountered by more complex hypotheses. Long ago, in the process of attacking the authority of numbers in textual criticism, Hort was constrained to confess: "A theoretical presumption indeed remains that a majority of extant documents is more likely to represent a majority of ancestral documents at each stage of transmission than *vice versa*."[8] In conceding this, he was merely affirming a truism of manuscript transmission. It was this: Under normal circumstances the older a text is than its rivals, the greater are its chances to survive in a plurality or a majority of the texts extant at any subsequent period. But the *oldest* text of all is the autograph. Thus it ought to be taken for granted that, barring some radical dislocation in the history of transmission, a majority of texts will be far more likely to represent correctly the character of the original than a small minority of texts. This is especially true when the ratio is an overwhelming 8:2. Under any reasonably normal transmissional conditions, it would be for all practical purposes quite impossible for a later text-form to secure so one-sided a preponderance of extant witnesses. Even if we push the origination of the so-called Byzantine text back to a date coeval with P^{75} and P^{66} (c. 200)—a time when already there must have been hundreds of manuscripts in existence—such mathematical proportions as the surviving tradition reveals could not be accounted for apart from some prodigious upheaval in textual history.

Statistical probability

This argument is not simply pulled out of thin air. What is involved can be variously stated in terms of mathematical probabilities. For this, however, I have had to seek the help of my brother, David M. Hodges, who received his B.S. from Wheaton College in 1957, with a major in mathematics. His subsequent experience in the statistical field includes service at Letterkenny Army Depot (Penna.) as a Statistical Officer for the U.S. Army Major Item Data Agency and as a Supervisory Survey Statistician for the Army Materiel Command Equipment Manuals Field Office (1963–67), and from 1967–70 as a Statistician at the Headquarters of U.S. Army Materiel Command, Washington, D.C. In 1972 he received an M.S. in Operations Research from George Washington University.

Below is shown a diagram of a transmissional situation in which one of three copies of the autograph contains an error, while two retain the correct reading. Subsequently the textual phenomenon known as "mixture" comes into play with the result that erroneous readings are introduced into good manuscripts, as well as the reverse process in which good readings are introduced into bad ones. My brother's statement about the probabilities of the situation follows the diagram in his own words.

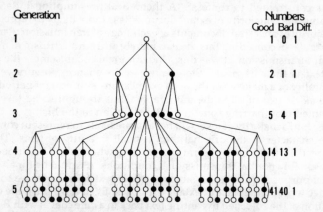

Generation	Numbers Good Bad Diff.
1	1 0 1
2	2 1 1
3	5 4 1
4	14 13 1
5	41 40 1

Provided that good manuscripts and bad manuscripts will be copied an equal number of times, and that the probability of introducing a bad reading into a copy made from a good manuscript is equal to the probability of reinserting a good reading into a copy made from a bad manuscript, the correct reading would predominate in any generation of manuscripts. The degree to which the good reading would predominate depends on the probability of introducing the error.

For purposes of demonstration, we shall call the autograph the first generation. The copies of the autograph will be called the second generation. The copies of the second generation manuscripts will be called the third generation and so on. The generation number will be identified as "n." Hence, in the second generation, $n=2$.

Assuming that each manuscript is copied an equal number of times, the number of manuscripts produced in any generation is k^{n-1}, where k is the number of copies made from each manuscript.

The probability that we shall reproduce a good reading from a good manuscript is expressed as p and the probability that we shall introduce an erroneous reading into a good manuscript is q. The sum of p and q is 1. Based on our original provisions, the probability of reinserting a good reading from a bad manuscript is q and the probability of perpetuating a bad reading is p.

The expected number of good manuscripts in any generation is the quantity $pkG_{n-1} + qkB_{n-1}$ and the expected number of bad manuscripts is the quantity $pkB_{n-1} + qkG_{n-1}$, where G_{n-1} is the number of good manuscripts from which we are copying and B_{n-1} is the number of bad manuscripts from which we are copying. The number of good manuscripts produced in a generation is G_n and the number of bad produced is B_n. We have, therefore, the formulas:

(1) $G_n = pkG_{n-1} + qkB_{n-1}$ and

(2) $B_n = pkB_{n-1} + qkG_{n-1}$ and

(3) $k^{n-1} = G_n + B_n = pkG_{n-1} + qkB_{n-1} + pkB_{n-1} + qkG_{n-1}$.

If $G_n = B_n$, then $pkG_{n-1} + qkB_{n-1} = pkB_{n-1} + qkG_{n-1}$ and $pkG_{n-1} + qkB_{n-1} - pkB_{n-1} - qkG_{n-1} = 0$.

Collecting like terms, we have $pkG_{n-1} - qkG_{n-1} + qkB_{n-1} - pkB_{n-1} = 0$ and since k can be factored out, we have $(p-q)G_{n-1} + (q-p)B_{n-1} = 0$ and $(p-q)G_{n-1} - (p-q)B_{n-1} = 0$ and $(p-q)(G_{n-1} - B_{n-1}) = 0$. Since the expression on the left equals zero, either $(p-q)$ or $(G_{n-1} - B_{n-1})$ must equal zero. But $(G_{n-1} - B_{n-1})$ cannot equal zero, since the autograph was good. This means that $(p-q)$ must equal zero. In other words, the expected number of bad copies can equal the expected number of good copies only if the probability of making a bad copy is equal to the probability of making a good copy.

If B_n is greater than G_n, then $pkB_{n-1} + qkG_{n-1} > pkG_{n-1} + qkB_{n-1}$. We can subtract a like amount from both sides of the inequality without changing the inequality. Thus, we have $pkB_{n-1} + qkG_{n-1} - pkG_{n-1} - qkB_{n-1} > 0$ and we can also divide k into both sides obtaining $pB_{n-1} + qG_{n-1} - pG_{n-1} - qB_{n-1} > 0$. Then, $(p-q)B_{n-1} + (q-p)G_{n-1} > 0$. Also, $(p-q)B_{n-1} - (p-q)G_{n-1} > 0$. Also $(p-q)(B_{n-1} - G_{n-1}) > 0$. However, G_{n-1} is greater than B_{n-1} since the autograph was good. Consequently, $(B_{n-1} - G_{n-1}) < 0$. Therefore, $(p-q)$ must also be less than zero. This means that q must be greater than p in order for the expected number of bad manuscripts to be greater than the expected number of good manuscripts. This also means that the probability of error must be greater than the probability of a correct copy.

The expected number is actually the mean of the binomial distribution. In the binomial distribution, one of two outcomes occur; either a success, i.e., an accurate copy, or a failure, i.e., an inaccurate copy.

In the situation discussed, equilibrium sets in when an error is introduced. That is, the numerical difference between the number of good copies and bad copies is maintained, once an error has been introduced. In other words, bad copies are made good at the same rate as good copies are made bad. The critical element is how early a bad copy appears. For example, let us suppose that two copies are made from each manuscript and that q is 25% or 1/4. From the autograph two copies are made. The probability of copy number 1 being good is 3/4 as is the case for the second copy. The probability that both are good is 9/16 or 56%. The probability that both are bad is $1/4 \times 1/4$ or 1/16 or 6%. The probability that one is bad is $3/4 \times 1/4 + 1/4 \times 3/4$ or 6/16 or 38%. The expected number of good copies is $pkG_{n-1} + qkB_{n-1}$ which is $3/4 \times 2 \times 1 + 1/4 \times 2 \times 0$ or 1.5. The expected number of bad copies is $2 - 1.5$ or .5. Now, if an error is introduced into the second generation, the number of good and bad copies would, thereafter, be equal. But the probability of this happening is 44%. If the probability of an accurate copy were greater than 3/4, the probability of an error in the second generation would decrease. The same holds true regardless of the number of copies and the number of generations so long as the number of copies made from bad manuscripts and the number from good manuscripts are equal. Obviously, if one type of manuscript is copied more frequently than the other, the type of manuscript copied most frequently will perpetuate its reading more frequently.

Another observation is that if the probability of introducing an incorrect reading differs from the probability of reintroducing a correct reading, the discussion does not apply.

This discussion, however, is by no means weighted in favor of the view we are presenting. The reverse is the case. A further statement from my brother will clarify this point.

Since the correct reading is the reading appearing in the majority of the texts in each generation, it is apparent that, if a scribe consults other texts at random, the majority reading will predominate in the sources consulted at random. The ratio of good texts consulted to bad will approximate the ratio of good texts to bad in the preceding generations. If a small number of texts are consulted, of course, a non-representative ratio may occur. But, in a large number of consultations of existing texts, the approximation will be representative of the ratio existing in all extant texts.

In practice, however, random comparisons probably did not occur. The scribe would consult those texts most readily available to him. As a result, there would be branches of texts which would be corrupt because the majority of texts available to the scribe would contain the error. On the other hand, when an error first occurs, if the scribe checked more than one manuscript he would find all readings correct except for the copy that introduced the error. Thus, when a scribe used more than one manuscript, the probability of reproducing an error would be less than the probability of introducing an error. This would apply to the generation immediately following the introduction of an error.

In short, therefore, our theoretical problem sets up conditions for reproducing an error which are somewhat too favorable to the error. Yet even so, in this idealized situation, the original majority for the correct reading is more likely to be retained than lost. But the majority in the fifth generation is a slender 41:40. What shall we say, then, when we meet the actual extant situation where (out of any given 100 manuscripts) we may expect to find a ratio of, say, 80:20? It at once appears that the probability that the 20 represent the original reading in any kind of normal transmissional situation is poor indeed.

Hence, approaching the matter from this end (i.e., *beginning* with extant manuscripts) we may hypothesize a problem involving (for mathematical convenience) 500 extant manuscripts in which we have proportions of 75% to 25%. My brother's statement about this problem is as follows:

Given about 500 manuscripts of which 75% show one reading and 25% another, given a one-third probability of introducing an error, given the same probability of correcting an error, and given that each manuscript is copied twice, the probability that the majority reading originated from an error is less than one in ten. If the probability of introducing an error is less than one-third, the probability that the erroneous reading occurs 75% of the time is even less. The same applies if three, rather than two copies are made from each manuscript. Consequently, the conclusion is that, given the conditions described, it is highly unlikely that the erroneous reading would predominate to the extent that the majority text predominates.

This discussion applies to an individual reading and should not be construed as a statement of probability that copied manuscripts will be error free. It should also be noted that a one-third probability of error is rather high, if careful workmanship is involved.

It will not suffice to argue in rebuttal to this demonstration that, of course, an error might easily be copied more often than the original reading in any particular instance. Naturally this is true, and freely conceded. But the problem is more acute than this. If, for example, in a certain book of the New Testament we find (let us say) 100 readings where the manuscripts divide 80 percent to 20 percent, are we to suppose that in every one of these cases, or even in most of them, that this reversal of probabilities has occurred? Yet this is what, *in effect,* contemporary textual criticism is saying. For the Majority text is repeatedly rejected in favor of minority readings. It is evident, therefore, that what modern textual critics are *really* affirming—either implicitly or explicitly—constitutes nothing less than a wholesale rejection of probabilities on a sweeping scale!

Surely, therefore, it is plain that those who repeatedly and consistently prefer minority readings to majority readings—especially when the majorities rejected are very large—are confronted with a problem. How can this preference be justified against the probabilities latent in any reasonable view of the transmissional history of the New Testament? Why should we reject these probabilities? What kind of textual phenomenon would be required to produce a Majority text diffused throughout 80 percent of the tradition, which nonetheless is more often wrong than the 20 percent which oppose it? And if we could conceptualize such a textual phenomenon, what proof is there that it ever occurred? Can anyone, logically, proceed to do textual criticism without furnishing a convincing answer to these questions?

I have been insisting for quite some time that the real crux of the textual problem is how we explain the overwhelming preponderance of the Majority text in the extant tradition. Current explanations of its origin are seriously inadequate (see below under "Objections"). On the other hand, the proposition that the Majority text is the natural outcome of the normal processes of manuscript transmission gives a perfectly natural explanation for it. The minority text-forms are thereby explained, *mutatis mutandis,* as existing in their minority form due to their comparative remoteness from the original text. The theory is simple but, I believe, wholly adequate on every level. Its adequacy can be exhibited also by the simplicity of the answers it offers to objections lodged against it. Some of these objections follow.

Objections

1. Since all manuscripts are not copied an even number of times, mathematical demonstrations like those above are invalid.

But this is to misunderstand the purpose of such demonstrations. Of course the diagram on page 162 is an "idealized" situation which does not represent what actually took place. Instead, it simply shows that all things being equal *statistical probability* favors the perpetuation in every generation of the original majority status of the authentic reading. And it must then be kept in mind that the larger the original majority, the more compelling this argument from probabilities becomes. Let us elaborate this point.

APPENDIX

If we imagine a stem as follows

in which A = autograph and (1) and (2) are copies made from it, it is apparent that, *in the abstract*, the error in (2) has an even chance of perpetuation in equal numbers with the authentic reading in (1). But, of course, *in actuality* (2) *may* be copied more frequently than (1) and thus the error be perpetuated in a larger number of later manuscripts than the true reading in (1). So far, so good. But suppose—

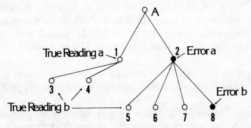

Now we have conceded that the error designated (a) is being perpetuated in larger numbers than the true reading (a), so that "error (a)" is found in copies 5-6-7-8, while "true reading (a)" is found only in copies 3 and 4. But when "error (b)" is introduced in copy 8, its rival ("true reading (b)") is found in copies 3-4-5-6-7.[9] Will anyone suppose that at this point it is at all likely that "error (b)" will have the same good fortune as "error (a)" and that manuscript 8 will be copied more often than 3-4-5-6-7 combined?

But even conceding this *far* less probable situation, suppose again—

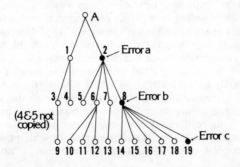

Will anybody believe that probabilities favor a repetition of the same situation for "error (c)" in copy 19?

Is it not transparent that as manuscripts multiply, and errors are introduced farther down in the stream of transmission, that the probability is drastically reduced that the error will be copied more frequently than the increasingly large number of rival texts?

Thus to admit that *some* errors might be copied more frequently than the rival, authentic reading in no way touches the core of our argument. The reason is simple: modern criticism repeatedly and systematically rejects majority readings on a very large scale. But, with every such rejection, the probability that this rejection is valid is dramatically reduced. *To overturn statistical probabilities a few times is one thing. To overturn them repeatedly and persistently is quite another!*

Hence, we continue to insist that to reject Majority text readings in large numbers without furnishing a credible overall rationale for this procedure is to fly blindly into the face of all reasonable probability.

2.   The Majority text can be explained as the outcome of a "process" which resulted in the gradual formation of a numerically preponderant text-type.

The "process" view of the Majority text seems to be gaining in favor today among New Testament textual scholars. Yet, to my knowledge, no one has offered a detailed explanation of what exactly the process was, when it began, or how—once begun—it achieved the result claimed for it. Indeed, the proponents of the "process" view are probably wise to remain vague about it because, on the face of the matter, it seems impossible to conceive of *any kind* of process which will be both historically credible and adequate to account for all the facts. The Majority text, it must be remembered, is relatively uniform in its general character with comparatively low amounts of variation between its major representatives.[10]

No one has yet explained how a long, slow process spread out over many centuries as well as over a wide geographical area, and involving a multitude of copyists, who often knew nothing of the state of the text outside of their own monasteries or scriptoria, could achieve this widespread uniformity out of the diversity presented by the earlier forms of text. Even an official edition of the New Testament— promoted with ecclesiastical sanction throughout the known world—would have had great difficulty achieving this result as the history of Jerome's Vulgate amply demonstrates.[11] But an unguided process achieving relative stability and uniformity in the diversified textual, historical, and cultural circumstances in which the New Testament was copied, imposes impossible strains on our imagination.

Thus it appears that the more clearly and specifically the "process" view may come to be articulated, the more vulnerable it is likely to be to all of the potential objections just referred to. Further, when articulation *is* given to such a view, it will have to locate itself definitely somewhere in history—with many additional inconveniences accruing to its defenders. For, be it remembered, just as history is silent about any "Syrian recension" (such as the one Hort imagined), so also history is silent about any kind of "process" which was somehow influencing or guiding the scribes as manuscripts were transmitted. Modern critics are the first to discover such a "process," but before accepting it we shall have to have more than vague, undocumented assertions about it.

It seems not unfair to say that the attempt to explain the Majority text by some obscure and nebulous "process" is an implicit confession of weakness on the part of contemporary criticism. The erosion of Westcott and Hort's view, which traced this text to an official, definitive recension of the New Testament, has created a vacuum very hard indeed to fill. More than ever, it appears, critics cannot reject the Majority text and at the same time also explain it. *And this is our point!* Rejection of the Majority text and credible explanation of that text are quite incompatible with each other. But acceptance of the Majority text immediately furnishes an explanation of this text and the rival texts as well! *And it is the essence of the scientific process to prefer hypotheses which explain the available facts to those which do not!*

Appendix D

Conflation or Confusion?[1]

Conflation is the theory that when a scribe or editor had before him two or more manuscripts that at a given point had different readings that might "properly" be combined to produce a more "full" reading, he might do so. The result would be called "conflation" according to Hort.

When evaluating a putative example of conflation, due consideration should be given to the possibility that the differences may have come about because of the accidental (or intentional) omission of different parts of a "complete" original reading.

The list that follows comprises possible examples of conflation found to date from all sources. (There may be quite a few more discoverable by a sharp eye.) These are presented to the reader for his own evaluation and decision. They range from cases of obvious conflation and obvious omission to cases of sheer confusion where it is highly doubtful that the mechanism "conflation" was at work. Accordingly, the examples are classified into two sets of two groups each:

1. True, or simple "conflation":
   a) Simple addition or telescoping of readings, or omission
   b) Addition plus simple coupling links, or omission.
2. Marginal "conflation" or confusion:
   a) Complicated by substitution, transposition or moderate internal changes, or omissions
   b) Substantial differences—"conflation" dubious.

The full extent of the confusion that exists will not be apparent to the reader since for most of the examples there are one or more further

171

variations not included here because they are not relevant to the possible instances of conflation.

The symbols in the critical apparatus are essentially those in general use. The abbreviations *pc*, *al*, *pm*, *pl*, and *rell* have the same meanings as in the Nestle editions. I have represented f¹ and f¹³ by the numbers only. Only one text-type symbol is used, Byz, which stands for the "Byzantine" manuscript tradition. I have used parentheses in two ways—enclosing a papyrus they mean there is doubt as to what reading is exhibited, enclosing any other kinds of witnesses they mean the witness(es) has a slight variation from the reading of the witness(es) not so enclosed. The reader cannot fail to note that the completeness of the apparatus varies considerably from example to example—this is a reflection of the sources that were available to me.

Group 1. a) Simple addition or telescoping of readings, or omission.

1. Matt. 3.12

αυτου εις την αποθηκην	Byz ℵ C K Δ 0233 1 *al* lat cop
εις την αποθηκην αυτου	L 892 *al* b ff¹ g¹ syᵖ·ʰ
αυτου εις την αποθηκην αυτου	B W *pc*

(This would appear to be a conflation on the part of B and W. Since Hort did not follow B here, he must have been of the same opinion.)

2. Matt. 5.41 σε

σε	Byz B *pl*
εαν	L
σε εαν	ℵ Δ 33 489

(This would appear to be a conflation on the part of Aleph. Since Hort did not follow Aleph here, he must have been of the same opinion.)

3. Matt. 20.21

δεξιων σου . . . ευωνυμων	D Θ 1 *pc* lat
δεξιων . . . ευωνυμων σου	ℵ B
δεξιων σου . . . ευωνυμων σου	Byz C L N W Z 085 13 *pm* syᵖ·ʰ

(Is this a "Byzantine" conflation of the "Western" and "Alexandrian" readings, or are the latter independent simplifications of the former? It should be noted that Aleph and B are alone in omitting the first σου.)

4. Matt. 23.25 ακρασιας   ℵ B D L Δ Π Θ 1 13 33 *al* it sy[h]

         αδικιας   Byz C K Γ *pm* f sy[p]

     ακρασιας αδικιας   W

(It seems clear that Codex W here conflates the "Alexandrian" and "Byzantine" readings.)

5. Matt. 24.38 εκειναις

         προ   D 253 *pc* it[pt] sy[h,pal]

     ταις προ   Byz ℵ L W Θ 067 0133 1 13 *pl* it[pt] vg bo

εκειναις ταις προ   B

(This would appear to be a conflation on the part of B. Since Hort used brackets here, he must have tended to the same opinion.)

6. Matt. 26.22

αυτω εἷς ἑκαστος   ℵ B C L Z 33 *pc* sa

αυτω   ἑκαστος αυτων   Byz (P[45]) A W Γ Δ Π Σ Ψ 074 1 13 *pl* sy[p]

αυτω εἷς ἑκαστος αυτων   M

     εἷς ἑκαστος αυτων   D Θ 69 *pc* bo

         ἑκαστος αυτων   P[37]

(This would appear to be a "Western" conflation of "Byzantine" and "Alexandrian" elements.)

7. Matt. 26.36 οὐ   Byz B E F G 067 *pm*

     αν   D K L W Δ Θ 074 1 69 *al*

   οὐ αν   P[53] A *pc*

(Before the advent of P[53] presumably all would agree that A has here conflated the "Byzantine" and "Western" readings. Although the papyrus antedates any extant witness to these two "text-types," I suggest that the proper conclusion is that the conflation is a very early one.)

8. Matt. 26.70 αυτων   K *al*
         παντων   ℵ B C[2] D E G L Z Θ 090 13 33 *al* lat sy[p,h]
    αυτων παντων   Byz A C W Γ Δ 0133 1 *pm*

(Shall we say that the "Byzantine" text has a conflation based on a handful of late MSS on the one hand and the combined "Alexandrian-Western" text-types on the other? It seems more probable that K etc. have simplified the "Byzantine" reading. In that event the "Alexandrian-Western" reading is best explained as a separate simplification of the original reading.)

9. Matt. 27.55 εκει   Byz B C *pl* lat
          και   D 56 aur d
     εκει και   F K L Π 33 sy[h,pal]
      κακει   ℵ (sy[p])

(Here we seem to have varied witnesses conflating the "Byzantine-Alexandrian" and "Western" readings.)

10. Mark 1.4
ὁ βαπτιζων εν τη ερημω   B 33 *pc*
  βαπτιζων εν τη ερημω και   Byz A K P W Π 1 13 *pl* f sy[h,pal]
  ὁ βαπτιζων εν τη ερημω και   ℵ L Δ *pc* bo
  (εν τη ερημω βαπτιζων και)   D Θ *pc* lat sy[p]

(Here we have "Alexandrian" witnesses conflating the "Byzantine" reading and that of Codex B. Although there has been no accretion of new evidence, UBS[3] seems to espouse this obvious conflation whereas UBS[1] did not.)

11. Mark 1.28 ευθυς   Byz A D E G H K M S U V Y Γ Δ Π
                             Σ Φ Ω 0104 *pm* lat sy[p,h]
       πανταχου W 579 *pc* b e q
    ευθυς πανταχου ℵ[c] B C L 0133 13 *pc*
         (omit)   ℵ Θ 1 *al* c ff[2] r[1] sy[s]

(Is this not an obvious "Alexandrian" conflation? Yet the UBS text adopts it without giving any indication that there are other readings.)

12. Mark 1.40 κυριε   C L W Θ *pc* e c ff sy^{pal}

           ὁτι   Byz ℵ A *pl* sy^h

      κυριε ὁτι   B

(This appears to be a clear conflation on the part of B. Since Hort did not follow B here he must have been of the same opinion.)

13. Mark 5.42

εξεστησαν   Byz P⁴⁵ A K W Θ Π 0133 1 13 *pl* e sy^{p,h}

εξεστησαν ευϑυς   ℵ B C L Δ 33 892 *pc* bo

εξεστησαν παντες   D it sa

(If the producers of the "Syrian" text followed a policy of conflation, why did they neglect this fine opportunity? Note that Hort's "late Syrian" reading now has the earliest attestation.)

14. John 4.29

παντα ὁσα   Byz P^{66,75} A D L W Γ Δ Θ Λ Π Ψ 086 1 13 *pl* lat sy^h

παντα   ἁ̈ ℵ B C e a d q sy^p cop

παντα ὁσα ἁ̈ 579

(This is an obvious conflation in one late MS. Note the strong early attestation for the "Byzantine" reading.)

15. John 5.37 εκεινος   P⁷⁵ ℵ B L W 213 *pc* a ff^a j sy^{p,h}

          αυτος   Byz P⁶⁶ A Γ Δ Θ Λ Π Ψ 063 1 13 *pl* lat

    εκεινος αυτος   D

(This appears to be a case of "Western" conflation. Note that Hort's "late Syrian" reading now has very early attestation.)

16. John 7.39

πνευμα   P^{66c,75} ℵ K N T Θ Π Ψ *pc* bo

πνευμα ἁγιον   Byz P⁶⁶ L W X Γ Δ Λ 0105 1 13 *pl*

πνευμα   δεδομενον   lat sy^{c,s,p} Eusebius

πνευμα ἁγιον δεδομενον   B 053 *pc* e q sy^{pal,h}

(το πνευμα το ἁγιον επ αυτοις)   D d f

(It would appear that B here conflates "Byzantine" and "Western" elements. Since Hort did not follow B here, he must have been of the same opinion. Note that Hort's "late Syrian" reading now has very early attestation.)

17. John 10.19

σχισμα ουν		D 1241 sy^s
σχισμα	παλιν	P$^{(45),75}$ ℵ B L W X 33 pc lat sa sy^p
σχισμα ουν παλιν		Byz P^{66} A Γ Δ Θ Λ Π Ψ 1 13 pl sy^h

(A century ago this could have been interpreted as a "Syrian" conflation, but now we can scarcely say that P^{66} conflated P^{75} and D. The possibility must at least be considered that Hort's "late Syrian" reading is in fact the earliest, the original.)

18. John 10.31

εβαστασαν		P^{45} Θ
εβαστασαν ουν		D 28 1780 pc lat sy^s bo
εβαστασαν	παλιν	(P^{75}) ℵ B L W 33 pc sy^p
εβαστασαν ουν παλιν		Byz P^{66} A X Π Ψ 1 13 565 pl f sy^h

(A century ago this could have been interpreted as a "Syrian" conflation, but now we can hardly say that P^{66} conflated B and D. The possibility must be entertained that Hort's "late Syrian" reading is in fact the earliest.)

19. John 11.22

αλλα	1780
και	P^{75} ℵ B C X 1 33 pc it^{pt}
αλλα και	Byz P^{45,66} ℵ^2 A C^3 D L W Θ Ψ Ω 0250 13 pl lat sy^{p,h} cop

(It seems obvious that the "Byzantine" reading cannot be a conflation of the "Alexandrian" reading and that of one late MS. 1780 has dropped part of the "Byzantine" reading. I suggest the same explanation for the "Alexandrian" reading. Observe that the "Byzantine" reading now has very early attestation.)

20. John 12.9

ὁ οχλος	πολυς	ℵ B L pc lat
οχλος ὁ πολυς		W 1010
ὁ οχλος ὁ πολυς		P^{66c}
οχλος	πολυς	Byz P^{66,75} A B^2 I Q X Θ Ψ 065 1 33 pl (cop)

(Conflation or confusion? Did P[66c] conflate B and W? Or should we say that P[66c] has the original reading that everyone else (including P[66*]!) simplified? Note that Hort's "late Syrian" reading now has the earliest attestation, with a vengeance!)

21. John 14.14 τουτο P[75] A B L Ψ 060 33 *al* c vg cop
                  εγω Byz P[66] ℵ D E G Q X Γ Δ Π *pm* it sy[p,h]
          τουτο εγω P[66c]

(This is an instructive conflation on the part of P[66c]. Note the early attestation for the "Byzantine" reading.)

22. John 16.4
αυτων μνημονευητε   ℵ[c] L 13 *al* lat
     μνημονευητε αυτων   Byz K Γ Δ Ψ 054 1 *pm* ff[2] sy[pal]
αυτων μνημονευητε αυτων   A B Θ Π 33 *al* sy[p,h]
     μνημονευητε   ℵ D a sy[s] cop

(This would appear to be a not very felicitous conflation on the part of B, etc.)

23. John 18.40 παλιν   P[60] ℵ B L W X 0109 *pc*
          παντες   G K N Ψ 1 13 33 *al* it sy[p,pal] cop
     παλιν παντες   Byz (P[66]) A Γ Δ Θ 054 0250 *pm* vg sy[h]
     παντες παλιν   D

(This could be a "Byzantine" conflation, but it could just as easily be the case that the two shorter readings are independent simplications of the longer one. Is the "Western" reading a conflation or simply a reversal of the word order?)

24. Acts 10.48 του κυριου   Byz H L P 049 056 *pm*
               Ιησου Χριστου   P[74] ℵ A B E 33 *al* cop
          του κυριου Ιησου   Lect. *al*
          του κυριου Ιησου Χριστου   D 81 d p

(This would appear to be a "Western" conflation of the "Byzantine" and "Alexandrian" readings.)

25. Acts 14.15 τον θεον   ζωντα   D *pc*
              θεον τον ζωντα   א
        τον θεον τον ζωντα   Byz P⁴⁵ H L P *pm*
             θεον   ζωντα   P⁷⁴ B C E 33 *al*

(A century ago this might have been interpreted as a "Syrian" conflation, but now we can hardly say that P⁴⁵ conflated Aleph and D. Why not say that Hort's "late Syrian" reading is not only the earliest but also the best? I would say that the "Alexandrian" reading is decidedly inferior in terms of the discourse structure of the text, the sort of thing that would appeal to scribes without native speaker control of Koine Greek.[2])

26. Acts 24.14 τοις   προφηταις   Byz א^c A *pm* syr bo
           εν τοις προφηταις   B C D *al*
        τοις εν τοις προφηταις   א E

(This seems to be a clear conflation on the part of Aleph.)

27. Acts 25.5 τουτω   Byz *pm*
           ατοπον   א A B C E 33 *al* lat
        τουτω ατοπον   Ψ 69 614 *al* syr bo

(This would appear to be a conflation of the "Byzantine" and "Alexandrian" readings.)

28. 1 Cor. 7.34
ἡ αγαμος και ἡ παρθενος   P¹⁵ B P *al* cop
    και ἡ παρθενος ἡ αγαμος   Byz D F G K L Ψ *pm* it syr
ἡ αγαμος και ἡ παρθενος ἡ αγαμος   P⁴⁶ א A 33 *pc*

(Although unquestionably early, this really does appear to be a conflation on the part of P⁴⁶, etc.)

29. Phil. 1.18 πλην   Byz D E K L *pm*
        ὅτι   B sy^p
    πλην ὅτι   P⁴⁶ א A F G P 048 33 *pc* sa

(Modern editors have tended to regard the long reading as original, but now that we know that the "Byzantine" text goes back at

least to the second century we should reconsider the possibility
that P⁴⁶, etc. have a conflation.)

30. 1 Thess. 5.27

τοις ἁγιοις		103 1984 1985
τοις	αδελφοις	ℵ B D E F G *pc* d e f g sa
τοις ἁγιοις αδελφοις		Byz (P⁴⁶) ℵᶜ A K L P Ψ 33 *pl* it syr bo

(The "Byzantine" reading can scarcely be a conflation based on
103, so 103 must have a simplification of the "Byzantine" reading. I suggest the same explanation for the "Alexandrian-
Western" reading.)

31. Heb. 7.22

και	920
κρειττονος	Byz P⁴⁶ ℵᶜ A Cᶜ D E K L P Ψ *pl* lat syr cop
και κρειττονος	ℵ B C 33 *pc*

(It is clear that B could not have a conflation based on 920, unless
it is the sole survivor of a very early tradition, but neither may
we say that P⁴⁶ is simplifying B. Note that here it is the
"Alexandrian" text that has the "fuller, smoother" reading.)

Group 1. b) Addition plus simple coupling links, or omission.

32. Matt. 4.3

αυτω ὁ πειραζων ειπεν	Byz C L P Θ 0233 *pm* k syʰ
ὁ πειραζων ειπεν αυτω	ℵ B W 1 13 33 *al* vg syᵖ bo
αυτω ὁ πειραζων και ειπεν αυτω	D it syᶜ,ˢ,ᵖᵃˡ

(Here we presumably have a "Western" conflation of the "Byzantine" and "Alexandrian" readings.)

33. Matt. 9.18

εἰς ελθων/εισελθων	Byz ℵ¹² C D E K M N S V W X Θ 1 33 *al* d f
προσελθων	ℵ 69 157 *pc* q syᵖ
εἰς προσελθων	ℵ¹ B lat *pc*
τις προσελθων	L 13 *al* k
τις ελθων	Γ *al*

(Codex B appears to have a conflation, an opinion with which the editors of the UBS texts evidently concur.)

34. Matt. 16.11 προσεχειν   Byz D^c W X *pm* sy^{c,s,h}
     προσεχετε   D Θ 13 124 *pc* lat sy^p
     προσεχετε δε   ℵ B C L 1 *pc* cop
  προσεχειν προσεχετε δε C^c 33 237 *al* q

(An evident conflation on the part of some later MSS, building on the "Byzantine" and "Alexandrian/Western" readings.)

35. Matt. 27.41

και πρεσβυτερων   A B L Θ 1 13^{pt} 33 *al* it^{pt} vg sa
και   Φαρισαιων   D W *pc* it^{pt} sy^s
και πρεσβυτερων και Φαρισαιων Byz Δ Φ 13^{pt} *pm* sy^{p,h} bo
              Diatessaron

(Here, at last, we seem to have a clear "Byzantine" conflation. The whole clause in the "Byzantine" text reads like this: οἱ αρχιερεις εμπαιξοντες μετα των γραμματεων και πρεσβυτερων και Φαρισαιων ελεγον. It really seems to be a bit too full; so much so that editors trained at Alexandria might well have been tempted to improve the style by shortening it. Might the "Western" reading be the result of parablepsis?)

36. Luke 24.53

αινουντες   D it^{pt}
  ευλογουντες   P^{75} ℵ B C L cop sy^{s,pal}
αινουντες και ευλογουντες Byz A C^2 K W X Δ Θ Π Ψ 063
             1 13 *pl* it^{pt} vg sy^{p,h} Diatessaron

(This is one of Hort's eight "Syrian conflations." According to Hort's own judgment Codex D has omitted 329 words from the genuine text of the last three chapters of Luke, plus adding 173, substituting 146, and transposing 243. Since the producer of D was on something of an omitting spree in these chapters, it is not unreasonable to suggest that D has simply dropped "and blessing" from the original reading, an easy instance of homoioteleuton. Nor is it hard to imagine that editors trained at Alexandria might reduce the longer reading to the proportions exhibited by the "Alexandrian" text-type.)

APPENDIX

37. 2 Cor. 11.3

$\tau\eta\varsigma\ \dot{\alpha}\pi\lambda o\tau\eta\tau o\varsigma$ Byz $\aleph^c$ H K P Ψ 0121

            0243 *pm* vg syr

    $\tau\eta\varsigma\ \dot{\alpha}\gamma\nu o\tau\eta\tau o\varsigma$ five early Fathers

$\tau\eta\varsigma\ \dot{\alpha}\pi\lambda o\tau\eta\tau o\varsigma\ \kappa\alpha\iota\ \tau\eta\varsigma\ \dot{\alpha}\gamma\nu o\tau\eta\tau o\varsigma$ P[46] $\aleph$ B G 33 *pc* it cop

$\tau\eta\varsigma\ \dot{\alpha}\gamma\nu o\tau\eta\tau o\varsigma\ \kappa\alpha\iota\ \tau\eta\varsigma\ \dot{\alpha}\pi\lambda o\tau\eta\tau o\varsigma$ D

(It appears that the "Alexandrian" and "Western" texts have separate conflations. From their use of brackets we may conclude that the editors of both the Nestle and UBS editions recognize the possibility.)

38. Eph. 2.5

$\tau o\iota\varsigma\ \pi\alpha\rho\alpha\pi\tau\omega\mu\alpha\sigma\iota\nu$ Byz $\aleph$ A D[2] *pl* cop

      $\tau\alpha\iota\varsigma\ \dot{\alpha}\mu\alpha\rho\tau\iota\alpha\varsigma$ D (G) lat

$\tau o\iota\varsigma\ \pi\alpha\rho\alpha\pi\tau\omega\mu\alpha\sigma\iota\nu\ \kappa\alpha\iota\ \tau\alpha\iota\varsigma\ \dot{\alpha}\mu\alpha\rho\tau\iota\alpha\varsigma$ Ψ

$\epsilon\nu\ \tau o\iota\varsigma\ \pi\alpha\rho\alpha\pi\tau\omega\mu\alpha\sigma\iota\nu\ \kappa\alpha\iota\ \tau\alpha\iota\varsigma\ \epsilon\pi\iota\vartheta\upsilon\mu\iota\alpha\iota\varsigma$ B

(Here we have separate conflations on the part of Ψ and B. Since Hort did not follow B here he must have been of the same opinion. The editors of the Nestle and UBS editions evidently agree as well.)

39. Col. 1.12

$\tau\omega\ \kappa\alpha\lambda\epsilon\sigma\alpha\nu\tau\iota$ D G 33 *pc* it sa

$\tau\omega$ $\iota\kappa\alpha\nu\omega\sigma\alpha\nu\tau\iota$ Byz P[46,(61)] $\aleph$ A C D[c] E

         K L P Ψ *pl* syr bo

$\tau\omega\ \kappa\alpha\lambda\epsilon\sigma\alpha\nu\tau\iota\ \kappa\alpha\iota\ \iota\kappa\alpha\nu\omega\sigma\alpha\nu\tau\iota$ B

(This obvious conflation on the part of Codex B was acknowledged by Hort [p. 240], a judgment with which the editors of the Nestle and UBS editions are in full agreement.)

Before going on to examples where the required phenomena for possible conflations are less clear, it will be well to pause and see what instruction may be gained from these clear possible examples.

Ignoring probabilities for the moment, I will tabulate the "possible" conflations.

	total	examples
Western text-type	3	6, 24, 32
Codex D	3	15, 23, 37
Alexandrian text-type	7	10, 11, 22, 28, 29, 31, 37
Codex B	7	1, 5, 12, 16, 33, 38, 39
Codex Aleph	2	2, 26
Byzantine text-type	10	3, 8, 17, 18, 19, 23, 25, 30, 35, 36

None of the Western "conflations" has early papyrus support, and I believe there is general agreement among scholars that all six of the "Western" instances are in fact conflations. None of the B or Aleph "conflations" has early papyrus support. I believe there is general agreement among scholars that all nine B and Aleph instances are in fact conflations. (Since Hort was evidently aware of these conflations in B, it is difficult to understand how he could affirm that to the best of his knowledge there were no "Neutral" conflations.) Three of the "Alexandrian" instances (28, 29, 37) have early papyrus attestation. Modern editors have tended to include all seven "Alexandrian" readings in their texts, although some express doubt about 31 and 37. One cannot help but suspect that they are still wearing hortian blinders, to use Colwell's phrase.

Six of the "Byzantine" instances (17, 18, 19, 23?, 25, 30?) now have early papyrus attestation. It follows that although modern editors continue to reject these readings, it can no longer be argued that they are late. If they are conflations then they happened in the second century. It is significant that in fully 28 of the 39 examples given (exceptions: 3, 8, 13, 17, 18, 19, 23, 25, 30, 35, 36), the "Byzantine" text is being conflated by other witnesses, not vice versa.

It is evident that all "text-types" have possible conflations and that "Western" and "Alexandrian" witnesses have actual conflations. I would argue that all the "Byzantine" instances are original, but in any case it should be clear that "conflation" may not responsibly be used to argue for a late "Byzantine" text-type. On the contrary, examples like 7, 13, 15, 16, 20, 21, 22, 28, 31, and 37 might reasonably be used to argue for a rather early "Byzantine" text-type.

Group 2. a) Complicated by substitution, transposition, moderate internal changes, or omissions.

40. Matt. 7.10 ἤ και   ιχϑυν αιτησει   א B C (1) 33 *pc*

          και εαν ιχϑυν αιτηση   Byz (LW) Θ *al* sy^{p,h}

      ἤ   εαν ιχϑυν αιτηση   lat sy^c

      ἤ και εαν ιχϑυν αιτηση   K^c 13 *al*

(This could be either a "Western" or an "Alexandrian" conflation,
but presumably not a "Byzantine.")

41. Matt. 7.18

ποιειν . . . ενεγκειν   א (alone of MSS)

ενεγκειν . . . ποιειν   B (alone of MSS)

ποιειν . . . ποιειν   Byz א^c C K L W X Z Δ Θ Π 0250 1

                       13 33 *pl* lat syr cop

(The editors of the UBS editions evidently agree that the "Byzantine" reading here is genuine.)

42. Matt. 8.1.   καταβαντι δε αυτω   Byz א K L (Δ) *al* (lat sy^{p,h})

           και καταβαντος   αυτου   Z sy^{c,pal}

           καταβαντος δε αυτου   B C 33 (lat sy^{p,h}) cop

(If anyone has conflated it would seem to be the "Alexandrians.")

43. Matt. 9.2 σου ἁι ἁμαρτιαι   א B C Δ W 1 33 *pc*

        σοι ἁι ἁμαρτιαι   D Δ^c *pc* k

        σοι ἁι ἁμαρτιαι σου   Byz L Θ 0233^v 13 *pm* lat sy^{s,p,h,pal}

        σου ἁι ἁμαρτιαι σου   M

(Codex M has evidently conflated, but should we say the same of
the "Byzantine" text? Or are the "Alexandrian" and "Western"
readings independent simplifications?)

44. Matt. 10.3

     Θαδδαιος   א

και Θαδδαιος   B *pc* vg cop

και Λεββαιος   D 122 d k

και Λεββαιος ὁ επικληϑεις Θαδδαιος   Byz C² K L W X Δ Θ

                                      Π 1 *pl* sy^{p,h,pal}

(The "Byzantine" reading does not really present the phenomena of a conflation. The reading of Aleph is clearly wrong. The "Western" reading could easily have resulted from homoioteleuton. It is not difficult to imagine that editors trained at Alexandria might prefer a shorter reading.)

45. Matt. 10.13 ει δε μηγη   D sy^s
        εαν δε μη ἡ αξια   Byz ℵ B *pl* lat sy^{p,h}
        ει δε μη αξια   L

(This appears to be a conflation on the part of Codex L.)

46. Matt. 12.4 εφαγεν ὅ   (P^{70}) D W 13 it sy$^{p,(c)}$
        εφαγον οὕς   ℵ
        εφαγον ὅ   B 481
        εφαγεν οὕς   Byz (p^{70}) C K L Δ Θ Π 0233 1 33 *pl*
                          vg sy^h cop

(Conflation or confusion?)

47. Matt. 12.46 ετι αυτου λαλουντος   ℵ B 33 *pc* lat
         λαλουντος δε αυτου   D L Z 892 sy^p
         ετι δε αυτου λαλουντος   Byz C W Θ 1 13 *pm* sy^h

(Is this a "Byzantine" conflation or are the other two readings independent simplifications?)

48. Matt. 13.28
οἱ δε αυτω λεγουσιν   B 157 *pc* cop
οἱ δε δουλοι ειπον αυτω   Byz L W Θ 1 13 *pm* vg sy^h
οἱ δε δουλοι αυτω λεγουσιν   C
λεγουσιν αυτω οἱ δουλοι   D it (sy^{c,s,p})
οἱ δε δουλοι λεγουσιν αυτω   ℵ

(Conflation or confusion? Both C and Aleph appear to have conflations, both based on the "Byzantine" reading plus B and D respectively. Surprisingly, the UBS text follows Aleph, without comment, while Nestle^{24} follows C. The reading of B would seem to be a clear error.)

49. Matt. 14.6

γενεσιων δε αγομενων   Byz W 0119 0136 13 *al* ff¹ sy^{h mg}
γενεσιοις δε γενομενοις   ℵ B D L Z *pc* (sy^{c,s,p,h})
γενεσιοις δε αγομενοις   1 *pc*
γενεσιων δε γενομενων   C K N Θ *al* (sy^{c,s,p,h})

(Codex C and f¹ appear to have separate conflations of the "Byzantine" and "Alexandrian" readings.)

50. Matt. 14.34 επι την γην Γεννησαρετ   C N 13 *al* sy^{pal}
       εις την γην Γεννησαρετ   Byz L 1 *pm* lat sy^{p,(c,s)}
       επι την γην εις Γεννησαρετ   ℵ B W Δ 0119 33 *pc* sy^h
       επι την γην εις Γεννησαρ   D 700

(Might this be an "Alexandrian/Western" conflation?)

51. Matt. 15.14

ὁδηγοι εισιν τυφλοι τυφλων   Byz C W X Δ Π 0106 *pm* q
ὁδηγοι εισιν τυφλοι   ℵ cop sy^c
τυφλοι εισιν ὁδηγοι   B D 0237
τυφλοι εισιν ὁδηγοι τυφλων   ℵ^c L Z Θ 1 13 33 *al* lat sy^{p,h}
ὁδηγοι εισιν τυφλων   K *pc* sy^s

(The "Alexandrian" reading appears to be a conflation of the "Byzantine" and "Western" readings. Codices Aleph and K appear to have separate reductions of the "Byzantine" reading, due to parablepsis.)

52. Matt. 17.7

προσελθων . . . ἡψατο αυτων και ειπεν   Byz C L W 1 *pm* sy^h
προσηλθεν . . . και ἁψαμενος αυτων ειπεν   ℵ B *pc*
προσελθων . . . και ἁψαμενος αυτων ειπεν   Θ 13 *pc*
προσηλθεν . . . και ἡψατο αυτων και ειπεν   D lat sy^{p,pal,(c)}

(The "Western" and "Caesarean" readings appear to be separate conflations of the "Byzantine" and "Alexandrian" readings.)

53. Matt. 19.9

μη επι πορ. και γαμ. αλλην μοιχαται   Byz ℵ C^c K L N (W) Z
                                        Δ Θ Π 078 *pm* vg sy^{s,p,h}

παρ. λογου πορ. ποιει αυ. μοιχευθηναι   (P²⁵) B 1 bo

παρ. λογου πορ. και γαμ. αλλην μοιχαται   D 13 33 *pc* it sy^{c,pal} sa

μη επι. πορ. και γαμ. αλλην ποιει αυ. μ.   C 1216 *pc*

(The "Western" text and Codex C have independent conflations
of the "Byzantine" and "Alexandrian" readings.)

54. Matt. 20.10 ελθοντες δε   Byz ℵ L W Z 1 *pm* sy^h bo
                  και ελθοντες   B C D Θ 085 13 33 *pc* e sy^{c,s,p}
                  ελθοντες δε και   N 473 *pc* lat arm

(An assortment of witnesses conflate the "Byzantine" and
"Alexandrian" readings.)

55. Matt. 20.21 η δε ειπεν   B *pc* (e) sa
                  λεγει αυτω   Byz ℵ C D Z *pl* (vg) sy^{c,s,p,(h)}
                  η δε λεγει αυτω   M (it)

(A few witnesses conflate the "Alexandrian" and "Byzantine"
readings.)

56. Matt. 22.13

αρατε αυτον ποδων και χειρων και β. α.   D it^{pt} sy^{c.s}

δησαντες αυτου ποδας και χειρας εκβ. α.   ℵ B L Θ 085 1 (13) *pc*
                                        it^{pt} vg sy^p cop

δησαντες αυτου ποδας και χειρας αρατε α.   Byz C W 0138 *pm*
και εκβ.   (M Φ *al*) sy^h

(Is this really a "Byzantine" conflation?)

57. Mark 4.5 και ότι   D W it^{pt} sy^{c,s}
                όπου   Byz ℵ A *pl* vg sy^{p,h}
                και όπου   B

(An evident conflation on the part of B.)

58. Mark 7.35

διηνοιχθησαν Byz P⁴⁵ A N X Γ Π 0131 13 *pm* lat sy^{s,p,h}

ηνοιγησαν ℵ B D Δ 0274 1 892

ηνοιχθησαν L

διηνοιγησαν W Θ *pc*

(Has P⁴⁵ conflated L and W, or have these managed independent conflations of the "Byzantine" and "Alexandrian" readings? Note that Hort's "late Syrian" reading now has the earliest attestation.)

59. Mark 9.49

πας γαρ πυρι ἁλισθησεται B L Δ 1 13 *pc* sy^s sa

πασα γαρ θυσια ἁλι ἁλισθησεται D *pc* it

πας γαρ πυρι ἁλισθησεται και Byz A K Π *pm* vg sy^{p,h}
πασα θυσια ἁλι ἁλισθησεται

(This is another of Hort's "Syrian conflations." But the "Alexandrian" reading could easily be the result of homoioteleuton, and a different bit of parablepsis could have given rise to the "Western" reading. Does not the presence of the article with "salt" at the beginning of vs. 50 suggest that "salt" has already been introduced in the prior context?)

60. Mark 12.17

και αποκριθεις W 258 *al*

  ὁ δε Ιησους ℵ B C L Δ Ψ 33 *pc* sy^{(p)} cop

και αποκριθεις ὁ Ιησους Byz P⁴⁵ A N X Γ Π Φ 1 13 *pm* sy^{(s),h}

αποκριθεις δε ὁ Ιησους D 700 *pc* lat

αποκριθεις δε Θ 565

(Who is conflating whom? It seems more likely that Theta has simplified the "Western" reading than that the latter builds on the former. But the "Western" reading may well be a conflation of the "Byzantine" and "Alexandrian" readings. It seems clear that P⁴⁵ cannot have conflated W and B, but might these have separate simplifications of the "Byzantine" reading? Note that Hort's "late Syrian" reading now has the earliest attestation.)

61. Luke 9.57

και πορευομενων	P⁴⁵,⁷⁵ ℵ B C L Θ Ξ 33 pc syᶜ,ˢ,ᵖ bo
εγενετο δε πορευομενων	Byz A W Ψ 1 pm lat syʰ
και εγενετο πορευομενων	D 13 a c e r¹

(This would appear to be a "Western" conflation.)

62. Luke 10.42

ἑνος δε εστιν χρεια	Byz P⁴⁵,⁷⁵ A C K P R W Γ Δ Θ
	Λ Π Ψ 13 pl lat syᶜ,ᵖ,ʰ sa
ολιγων δε χρεια εστιν ἤ ενος	B
ολιγων δε εστιν χρεια ἤ ενος	P³ L C² 1 33 pc syʰᵐᵍ bo
ολιγων δε εστιν ἤ ενος	ℵ

(The MSS usually associated with the "Alexandrian" text-type are
rather scattered here. Codex L and company might be said to
conflate the "Byzantine" reading and that of B. Note that Hort's
"late Syrian" reading now has the earliest attestation, with a
vengeance.)

63. Luke 11.12

ἤ και	P⁷⁵ ℵ B L 1 13 33 cop
εαν δε και	D
ἤ και εαν	Byz P⁴⁵ R W X Γ Δ Θ Π Ψ pl syʰ

(Should we say that "Syrian" editors conflated the "Alexandrian"
and "Western" readings, or is Hort's "late Syrian" reading really
the original?)

64. Luke 12.30

ζητει	D it
επιζητουσιν	P⁷⁵ ℵ B L X 070 13 33 pc
επιζητει	Byz P⁴⁵ A Q W Γ Δ Θ Λ Π Ψ 1 pl

(Conflation or confusion? Note that Hort's "late Syrian" reading
now has very early attestation.)

65. Luke 13.2

ὁτι ταυτα	ℵ B D L pc d e r¹
τα τοιαυτα	69 pc
ὁτι τοιαυτα	Byz P⁷⁵ A W X Γ Δ Θ Λ Π Ψ 070 1 pm lat sy⁽ᶜ,ˢ,ᵖ⁾,ʰ

(Did P⁷⁵ conflate B and 69? Note that Hort's "late Syrian" reading now has the earliest attestation.)

66. John 5.15 ανηγγειλεν   Byz P⁶⁶,⁷⁵ A B Γ Θ Λ Π Ψ
                                      063 1 *pm* sa (lat syʰ)
             ειπεν   ℵ C L *pc* e q syᶜ,ˢ,ᵖ bo
   ανηγγειλεν και ειπεν αυτοις W
   απηγγειλεν   D K U Δ 13 33 *al* (lat syʰ)

(Codex W appears to have a conflation involving the "Byzantine" and "Alexandrian" readings. Note that the "Byzantine" reading, which Hort tentatively rejected in spite of B, now has strong early attestation.)

67. John 6.69 ὁ ἅγιος του θεου   P⁷⁵ ℵ B C D L W
    ὁ Χριστος ὁ υἱος του θεου   Byz K Π Ψ 0250 13 (Δ Θ 1 33)
                                     Diatessaron *pl* lat syr
    ὁ Χριστος ὁ ἅγιος του θεου   P⁶⁶ cop

(An instructive conflation on the part of P⁶⁶.)

68. John 7.41
αλλοι ελεγον   Byz P⁶⁶ ℵ D W Γ Δ Π Ψ 0105 13 *pm* syᶜ,ᵖ,ʰ
οἱ δε ελεγον   P⁶⁶ᶜ,⁷⁵ B L N T X Θ 33 *al* lat
αλλοι δε ελεγον   1 *pc* e bo

(Is this a "Caesarean" conflation? Note the very early attestation for the "Byzantine" reading.)

69. John 9.6 επεθηκεν   B *pc*
          εχρισεν   661
          επεχρισεν   Byz P⁶⁶,⁷⁵ ℵ A C D K L W Δ Θ Π Ψ 0124
                               0216 1 13 *pl* lat syr cop

(Presumably no one would wish to suggest that the "Byzantine" reading is a conflation of B and 661, even before the advent of P⁶⁶,⁷⁵! And yet, Hort followed B.)

70. John 9.8 τυφλος ἦν   Byz C³ Γ Δ *pm*
      προσαιτης ἦν   P⁶⁶,⁷⁵ ℵ B C D *al* lat cop syˢ,ᵖ,ʰ
      τυφλος ἦν και προσαιτης   69 *pc* e syᵖᵃˡ

(An evident conflation on the part of a few MSS.)

71. John 11.44 αυτοις   157
          ὁ Ιησους   700 sy^s
      αυτοις ὁ Ιησους   Byz P^{45,66} ℵ A C² D X Γ Δ Θ Λ Π Ψ
                                 0250 1 13 *pl* it

        ὁ Ιησους αυτοις   L W
          Ιησους αυτοις   P^{75} B C cop

(157 and 700 have separate simplifications of the "Byzantine" reading. I suggest the same explanation for the "Alexandrian" reading—the editors of the UBS text evidently agree, whereas Hort did not.)

72. John 13.24
πυθεσθαι τις αν ειη π. οὖ λ.   Byz P^{66} A K W Γ Δ Λ
                                     Π 1 13 *pl* syr cop

πυθεσθαι τις αν ειη οὗτος π. οὖ λ.   D
και λεγει αυτω ειπε τις εστιν π. οὖ λ.   B C I L X 068 33 *pc*
πυθεσθαι τις αν ειη περι οὖ ελεγεν και   ℵ
λεγει αυτω ειπε τις εστιν π. οὖ λ.

(This would appear to be an unusually blatant conflation on the part of Aleph, conflating the "Byzantine" and "Alexandrian" readings.)

73. John 13.36
απεκριθη   B C L *pc* lat cop
λεγει αυτω   D
απεκριθη αυτω   Byz P^{66} ℵ A C³ K W X Γ Δ Θ Λ Π Ψ 1 13 *pl*

(A century ago this might have been interpreted as a "Syrian" conflation of the "Alexandrian" and "Western" readings, but now the presence of P^{66} rather encourages the opposite conclusion.)

74. Acts 11.7 ηκουσα δε   Byz L P *pm*
          και ηκουσα   D *pc* sy^s
        ηκουσα δε και   ℵ A B E *al* cop

(Might this be an "Alexandrian" conflation?)

75. Acts 20.28 $\tau o v$ $\kappa v \rho \iota o v$ P[74] A C D E Ψ 33 *al* cop

    $\tau o v$ $\vartheta \epsilon o v$ ℵ B 056 0142 *al* syr

    $\tau o v$ $\kappa v \rho \iota o v$ $\kappa \alpha \iota$ $\vartheta \epsilon o v$ Byz L P 049 *pm*

(Here we have a fine candidate for a "Byzantine" conflation, provided that the opposite interpretation is rejected.)

76. Acts 23.9 $\tau \iota \nu \epsilon \varsigma$ P[74] A E 33 *pc* bo

    $o \iota$ $\gamma \rho \alpha \mu \mu \alpha \tau \epsilon \iota \varsigma$ Byz *pm*

    $\tau \iota \nu \epsilon \varsigma$ $\tau \omega \nu$ $\gamma \rho \alpha \mu \mu \alpha \tau \epsilon \omega \nu$ ℵ B C *al* sa

(Might this be an "Alexandrian" conflation?)

77. Rom. 6.12 $\alpha v \tau \eta$ P[46] D E F G d f g m

    $\tau \alpha \iota \varsigma$ $\epsilon \pi \iota \vartheta \upsilon \mu \iota \alpha \iota \varsigma$ $\alpha v \tau o v$ ℵ A B C *al* lat cop

    $\alpha v \tau \eta$ $\epsilon \nu$ $\tau \alpha \iota \varsigma$ $\epsilon \pi \iota \vartheta \upsilon \mu \iota \alpha \iota \varsigma$ $\alpha v \tau o v$ Byz K L P Ψ *pm*

(Here is another fine candidate for a "Byzantine" conflation, unless the other two readings are independent simplifications. If the "Western" reading were original, however could the "Alexandrian" reading have come into being, and vice versa? But if the "Byzantine" reading is original the other two are easily explained.)

78. 2 Cor. 7.14 $\epsilon \pi \iota$ $\tau \iota \tau o v$ $\alpha \lambda \eta \vartheta \epsilon \iota \alpha$ ℵ B *pc*

    η $\pi \rho o \varsigma$ $\tau \iota \tau o v$ $\alpha \lambda \eta \vartheta \epsilon \iota \alpha$ D E F G P Ψ *pc* lat syr cop

    η $\epsilon \pi \iota$ $\tau \iota \tau o v$ $\alpha \lambda \eta \vartheta \epsilon \iota \alpha$ Byz P[46] ℵ[c] C K L 0243 *pl*

(A century ago this might have been interpreted as a "Syrian" conflation, but P[46] now makes the "Byzantine" reading the earliest and enhances its claim to be the original—a claim with which the editors of the UBS text evidently concur.)

79. 1 Thess. 3.2

$\kappa \alpha \iota$ $\delta \iota \alpha \kappa o \nu o \nu$		$\tau o v$ $\vartheta \epsilon o v$	ℵ A P Ψ *pc* lat cop
$\kappa \alpha \iota$	$\sigma v \nu \epsilon \rho \gamma o \nu$		B 1962
$\kappa \alpha \iota$	$\sigma v \nu \epsilon \rho \gamma o \nu$ $\tau o v$ $\vartheta \epsilon o v$		D 33 b d e mon
$\delta \iota \alpha \kappa o \nu o \nu$ $\kappa \alpha \iota$ $\sigma v \nu \epsilon \rho \gamma o \nu$ $\tau o v$ $\vartheta \epsilon o v$			G f g
$\kappa \alpha \iota$ $\delta \iota \alpha \kappa o \nu o \nu$ $\tau o v$ $\vartheta \epsilon o v$ $\kappa \alpha \iota$ $\sigma v \nu \epsilon \rho \gamma o \nu$ $\eta \mu \omega \nu$			Byz K *pl* sy[p,h]

(Codex G evidently has a conflation and Codex D might be said to have one. Is the "Byzantine" reading a conflation, or is it the original with which all the others have tampered in one way or another?)

80. 2 Thess. 3.4

και εποιησατε και ποιειτε	G
και ποιειτε και ποιησετε	Byz א︎ᶜ Dᶜ Ψ *pl*
ποιειτε και ποιησετε	א︎ A *pc*
ποιειτε και ποιησατε	D
και εποιησατε και ποιειτε και ποιησετε	B sa

(This would appear to be a conflation on the part of B, which is abandoned by both the Nestle and UBS texts.)

Group 2. b) Substantial differences—conflation dubious.

81. Matt. 10.23

φευγετε εις την αλλην	Byz C K X Δ Π *pl*
φευγετε εις την ετεραν	א︎ B W 33 *pc*
φευγετε εις την αλλην καν εκ ταυτης διωκωσιν	Θ (D L 1 13) *pc*
ὑμας φευγετε εις την ετεραν	

(The "Western" reading here seems to include a conflation of the "Byzantine" and "Alexandrian" readings.)

82. Matt. 27.23

ὁ δε εφη	א︎ B Θ 13 33 *pc* sa
λεγει αυτοις ὁ ἡγεμων	D L 1 *pc* it syᵖ bo
ὁ δε ἡγεμων εφη	Byz A W 064 0250 *pm*

(Conflation or confusion?)

83. Mark 6.33

εκει και προηλθον αυτους	א︎ B *pc* lat cop
εκει και προσηλθον αυτους	L *pc*
εκει και προσηλθον αυτοις	Δ Θ
εκει και συνηλθον αυτου	D b
προς αυτους και συνηλθον προς αυτον	33
εκει και προηλθον αυτους και συνηλθον προς αυτον	Byz (A) K Π (13

192

(Conflation or confusion? This is one of Hort's eight "Syrian conflations," but unless one is prepared to argue that the "Byzantine" reading is based on 33 it does not meet the requirements for a conflation and may properly be viewed as the original that all the others have simplified.)

84. Mark 8.26

μη εις την κωμην εισελθης	ℵ W
μηδε εις την κωμην εισελθης	ℵ^c B L 1 pc cop sy^s
ὑπαγε εις τον οικον σου και μηδενι	D d q
ειπης εις την κωμην	
μηδε εις την κωμην εισελθης μηδε	Byz A C K X Δ Π 33
ειπης τινι εν τη κωμη	pl sy^{p,h}
ὑπαγε εις τον οικον σου και εαν εις	13 (Θ pc lat)
την κωμην εισελθης μηδενι ειπης	
μηδε εν τη κωμη	

(Conflation or confusion? This is another of Hort's eight "Syrian conflations," but the "Byzantine" reading does not meet the requirements for a conflation and may reasonably be viewed as the original.)

85. Mk 9:38

ὅς ουκ ακολουθει μεθ ὑμων και εκωλυομεν αυτον	D
ὅς ουκ ακολουθει ἡμιν και εκωλυσαμεν αυτον	X (W 1) 13 pc lat
και εκωλυομεν αυτον ὅτι ουκ ηκολουθει ἡμιν	ℵ B (L Ψ) Δ Θ
	0274 pc aur f
και εκωλυσαμεν αυτον ὅτι ουκ ακολουθει ἡμιν	C pc cop
ὅς ουκ ακολουθει ἡμιν και εκωλυσαμεν αυτον ὅτι	Byz A K Π
ουκ ακολουθει ἡμιν	pm sy^h

(Conflation or confusion? Here is another of Hort's eight "Syrian conflations." If this is a "Byzantine" conflation, it is built on the lesser "Western" and "Alexandrian" witnesses, and in that event, where did D and B get their readings? Is it not more reasonable to regard the "Byzantine" reading as the original that the others have variously simplified? Nestle[24] seems to reflect essentially this opinion.)

86. Luke 9.10

τοπον ερημον	ℵ *al* sy^c
κωμην λεγομενην Βηδσαιδα	D
πολιν καλουμενην Βηδσαιδα	P^{75}
πολιν καλουμενην Βηθσαιδα	ℵ^c B L Ξ 33
	pc cop
κωμην καλουμενην Βηθσαιδαν εις τοπον ερημον	Θ
τοπον ερημον πολεως καλουμενης Βηθσαιδαν	Byz A C W (1)
	13 *pm* sy$^{(p),h}$

(Conflation or confusion? This is yet another of Hort's eight "Syrian conflations," but the "Byzantine" reading does not meet the requirements for a conflation and may reasonably be viewed as the original. Codex Theta appears to have conflated elements from all four of the other readings!)

87. Luke 9.34

εισελθειν	P^{75} S
εισελθειν αυτους	ℵ B L *pc* bo
εισελθειν εκεινους	*pc*
αυτους εισελθειν	C *pc*
εκεινους εισελθειν	Byz P^{45} A D P R W X Γ Δ Θ Λ Π
	Ψ 1 13 *pl* sa

(Conflation or confusion? Note that the "Byzantine" reading now has very early attestation.)

88. Luke 11.54

ενεδρευοντες αυτον θηρευσαι τι εκ του στοματος αυτου	P^{75} (ℵ) B L *pc* cop
ζητουντες αφορμην τινα λαβειν αυτου ινα εὑρωσιν κατηγορησαι αυτον	D (Θ it sy^{s,c})
ενεδρευοντες αυτον ζητουντες θηρευσαι τι εκ του στοματος αυτου ινα κατηγορησωσιν αυτου	Byz A C W (Ψ 1) 13 *pm* (lat sy^p)

194

(Conflation or confusion? This is another of Hort's eight "Syrian conflations," which clearly does not meet the requirements for a conflation. The solution of this problem is linked to textual choices in verse 53, but I submit that the "Byzantine" reading here is a serious candidate for the original.)

89. Luke 12.18

παντα τα γενηματα μου	ℵ D it (sy^{s,c})
παντα τον σιτον και τα αγαθα μου	P^{75c} B L 070 1
	(13) pc cop
παντα τα γενηματα μου και τα αγαθα μου	Byz A Q W Θ Ψ
	pm vg sy^{p,h}

(Conflation or confusion? This is the last of Hort's eight "Syrian conflations." The "Western" reading could easily have arisen through homoioteleuton and the "Alexandrian" reading be the result of a stylistic retouching.)

90. Luke 24.47

αρξαμενον	Byz P^{75} A F H K M U V W Γ Δ Λ Π 063 1 13 pm syr
αρξαμενοι	ℵ B C L N X 33 pc cop
αρξαμενος	Θ Ψ 028 pc
αρξαμενων	D pc lat

(Conflation or confusion? Note that Hort's "late Syrian" reading now has the earliest attestation.)

91. John 2.15

ανετρεψεν	P^{66} B W X Θ 0162 pc
κατεστρεψεν	P^{59} ℵ 13 pc
ανεστρεψεν	Byz P^{75} A G K L P Γ Δ Λ Π Ψ 1 pl

(Conflation or confusion? Note that Hort's "late Syrian" reading now has very early attestation.)

92. John 8.51

τον λογον μου	433 pc
τον εμον λογον	P^{75} ℵ B C D L X W Ψ 0124 33 al cop
τον λογον τον εμον	Byz P^{66} E G K Γ Δ Θ Λ Π 1 13 pm lat syr

(Conflation or confusion? Note that Hort's "late Syrian" reading now has very early attestation.)

93. John 9.28 ελοιδορησαν   Byz P⁶⁶ A E G K S X Γ Δ Λ 13 *pm* lat
         και ελοιδορησαν   P⁷⁵ ℵ B W 0124 *pc*
         οἱ δε ελοιδορησαν   ℵ ᶜ D L N Θ Ψ 0250 1 33 *pc* syr bo
         ελοιδορησαν ουν   69 *pc*

(Conflation or confusion? Note that Hort's "late Syrian" reading now has very early attestation, and is also the shortest.)

94. John 10.32 καλα εργα εδειξα ὑμιν   Byz P⁶⁶ D L X Γ Δ 13 *al*
         εργα καλα εδειξα ὑμιν   (P⁴⁵) ℵ A K Λ Π Ψ 1 33 *al* lat
         εργα εδειξα ὑμιν   W
         εργα εδειξα ὑμιν καλα   B 1170 pc
         εδειξα ὑμιν εργα καλα   (P⁷⁵)

(Conflation or confusion? Note the very early attestation for the "Byzantine" reading.)

95. John 11.21
ὁ αδελφος μου ουκ αν απεθανεν   P⁴⁵,⁶⁶ K 0250
ὁ αδελφος μου ουκ αν ετεθνηκει   Byz E G U Γ Δ Θ Λ Π Ω 13 *pm*
ουκ αν απεθανεν ὁ αδελφος μου   P⁷⁵ ℵ B C L W *pc*
ουκ αν απεθανεν μου ὁ αδελφος   (Ψ) 1 33 565 *pc*
ουκ αν ὁ αδελφος μου απεθανεν   (A) D *pc*

(Conflation or confusion? Note that Hort's "late Syrian" order now has very early attestation.)

96. John 11.32
απεθανεν μου ὁ αδελφος   Byz P⁴⁵ A E G K S X Γ Λ Π 1 *pl*
μου απεθανεν ὁ αδελφος   P⁶⁶,⁷⁵ ℵ B C L W Δ Θ 33 *pc*
απεθανεν ὁ αδελφος μου   69 lat
μου ὁ αδελφος απεθανεν   D

(Conflation or confusion? Note that Hort's "late Syrian" reading now has very early attestation.)

97. John 13.26
και εμβαψας   Byz P⁶⁶ᶜ A K W Γ Δ Θ Λ Π Ψ 1 13 *pl* lat syr cop
βαψας ουν   ℵ B C L X 33 *pc*
και βαψας   D *pc*

(Is this a "Western" conflation? Note that the "Byzantine" reading now has the earliest attestation.)

98. John 14.5

δυναμεθα την όδον ειδεναι	Byz P⁶⁶ A L N Q W X Γ Δ Θ Λ Π Ψ 1 13 *pl* lat syr cop
την όδον ειδεναι δυναμεθα	ℵ K
οιδαμεν την όδον	B C a b e
την όδον οιδαμεν	D

(Conflation or confusion? Note that Hort's "late Syrian" reading now has the earliest attestation. The editors of the UBS text evidently agree that it is the original.)

99. Acts 25.6

πλειους	ή δεκα	Byz Ψ *pm*
	οκτω ή δεκα	2147 *pc* syr
πλειους οκτω ή δεκα		E *al*
ου πλειους οκτω ή δεκα		(P⁷⁴ ℵ) B A C 33 *pc* lat bo

(Is this an "Alexandrian" conflation?)

100. 1 Cor. 9.21

κερδησω	ανομους	Byz ℵᶜ K L Ψ *pl*
κερδησω τους ανομους		P⁴⁶
κερδανω	ανομους	F G
κερδανω τους ανομους		ℵ A B C P 33 *pc*
τους ανομους κερδησω		D E

(Might this be a "Western" conflation?)

101. Phil. 1.14

λογον λαλειν	Byz P⁴⁶ Dᶜ K *pm*
λογον του θεου λαλειν	ℵ A B P Ψ 33 *al* lat syr cop
λογον λαλειν του θεου	D d e
του θεου λογον λαλειν	42 234 483
λογον κυριου λαλειν	F G g

(Conflation or confusion? Note that Hort's "late Syrian" reading now has the earliest attestation. The editors of the UBS text give tentative preference to it.)

102. Heb. 10.38 εκ πιστεως   Byz P¹³ Dᶜ E I K L P Ψ *pl* b t z bo

        μου εκ πιστεως   P⁴⁶ ℵ A H 33 *pc* lat sa

        εκ πιστεως μου   D *pc* d e syᵖ·ʰ

(Why did the "conflating Syrians" miss this opportunity to fill out their text? Note that Hort's "late Syrian" reading now has very early attestation.)

103. 1 Pet. 5.8 τινα καταπιη   Byz P⁷² A 056 *al* lat syr

        τινα καταπιν   ℵ

        τινα καταπιειν   ℵᶜ K L P 049 *al* bo

        τινα καταπιει   0142 *pc*

        καταπιειν   B Ψ 0206 1175 *pc*

        καταπιη τινα   33 *al*

(Conflation or confusion? Note that the "Byzantine" reading now has the earliest attestation.)

Although many of the examples in Group 2 scarcely offer the required phenomena for possible conflation, others do, to a greater or lesser extent. I will make some observations and draw some conclusions while recognizing that the evidence is not as clear as in the first section.

Ignoring probabilities for the moment, I will tabulate the "possible" conflations (many of which are entirely improbable).

	total	examples
Western text-type	9	40, 52, 53, 60, 61, 79, 81, 97, 100
Alexandrian text-type	7	40, 42, 50, 51, 74, 76, 99
Codex B	2	57, 80
Codex Aleph	2	48, 72
Byzantine text-type	26	
with early attestation	10	60, 63, 64, 65, 69, 71, 73, 78, 91, 92
lacking phenomena	5	44, 83, 84, 86, 88
really possible	11	41, 43, 47, 56, 59, 75, 77, 79?, 82?, 85?, 89

None of the Western "conflations" has early papyrus support, and I believe there is general agreement among scholars that none of the "Western" instances, except 79, is original, whether or not the mechanism that gave rise to the readings was actually conflation in every case.

None of the Alexandrian "conflations" (including those of B and Aleph) has early papyrus support. I believe that both B's instances and one of Aleph's are universally rejected (the UBS text follows Aleph in 48). Modern editors continue to adopt the "Alexandrian" instances.

Ten of the Byzantine "conflations" have early papyrus attestation (and in only five of the instances do any of the other readings have such support), so they may not be used to argue for a late "Byzantine" text-type. Of the sixteen cases without early papyrus attestation, in only four of them do any other readings have such support (77, 86, 88, 89). I submit that in at least five instances (I think 79, 82, and 85 should also be included) the "Byzantine" reading does not exhibit the required phenomena for a conflation. Most of these are among Hort's eight "Syrian conflations," so I felt obliged to include them lest I be accused of suppressing unfavorable evidence. With reference to the remaining eight instances that may fairly be described as possible conflations, I believe they are most reasonably explained as being the original readings (see the comments under each one). It is significant that in thirty-three of the examples given in Group 2 the "Byzantine" text is being possibly conflated by other witnesses and in twenty-four examples (not necessarily the same ones) the "Byzantine" reading has early papyrus support.

Conclusion

The evidence presented in this appendix justifies the following statements: "Western" witnesses have clear, undoubted conflations; "Alexandrian" witnesses have clear, undoubted conflations; many putative conflations build upon "Byzantine" readings; numerous readings that were once thought to be late "Syrian conflations" now have early papyrus attestation. It follows that Hort's statement and use of "conflation" are erroneous.

It has been customary to refer to the "Byzantine" text as "the later, conflated text,"[3] as if "conflation" were a pervading characteristic of this text. The evidence presented above scarcely supports such a characterization since in fully sixty percent of the examples the "Byzantine" text is being built upon and not vice versa. Reference has already been made to Hutton's *Atlas* (on p. 59) which provides evidence that there are over eight hundred places where the producers of the "Byzantine" text could have conflated "Western" and "Alexandrian" readings (following Hort's hypothesis) but did not.

I trust that the reader will not judge me to be unreasonable if I express the hope that all concerned will loyally concede that the specter of "Syrian conflation" has been laid to rest. Henceforth no one may reasonably or responsibly characterize the "Byzantine" text-type as being "conflate" nor argue therefrom that it must be late.[4]

Appendix E

Text Determination in the "Plucking Grain on the Sabbath" Pericope

(Matthew 12:1-8; Mark 2:23-28; Luke 6:1-5)

by Dr. Jakob Van Bruggen (The Netherlands)[1]

Introduction

Between the Authorized Version and the modern English translations there are various differences which go back to differences in the basic text followed. Sometimes Nestle[25] (N25) places the siglum p) beside the reading now abandoned, to indicate the opinion that these readings have "probably crept in from one of the other Gospels" (Preface N25 p. 80*). In total N25 mentions six cases of parallelising readings in the Koine-text (K-text) (see *table I*). This arouses suspicion about the K-text in general and against the readings at issue in particular. Thus Metzger in his *Textual Commentary* writes at Matthew 12:4: "Although ἔφαγον is supported by only ℵ B and 481, as the non-parallel reading it is more likely to have been altered to ἔφαγεν than vice-versa."

Comparison with the Critical Apparatus in Aland's *Synopsis Quattuor Evangeliorum* (1964) shows that the suspicion about the abandoned readings does not always remain. Twice the Synopsis allows the qualifying designation p) to drop out and in one of these cases it also abandons the hesitation about the correctness of the text originally followed (in Mark 2:26 the square brackets around πῶς disappear; in UBS[3] they do not reappear). On the other hand a variant not mentioned in N25 is included as a p)-variant to the discredit of the K-text (see *table II*).

Number and distribution of the p)-variants

A study of the readings which can be qualified as p) leads to the result that all types of text include such readings.

In the list of possible p)-variants (see *table III*) the two readings which were qualified in N25 (but not in the Synopsis) as p)-readings are included. Also included was the variant $+\delta\epsilon\upsilon\tau\epsilon\rho o\pi\rho\omega\tau\omega$ from Luke 6:1 (omission of this word is very similar to the omission of the words $\epsilon\pi\iota$ Αβιαθαρ αρχιερεως in Mark 2:26; this last case is qualified as p) by Aland in the Synopsis). Also, the insertion of $\tau\omega\nu$ in Luke 6:1 was considered as a p)-variant. So, four other variants were included, besides the nineteen mentioned by Aland in the Synopsis as p)-variants, according to the criteria which Aland evidently had used in the other nineteen cases. Inclusion of these four readings (numbers 2, 11, 12, and 13) is more to the detriment of the K-text than to its advantage; B has only one while the K-text has three of the four variants indicated as p). The distribution of these possible p)-variants and their number per manuscript or group can be found on the left half of *table III*.

The complete list of p)-variants must now be closely examined. If of two readings the one is similar to parallel-gospel I and the other to parallel-gospel II, none of the two readings can be qualified as p) (see numbers 10, 17, 23). In the case of number 11, there are special reasons for not using the description p): if BD have the original text, one must admit that at some moment, simultaneously, $\pi\tilde{\omega}\varsigma$ was inserted in Mark and $\dot{\omega}\varsigma$ in Luke. In addition, there are still a number of unclear cases: in numbers 14, 16, and 21, the possible assimilation to another gospel is only present in one manuscript, or it is accompanied by simultaneous dissimilation. When we look at the variants which remain as serious candidates for the title p), it appears that these harmonising readings occur *the least* in the K-text (see the right half of *table III*).

Internal and external criticism

The omission of all the p)-variants would lead to a text which sometimes follows B (numbers 2, 3, and 13) and sometimes the K-text (numbers 4, 12, 19, and 20). The remaining five points of difference between B and the K-text (numbers 10, 11, 17, 21, and 22) could be solved on external grounds. In four of these five cases the Koine-reading is not a specific K-lectio but also occurs in D (10, 21), W (10, 11, 17), or Sinaiticus (11, 17, 21). In these four cases the K-lectio may be chosen. This means that B is followed three times against eight times for the K-text. There is reason to ask whether the K-text should not be followed in number 23 as well: it also is not a specific K-lectio.

In the Synopsis of Aland, B is followed eight times (2, 3, 10, 12, 13, 17, 21, 23) and the K-text four times (4, 11, 19, 20) in the twelve differences between B and K-text now being discussed. In the text of UBS³ the K-text has also been abandoned in number 19 and has been placed between square brackets in number 20. Thus B has been subscribed to nine or ten times and the K-text three or two times. This means that the number of readings in the text of UBS³ qualified as p) increases by two or three (12, 19 and (20)). This increase in the amount of assimilating readings in the text of the United Bible Societies is the result of the abandonment of K-readings under the influence of P⁴ (this papyrus evidently turned the scale in favor of an altered point of view in Luke 6:3; also in Luke 6:4 the first word ὡς is placed between square brackets under the influence of P⁴). Is assimilation objectionable when it is found in the K-text and not when it occurs in a papyrus?

Or is a reading no longer called assimilating when it appears in a papyrus? This suggestion finds support in the strange fact that the designation p) for the reading εφαγεν in Matthew 6:4 is abandoned in Aland's Synopsis as soon as P⁷⁰ is also mentioned as a witness to this reading. Such a proceeding raises questions concerning the applicability of the rule of internal criticism that a nonparallel reading deserves preference.

Are p)-variants really p)-variants?

From the presupposition that in the transmission of the text there was a process of assimilation and harmonization, scholars began to distinguish between so-called parallel and nonparallel readings. The question arises whether a framework has not been pressed upon the data (see last paragraph).

Example (number 2):

The reading εφαγεν seems to be a complete formal assimilation to Mark and Luke. As an assimilating reading it must, however, be of a later date. How can it then appear in P⁷⁰? Aland, Synopsis, now abandons the sign p) with this reading. But surely the nature of readings does not change when they occur in papyri? Aland's omission of the designation p) makes us ask for a different kind of approach to these and other readings. Now the apparent nonparallel reading εφαγον can be described as internal (inside Matthew) assimilating. It gives a better association with the words directly preceding it (επεινασεν και οι μετ'αυτου), and the words directly following it (αυτω . . . . ουδε τοις μετ'αυτου). However, while the reading εφαγεν does correspond formally with Mark and Luke, it does not do so materially, for by means of this reading the emphasis lies more on *David's* deed ("they that were with him" now stands in the shadow). It appears to be characteristic and specific for Matthew that he places the emphasis in this pericope more on (David and) Christ personally (cf. Matt. 12:5-7, but not in Mark and Luke). The notion of "giving to those who were with David" is absent in Matthew. This implies that the reading εφαγον can be described as an alteration of the text with the purpose of improving it philologically, but with the effect that it becomes more vague in content and more assimilated to Mark and Luke, where the eating is explicitly related to Jesus *and* the disciples, to David *and* the people in his company.

A new look at the readings which have by now been selected as real p)-variants leads to the conclusion that these variants can also be explained without the p)-model.

1. A number of readings can be interpreted as the making explicit of a preposition (number 1), subject (number 5), article (number 13) or prepositional object (number 15); in all these cases it is clear from the context that these are meant. Regarded as p)-variants these readings would be secondary, but as explicit-making readings they can be authentic: (1) because of the more "Semitic" character; (2) because of the circumstance that with the dictation of a text the omission of apparent dispensable details is more acceptable than insertion by the writers.

2. In one case the thought of mutual influence between the Gospels seems acceptable because this influence is reciprocal (numbers 7 and 18 vice versa).

3. In a reasonably large number of cases variants can be regarded as the result of philological improvement of the text:

> Numbers 2 (see discussion above).
>
> 3 (Mark-Luke: ούς ούκ έξεστιν Mt: ὁ ούκ έξον ἦν).
>
> 4 (διαπορευεσθαι in connection with δια των σποριμων).
>
> 9 (omission of a difficult, apparently incorrect, and also dispensable element).
>
> 12 (like 9).
>
> 19 (ότε in this case better Greek than όποτε).
>
> 20 (omission of ὀντες as the removal of needless redundancy).

22 (the sentence does not run well; this is solved by the omission of λαβων (Sinaiticus D W), or by the omission of ὡς (P⁴BD), cf. number 11).

A review of the distribution of the readings placed in the right column of *table III* as real p)-variants according to the evaluation now offered in three groups leads to the conclusion that the ph)-variants (philological improvement variants) are totally absent in the K-text (see *table IV*).

The application of the p)-criterion led to confusion; the application of the ph)-model leads to the coincidence of internal criteria and external data. The absence of ph)-variants in the K-text gives us occasion to grant this text our trust.

Text-determination

With the K-text as a basis it is possible to explain the divergent variants (more explicit, assimilating, philological improvement), but it is not possible to explain from the B-text or the D-text how a K-text originated (especially where the readings in the K-text are definitely *not* philological improvements).

If N25 gives the impression that a non-K-text can be taken as a basis, this is due to the fact that N25 neither follows B completely nor D; if all the variants from B rejected as p) had been maintained in the text, no model could be developed for the explanation of the variant-groups.

Example: If in Luke 6:4 ὡς πῶς was originally absent and λαβων was to be found there, then it would be inexplicable why πῶς was added (via assimilation to Mark?) without a simultaneous omission of the consequently difficult λαβων also by assimilation to Mark. If the K-text is followed then the embellishment of the somewhat paratactically jerky ἐλαβεν και to λαβων calls for measures regarding ὡς.

Another example is the choice of the reading ὁτε by UBS³ in Luke 6:3. How can one explain that this reading would ever at a later time be substituted by the reading ὁποτε which deviates from Matthew and Mark and is poorer Greek?

Conclusion

For the pericopes under consideration the K-text is evidently the most recommendable. This conclusion may not automatically be transferred to other pericopes. Yet, in applying the model presently in use for the selection and evaluation of readings elsewhere, it does induce one to test it critically against the totality of a literary text-unit, as well as the variation of readings occurring within. Atomistic treatment of variants is not the same as text-determination.

Table I. List of readings which are qualified as p) in N25 and belong to the K-text

	N25	K-text	Parallel passage
Matthew 12:4	B ℵ 481 ἐφαγον	rell. ἐφαγεν	Mark 2:26; Luke 6:4 ἐφαγεν
Matthew 12:4	BDφ it ὁ	ℵ C ℜ Θ pl οὕς	Mark 2:26 οὕς
Mark 2:26	BD --	ℵ C ℜ Θ pl πῶς	Matthew 12:4 πῶς
Luke 6:2	P75vid B(D)pc lat --	ℵ C ℜ Θ pl ποιειν	Matthew 12:2 ποιειν
Luke 6:4	B al --	ℵ ℜ D Θ pm και	Mark 2:26 και
Luke 6:5	B ℵ του σαββ.ὁ υἱος τ.ἀνθρ.	ℜ (D)Θpl ὁ υἱος τ.ἀ. και τ.σαβ.	Mark 2:28 ὁ υἱος τ. ἀ. και τ.σαβ.

Table II. Differences between Aland (Synopsis) and N25 regarding the so-called p)-variants in the K-text

Matthew 12:4	the qualification p) abandoned with the reading ἐφαγεν
Mark 2:26	square brackets around πῶς disappear; designation p) in critical apparatus abandoned
Mark 2:26	variant τους ἱερευσιν (C ℵ ADWΘ pm lat) included as p)-reading

ℵ	B	W	D	𝔐	Numbers · Text	Variant	Evaluation	ℵ	B	W	D	𝔐
	x		x		1. Matthew 12,1	+ εν [τους σαββ.]	// Mark			x		
	x	x		x	2. Matthew 12,4	εφαγεν (pro εφαγον)	// Mark-Luke			x	x	
x			x		3. Matthew 12,4	ους (pro ο)	// Mark-Luke	x			x	x
	x				4. Mark 2,23	διαπορευεσθαι (pro παρα-)	// Luke		x			
	x	x			5. Mark 2,24	+ οι μαθηται σου	// Matthew				x	x
		x			6. Mark 2,24	+ ποιειν	// Matthew -(Luke)					
x			x		7. Mark 2,25	ουδε τουτο (pro ουδεποτε)	// Luke				x	
		x	x		8. Mark 2,25	om. χρειαν εσχεν και	// Matthew-Luke				x	x
	x	x	x		9. Mark 2,26	om. επι Αβιαθαρ αρχιερεως	// Matthew-Luke			x	x	
x		x	x		10. Mark 2,26	τους ιερευσιν (pro τους ιερεις)	// Matthew-Luke			x	-	-
x			x		11. Mark 2,26	+ πως	// Matthew; /| Luke BD: om. πως (Mark), ως (Luke) alii: Matthew: πως Luke: ως	-			-	-
	x	x			12. Luke 6,1	om. δευτεροπρωτω	// Matthew-Mark	x		x		
		x	x		13. Luke 6,1	των [σπορμων]	// Matthew-Mark			x	x	
		x	x		14. Luke 6,1	ηρξαντο τιλλειν (pro ετιλλον)	in D // Mark				?	
			x		15. Luke 6,2	+ αυτω	// Matthew-Mark			x		
		x			16. Luke 6,2	ιδε, τι ποιουσιν οι μαθ. ο ουκ εξ. σον τος σαββ.	in D // Mark				?	
(x)			x		17. Luke 6,2	+ ποιειν εν/(ποιειν)	// Matthew; /| Mark					-
		x			18. Luke 6,3	ουδεποτε (pro ουδε τουτο)	// Mark			x		x
x		x	x		19. Luke 6,3	οτε (pro οποτε)	// Matthew-Mark		x	x	x	x
x	x	x	?	x	20. Luke 6,3	om. οντες	// Matthew-Mark	?		x	?	?
x			x		21. Luke 6,4	+ και [τους μετ' αυτου]	partim // Mark				x	
x		x	x		22. Luke 6,4	om. λαβων/ελαβεν και οτι [κυριος εστιν] ο υιος τ.ανθρωπον και τον σαββ.	// Matthew-Mark			x	x	x
			x		23. Luke 6,5	(pro [κυριος εστιν] τον σαββατον ο υιος τ.ανθρ.)	// Mark; /| Matthew	-				-
Total: 7	4	11	14	8				**Total:** 5	4	9	10	3
(8?)		(12)						(6?)		(13?)		(4?)

Present in: ℵ B W D 𝔐 (both flanking column groups)

THE IDENTITY OF THE NEW TESTAMENT TEXT

Table IV. Distribution of the possible p)-variants according to another evaluation-system					
א	B	W	D	**𝕽**	
-	-	1	3	1	more explicit
-	-	1	1	-	assimilating
5	6	5(6)	6	-	philological improvement

Footnotes

Chapter 1

[1]F. H. A. Scrivener, ed., *The New Testament in the Original Greek, together with the variations adopted in the Revised Version* (Cambridge: Cambridge University Press, 1880). In spite of the differences between the printed editions of the Greek text in general use, they are all agreed as to the identity of about 90 percent of the Text.

[2]For instance, Tasker says of the NEB translators, "Every member of the Panel was conscious that some of its decisions were in no sense final or certain, but at best tentative conclusions, . . ." *The Greek New Testament* (being the text translated in the New English Bible) ed. R. V. G. Tasker (Oxford: Oxford University Press, 1964), p. viii. See also B. M. Metzger, *Historical and Literary Studies*, NTTS, VIII (Grand Rapids: Wm. B. Eerdmans, 1968), pp. 160-61.

[3]Bruce M. Metzger is one of the senior New Testament scholars of North America. He has been a Professor at Princeton University for many years and has authored many scholarly works including the standard textbook, *The Text of the New Testament*.

[4]B. M. Metzger, *The Text of the New Testament* (London: Oxford University Press, 1964), p. 210.

[5]K. Aland, M. Black, C. M. Martini, B. M. Metzger, and A. Wikgren, eds. *The Greek New Testament*, third edition (New York: United Bible Societies, 1975), p. viii. Although this edition is dated 1975, Metzger's *Commentary* upon it appeared in 1971. The second edition is dated 1978. It thus appears that in the space of three years, with no significant accretion of new evidence, the same group of five scholars changed their mind in over five hundred places. It is hard to resist the suspicion that they are guessing.

[6]Even where there is unanimous testimony for the wording of the Text, the canons of internal evidence do not preclude the possibility that that unanimous testimony might be wrong. Once internal evidence is accepted as *the* way to determine the text there is no basis *in principle* for objecting to conjectural emendation. Hence no part of the Text is safe. (Even if it is required that a proposed reading be attested by at least one manuscript, a new Papyrus may come to light tomorrow with new variants to challenge the unanimous witness of the rest, and so on.)

[7]R. M. Grant, *A Historical Introduction to the New Testament* (New York: Harper and Row, 1963), p. 51.

[8]K. W. Clark, "The Theological Relevance of Textual Variation in Current Criticism of the Greek New Testament," *Journal of Biblical Literature*, LXXXV (1966), p. 15.

[9]Grant, "The Bible of Theophilus of Antioch," *Journal of Biblical Literature,* LXVI (1947), 173. For a most pessimistic statement see E. C. Colwell, "Biblical Criticism: Lower and Higher," *Journal of Biblical Literature,* LXVII (1948), 10-11. See also G. Zuntz, *The Text of the Epistles,* 1953, p. 9; K. and S. Lake, *Family 13 (The Ferrar Group),* 1941, p. vii; F. C. Conybeare, *History of New Testament Criticism,* 1910, p. 129.

[10]In ordinary usage the term "eclecticism" refers to the practice of selecting from various sources. In textual criticism there is the added implication that the sources are disparate. Just what this means in practice is spelled out in the section "What is it?" in Chapter 2.

Chapter 2

[1]E. J. Epp, "The Twentieth Century Interlude in New Testament Textual Criticism," *Journal of Biblical Literature,* XCIII (1974), p. 403.

[2]E. C. Colwell, "Hort Redivivus: A Plea and a Program," *Studies in Methodology in Textual Criticism of the New Testament,* E. C. Colwell (Leiden: E. J. Brill, 1969), pp. 152-53. Tasker records the principles followed by the NEB translators: "The Text to be translated will of necessity be eclectic, . . ." (p. vii).

[3]Metzger, *The Text,* pp. 175-76.

[4]The late Ernest Cadman Colwell might well have been described as the dean of New Testament textual criticism in North America during the 1950s and 1960s. He was associated with the University of Chicago for many years as Professor and President. Some of his important articles have been collected and reprinted in *Studies in Methodology in Textual Criticism of the New Testament.*

[5]Colwell, "Biblical Criticism," pp. 4-5. For words to the same effect see also K. Lake, *The Text of the New Testament,* sixth edition revised by Silva New (London: Rivingtons, 1959), p. 10 and Metzger, *The Text,* pp. 216-17.

[6]Colwell, "Hort Redivivus," p. 154. Cf. pp. 149-54.

[7]J. K. Elliott, *The Greek Text of the Epistles to Timothy and Titus,* ed., Jacob Geerlings, *Studies and Documents,* XXXVI (Salt Lake City: University of Utah Press, 1968), pp. 10-11. Cf. K. Aland, "The Significance of the Papyri for Progress in New Testament Research," *The Bible in Modern Scholarship,* ed. J. P. Hyatt (New York: Abingdon Press, 1965), p. 340, and Tasker, p. viii.

[8]Elliott, p. 11.

[9]Epp, p. 404.

[10]Colwell, "Scribal Habits in Early Papyri: A Study in the Corruption of the Text," *The Bible in Modern Scholarship,* ed. J. P. Hyatt (New York: Abingdon Press, 1965), pp. 371-72.

[11]Frederick G. Kenyon was an outstanding British scholar during the first half of this century. He was Director and Principal Librarian of the British Museum and his *Handbook to the Textual Criticism of the New Testament* is still a standard textbook.

[12]F. G. Kenyon, *Handbook to the Textual Criticism of the New Testament,* 2nd ed., 1926, p. 3.

[13]Epp, pp. 403-4. Cf. K. W. Clark, "The Effect of Recent Textual Criticism upon New Testament Studies," *The Background of the New Testament and its Eschatology,* ed. W. D. Davies and D. Daube (Cambridge: The Cambridge University Press, 1956), p. 37.

[14]A. F. J. Klijn is a well-known textual scholar who has specialized in the study of the "Western text-type."

[15]A. F. J. Klijn, *A Survey of the Researches into the Western Text of the Gospels and Acts; part two 1949-1969* (Leiden: E. J. Brill, 1969), p. 65.

[16]Epp, pp. 391-92.

[17]*Ibid.*, pp. 398-99.

[18]Metzger states that "Westcott and Hort's criticism is subjective." *The Text*, p. 138. See also Colwell, *Studies in Methodology in Textual Criticism of the New Testament* (Leiden: E. J. Brill, 1969), pp. 1-2.

[19]Elliott, pp. 5-6.

[20]Tasker, p. vii.

[21]Metzger, *The Text*, p. 175.

[22]Epp, p. 403.

[23]Colwell, "Hort Redivivus," p. 149.

[24]See K. W. Clark, "Today's Problems with the Critical Text of the New Testament," *Transitions in Biblical Scholarship*, ed. J. C. R. Rylaarsdam (Chicago: The University of Chicago Press, 1968), pp. 159-60, for facts and figures. Also see Epp, pp. 388-90.

[25]Epp, 390-91. Cf. G. Zuntz, *The Text of the Epistles* (London: Oxford University Press, 1953), p. 8. Epp reinforces an earlier statement by Aland: "It is clear that the situation with which our present day method of establishing the New Testament text confronts us is most unsatisfactory. It is not at all the case that, as some seem to think, everything has been done in this field and we can for practical purposes rest satisfied with the text in use. On the contrary, the decisive task still lies ahead." "The Present Position of New Testament Textual Criticism," *Studia Evangelica*, ed. F. L. Cross and others (Berlin: Akademie—Verlag, 1959), p. 731.

[26]Clark, "Today's Problems," p. 159.

[27]*Ibid.*, pp. 158-60. Cf. M. M. Parvis, "Text, NT.," *The Interpreter's Dictionary of the Bible* (4 Vols.; New York: Abingdon Press, 1962), IV, 602, and D. W. Riddle, "Fifty Years of New Testament Scholarship," *The Journal of Bible and Religion*, X (1942), 139.

[28]Cf. Clark, "Today's Problems," p. 166, and especially Colwell, "Scribal Habits," pp. 170-71.

[29]Elliott's results are interesting in a further way. He does his reconstruction "untrammeled" by considerations of manuscript support and then traces the performance of the principal manuscripts. Summarizing his statement of the results, considering only those places where there was variation, codex Aleph was right 38% of the time, A was right 38% of the time, C right 41%, D right 35%, F, G right 31%, and the bulk of the minuscules (Byzantine) was right 35% of the time (pp. 241-43). He claims that doing a reconstruction his way then enables one to trace the behavior of individual MSS and to show their "illogical fluctuations." Such a tracing is based upon his own subjective evaluation of readings but the illogical fluctuations can be seen empirically by comparing the collations of a variety of MSS.

[30]See, for example, K. Aland, "The Significance of the Papyri," p. 325; Colwell, "Scribal Habits," p. 370; Metzger, *The Text*, p. 137; V. Taylor, *The Text of the New Testament* (New York: St. Martin's Press Inc., 1961), p. 49; K. Lake, p.

67; F. G. Kenyon, *Handbook to the Textual Criticism of the New Testament* (2nd ed.; Grand Rapids: Wm. B. Eerdmans Publishing Co., 1951), p. 294; Epp, p. 386, and Riddle, Parvis and Clark, noted above (fn. 27).

[31]J. H. Greenlee, *Introduction to New Testament Textual Criticism* (Grand Rapids: Wm. B. Eerdmans Publishing Co., 1964), p. 78.

Chapter 3

[1]F. J. A. Hort and B. F. Westcott were highly respected and influential Anglican churchmen of the past century—especially during the 70s and 80s. Westcott was Bishop of Durham and Hort a Professor at Cambridge. The Greek text of the N.T. prepared by them was adopted (essentially) by the committee that produced the English Revised Version of 1881. Westcott wrote a number of commentaries on N.T. books which are still considered to be standard works. His prestige and influence were important to the success of their (W-H) undertaking.

[2]B. F. Westcott and F. J. A. Hort, *The New Testament in the Original Greek* (2 Vols.; London: Macmillan and Co., 1881).

[3]A. F. Hort, *Life and Letters of Fenton John Anthony Hort* (2 Vols.; London: Macmillan and Co. Ltd., 1896), I, 211.

[4]*Ibid.*, p. 240.

[5]*Ibid.*, p. 264.

[6]The expression *"Textus Receptus"* properly refers to some one of the printed editions of the Greek text of the N.T. related in character to the text prepared by Erasmus in the sixteenth century. (Of over thirty such editions, few are identical.) It is not identical to the text reflected in the AV (though it is quite close) nor yet to the so-called "Syrian" or "Byzantine" text (these terms will be introduced presently). The critical edition of the "Byzantine" text being prepared by Zane C. Hodges, Professor of New Testament Literature and Exegesis at the Dallas Theological Seminary, Arthur Farstad, and others, and to be published by Thomas Nelson, will differ from the *Textus Receptus* in over a thousand places.

[7]Colwell, "Hort Redivivus," p. 158.

[8]Colwell, "Genealogical Method: Its Achievements and its Limitations," *Journal of Biblical Literature*, LXVI (1947), 111.

[9]In fact, Hort did not hold to a high view of inspiration. Cf. A. F. Hort, I, 419-21 and Westcott and Hort, II, "Introduction," 280-81.

[10]Westcott and Hort, p. 73.

[11]*Ibid.*, p. 282.

[12]*Ibid.*, p. 57.

[13]Colwell, "Genealogical Method," p. 111.

[14]Westcott and Hort, pp. 178-9. Note that Hort made use of only a small fraction of the manuscripts extant in his day. Cf. K. Aland, "The Significance of the Papyri," pp. 327-28. A check of W-H's "Notes on Select Readings" in volume 2 of their *The New Testament in the Original Greek* suggests that Aland is probably generous.

[15]Westcott and Hort, p. 49.

[16]*Ibid.*, p. 106. This seems obvious enough, since the materials used in

manufacture must of necessity exist before the resulting product. A clear putative example occurs in Luke 24:53. The "Western" text has "praising God," the "Neutral" text has "blessing God" and the "Syrian" text has "praising and blessing God." According to Hort's hypothesis the longest reading was constructed out of the two shorter ones. Note that the use of the word "conflation" embodies the rejection of the possibility that the longer reading is original.

[17]Mark 6:33; 8:26; 9:38; 9:49; Luke 9:10; 11:54; 12:18; 24:53.

[18]Westcott and Hort, p. 106.

[19]Cf. Kenyon, p. 302; E. F. Harrison, *Introduction to the New Testament* (Grand Rapids: Wm. B. Eerdmans Publishing Co., 1964), p. 73; and Metzger, *The Text*, pp. 135-6.

[20]Taylor, p. 53.

[21]Lake, p. 68.

[22]Westcott and Hort, p. 115.

[23]*Ibid.*, p. 91.

[24]F. G. Kenyon, *Recent Developments in the Textual Criticism of the Greek Bible* (London: Oxford University Press, 1933), pp. 7-8.

[25]Lake, p. 72.

[26]Westcott and Hort, pp. 134-5.

[27]*Ibid.*, pp. 115-16.

[28]See, for example, Kenyon, *Recent Developments*, p. 66, Metzger, *The Text*, p. 131, and Greenlee, p. 91.

[29]Westcott and Hort, p. 133.

[30]*Ibid.*, p. 137.

[31]F. C. Burkitt, *Evangelion da-Mepharreshe* (2 vols.; Cambridge: Cambridge University Press, 1904), II, 161.

[32]H. C. Thiessen, *Introduction to the New Testament* (Grand Rapids: Wm. B. Eerdmans Publishing Co., 1955), pp. 54-55.

[33]See footnote 30, Chapter 2.

[34]Colwell, "Scribal Habits," p. 370.

[35]Cf. Colwell, "External Evidence and New Testament Criticism," *Studies in the History and Text of the New Testament*, eds. B. L. Daniels and M. J. Suggs (Salt Lake City: University of Utah Press, 1967), p. 3; Colwell, "Hort Redivivus," p. 162; Clark, "Today's Problems," pp. 159-60; Epp, p. 390.

[36]Westcott and Hort, p. 225. Cf. pp. 212-13.

[37]*Ibid.*, p. 276. And, "B very far exceeds all other documents in neutrality of text," p. 171.

[38]*Ibid.*, pp. 109-10.

[39]J. N. Birdsall, "The Text of the Gospels in Photius," *Journal of Theological Studies*, VII (1956), p. 43. Some scholars seem even to reflect the emotion of the twenty-three-year-old Hort—not long ago Epp spoke of "the tyrannical *textus receptus*" (p. 386).

[40]Clark, "The Effect of Recent Textual Criticism," p. 50.

Chapter 4

[1]Metzger, *The Text*, p. 201. For actual examples from Irenaeus, Clement, Tertullian, and Eusebius, please see Sturz (pp. 86-89), who also has a good discussion of their significance. As he says, "While scribal blunders were

recognized by them as one cause of variation, the strongest and most positive statements, by the Fathers, are in connection with the changes introduced by heretics" (p.89).

[2]J. W. Burgon, *The Revision Revised* (London: John Murray, 1883), p. 323.

[3]Colwell, "The Origin of Textypes of New Testament Manuscripts." *Early Christian Origins,* ed. Allen Wikgren (Chicago: Quadrangle Books, 1961), p. 130.

[4]J. W. Burgon, *The Causes of the Corruption of the Traditional Text of the Holy Gospels,* arranged, completed and edited by Edward Miller (London: George Bell and Sons, 1896), pp. 211-12. Cf. Martin Rist, "Pseudepigraphy and the Early Christians," *Studies in New Testament and Early Christian Literature,* ed. D. E. Aune (Leiden: E. J. Brill, 1972), pp. 78-79.

[5]Colwell, *What is the Best New Testament?* (Chicago: The University of Chicago Press, 1952), p. 53. Observe that Colwell flatly contradicts Hort. Hort said there were no theologically motivated variants; Colwell says they are in the majority. But, in the next quote, Colwell uses the term "deliberately," without referring to theology (both quotes come from the same work, five pages apart). What is Colwell's real meaning? We may no longer ask him personally, but I will hazard the following interpretation on my own.

The MSS contain several hundred thousand variant readings. The vast majority of these are misspellings or other obvious errors due to carelessness or ignorance on the part of the copyists. As a sheer guess I would say there are between ten thousand and fifteen thousand that cannot be so easily dismissed—i.e., a maximum of five percent of the variants are "significant." It is to this five percent that Colwell (and Kilpatrick, Scrivener, Zuntz, etc.) refers when he speaks of the "creation" of variant readings. A fair number of these are probably the result of accident also, but Colwell affirms, and I agree, that most of them were created deliberately.

But why would anyone bother to make deliberate changes in the text? Colwell answers, "because they were the religious treasure of the church." Some changes would be "well intentioned"—many harmonizations presumably came about because a zealous copyist felt that a supposed discrepancy was an embarrassment to his high view of Scripture. The same is probably true of many philological changes. For instance, the plain Koine style of the New Testament writings was ridiculed by the pagan Celsus, among others. Although Origen defended the simplicity of the New Testament style, the space that he gave to the question indicates that it was a matter of some concern (*Against Celsus,* Book VI, chapters 1 and 2), so much so that there were probably those who altered the text to "improve" the style. Again, their motive would be embarrassment, deriving from a high view of Scripture. Surely Colwell is justified in saying that the motivation for such variants was theological even though no obvious doctrinal axe is being ground.

To judge by the emphatic statements of the early Fathers, there were many other changes that were not "well intentioned." It seems clear that numerous variants existed in the second century that have not survived in any extant MS. Metzger refers to Gwilliam's detailed study of chapters 1–14 of Matthew in the Syriac Peshitta as reported in "The Place of the Peshitta Version in the Apparatus Criticus of the Greek N.T.," *Studia Biblica et Ecclesiastica V,* 1903,

187-237. From the fact that in thirty-one instances the Peshitta stands alone (in those chapters), Gwilliam concluded that its unknown author "revised an ancient work by Greek MSS which have no representative now extant (p. 237)" (*The Early Versions of the New Testament*, Oxford, 1977, p. 61). In a personal communication, Peter J. Johnston, a member of the IGNT editorial panel working specifically with the Syriac Versions and Fathers, says of the Harklean Version: "Readings confidently referred to in the Harklean margin as in 'well-approved MSS at Alexandria' have sometimes not come down to us at all, or if they have, they are found only in medieval minuscule MSS." In commenting upon the discrepancies between Jerome's statements of MS evidence and that extant today, Metzger concludes by saying, "the disquieting possibility remains that the evidence available to us today may, in certain cases, be totally unrepresentative of the distribution of readings in the early church" ("St. Jerome's explicit references to variant readings in manuscripts of the New Testament," *Text and Interpretation: Studies in the New Testament presented to Matthew Black*, edited by Best and McL. Wilson, Cambridge: University Press, 1979, p. 188).

Some of my critics seem to feel that the extant evidence from the early centuries is representative. However, there is good reason for believing that it is not, and in that event the extant MSS may preserve some random survivors from sets of alterations designed to grind one doctrinal axe or another. The motivation for such a reading in isolation would not necessarily be apparent to us today.

I would go beyond Colwell and say that the disposition to alter the text, even with "good motives," itself bespeaks a mentality which has theological implications.

[6]Colwell, *What is the Best New Testament?*, p. 58.

[7]M. Black, *An Aramaic Approach to the Gospels and Acts* (Oxford: Oxford University Press, 1946), p. 214.

[8]H. H. Oliver, "Present Trends in the Textual Criticism of the New Testament," *The Journal of Bible and Religion*, XXX (1962), 311-12. Cf. C. S. C. Williams, *Alterations to the Text of the Synoptic Gospels and Acts* (Oxford: Basil Blackwell, 1951), pp. 14-17.

[9]The "inconvenience" referred to is virtually fatal to the W-H theory, at least as formulated in their "Introduction." The W-H theory is much like a multistoried building—each level depends on the one below it. Thus, Hort's simplistic notion of "genealogy" absolutely depends upon the allegation that there was no deliberate alteration of the Text, and his notion of "text-types" absolutely depends upon "genealogy," and his arguments concerning "conflation" and "Syrian" readings before Chrysostom absolutely depend upon those "text-types." The foundation for the whole edifice is Hort's position that the New Testament was an ordinary book that enjoyed an ordinary transmission. With its foundation removed, the edifice collapses.

[10]Further, if a genealogical reconstruction ends up with only two immediate descendants of the Original, as in Hort's own reconstruction, then the genealogical method ceases to be applicable, as Hort himself recognized. Westcott and Hort, p. 42.

[11]Colwell, *What is the Best New Testament?*, p. 49.

[12]Codex Claromontanus apparently has a "child" three centuries younger than it (also, minuscule 205 may have been copied from 208). Codices F and G containing Paul's Epistles appear to be almost twin brothers, and groups like family 1 and family 13 are clearly closely related. Also, in the Apocalypse Hoskier has identified a number of related groups.

[13]Parvis, p. 611.

[14]Colwell, "Genealogical Method," pp. 111-12.

[15]Westcott and Hort, p. 63.

[16]*Ibid.*

[17]Colwell, "Genealogical Method," p. 114. The sort of genealogical diagram that one always sees is like a family tree that shows only male parents. Because of mixture the diagrams should be like a family tree that shows *both* parents, at every level—the farther back you go to the more hopelessly complicated it gets.

[18]Zuntz, p. 155.

[19]L. Vaganay, *An Introduction to the Textual Criticism of the New Testament*, translated by B. V. Miller (London: Sands and Company, 1937), p. 71.

[20]Aland, "The Significance of the Papyri," p. 341.

[21]Colwell, "External Evidence," p. 4.

[22]Westcott and Hort, p. 287.

[23]Colwell, "Genealogical Method," p. 124.

[24]Colwell, "The Complex Character of the Late Byzantine Text of the Gospels," *Journal of Biblical Literature*, LIV (1935), 212-13.

[25]Colwell, "Genealogical Method," p. 109.

[26]Colwell, "Scribal Habits," pp. 370-71.

[27]Burgon, *The Revision Revised*, p. 358. Burgon's own index of the Fathers is no doubt still the most extensive in existence—it contains 86,489 quotations.

[28]G. Salmon, *Some Thoughts on the Textual Criticism of the New Testament* (London, 1897), p. 33.

[29]M. M. Parvis, "The Nature and Task of New Testament Textual Criticism," *The Journal of Religion*, XXXII (1952), 173.

[30]A. Wikgren, "Chicago Studies in the Greek Lectionary of the New Testament," *Biblical and Patristic Studies in Memory of Robert Pierce Casey*, ed. J. N. Birdsall and R. W. Thomson (New York: Herder, 1963), pp. 96-121.

[31]Colwell, "The Origin of Texttypes," p. 135.

[32]Zuntz, p. 240.

[33]Klijn, p. 36.

[34]*Ibid.*, p. 66.

[35]Metzger, *Chapters in the History of New Testament Textual Criticism* (Grand Rapids: Wm. B. Eerdmans Publishing Co., 1963), p. 67.

[36]Klijn seems to be of this opinion (pp. 33-34).

[37]Cf. Burgon, *The Revision Revised*, p. 380.

[38]H. C. Hoskier, *A Full Account and Collation of the Greek Cursive Codex Evangelium 604* (London: David Nutt, 1890), Introduction, pp. cxv-cxvi.

[39]Kenyon, *Handbook*, p. 356.

[40]Colwell, "The Greek New Testament with a Limited Critical Apparatus: its Nature and Uses," *Studies in New Testament and Early Christian Literature*, ed. D. E. Aune (Leiden: E. J. Brill, 1972), p. 33.

FOOTNOTES

[41]Metzger, *The Text*, p. 141.

[42]Klijn, p. 64.

[43]Colwell, "The Significance of Grouping of New Testament Manuscripts," *New Testament Studies*, IV (1957-1958), 86-87. Cf. also Colwell, "Genealogical Method," pp. 119-123.

[44]H. C. Hoskier, *Codex B and its Allies* (2 vols.; London: Bernard Quaritch, 1914), II, 1.

[45]Zuntz, "The Byzantine Text in New Testament Criticism," *The Journal of Theological Studies*, XLIII (1942), 25.

[46]Clark, "The Manuscripts of the Greek New Testament," *New Testament Manuscript Studies*, ed. M. M. Parvis and A. P. Wikgren (Chicago: The University of Chicago Press, 1950), p. 12.

[47]K. Lake, R. P. Blake and Silva New, "The Caesarean Text of the Gospel of Mark," *Harvard Theological Review*, XXI (1928), 348-9.

[48]John William Burgon was Dean of Chichester from 1876 until his death in 1888. His biographer declared him to be "the leading religious teacher of his time" in England (E. M. Goulburn, *Life of Dean Burgon*, 2 Vols.; London: John Murray, 1892, I, vii). Clark lists Burgon along with Tregelles and Scrivener as "great contemporaries" of Tischendorf, whom he calls "the colossus among textual critics" ("The Manuscripts of the Greek New Testament," p. 9). As a contemporary of Westcott and Hort, Burgon strenuously opposed their text and theory and is generally acknowledged to have been the leading voice in the "opposition" (cf. A. F. Hort, II, 239).

[49]J. W. Burgon, *The Traditional Text of the Holy Gospels Vindicated and Established*, arranged, completed, and edited by Edward Miller (London: George Bell and Sons, 1896), pp. 46-7.

[50]Kurt Aland, the Director of the Institut für neutestamentliche Textforschung at Münster, is perhaps the leading textual critic in Europe. He is a co-editor of both of the most popular editions of the Greek N.T.—Nestle and U.B.S. He is the one who catalogs each new MS that is discovered.

[51]Aland, "The Significance of the Papyri," pp. 334-7.

[52]Colwell, "Hort Redivivus," pp. 156-7.

[53]Epp, pp. 396-7.

[54]*Ibid.*, p. 398.

[55]*Ibid.*, p. 397.

[56]*Ibid.*, pp. 394-6.

[57]*Ibid.*

[58]Cf. Metzger, *A Textual Commentary on the Greek New Testament* (London: United Bible Societies, 1971), p. xviii.

[59]Klijn, pp. 45-8.

[60]*Ibid.*

[61]G. D. Fee, *Papyrus Bodmer II (P⁶⁶): Its Textual Relationships and Scribal Characteristics* (Salt Lake City: University of Utah Press, 1968), p. 56.

[62]*Ibid.*, p. 14.

[63]J. N. Birdsall, *The Bodmer Papyrus of the Gospel of John* (London, 1960), p. 17.

[64]C. H. Turner, "Historical Introduction to the Textual Criticism of the New Testament," *Journal of Theological Studies*, Jan. 1910, p. 185.

[65]Metzger, *The Text*, p. 247; Epp, p. 397.

[66]Hoskier, *Codex B*, p. xi.

[67]Fee, pp. 12-13.

[68]A hurried count using Nestle's (24th) critical apparatus (I assume that any agreement of ℵ and B will infallibly be recorded) shows them agreeing 3,007 times, where there is variation. Of these roughly 1,100 are against the "Byzantine" text, with or without other attestation, while the rest are against a small minority of MSS (several hundreds being singular readings of Codex D, one of the papyri, etc.). It appears that B and Aleph do not meet Colwell's requirement of 70 percent agreement in order to be classified in the same text-type.

[69]This is one of the central features in the method proposed by Colwell and E. W. Tune in "The Quantitative Relationships between MS Text-Types," *Biblical and Patristic Studies in Memory of Robert Pierce Casey*, eds. J. N. Birdsall and R. W. Thomson (Freiberg: Herder, 1963).

[70]See the section with that heading in Chapter 6.

[71]Colwell, "Genealogical Method," p. 118.

[72]Harrison, p. 73.

[73]Kenyon, *Handbook*, p. 302; Lake, p. 68.

[74]Burgon, *The Traditional Text*, p. 229.

[75]Westcott and Hort, p. 94 and pp. 240-1. (Since Hort regarded D and B as adequate to represent the "Western" and "Neutral" texts elsewhere, he should not object here.)

[76]Colwell, "The Origin of Texttypes," pp. 130-31.

[77]Hoskier, *Codex B*, I, 465.

[78]Burgon, *The Revision Revised*, pp. 257-65.

[79]Westcott and Hort, p. 95.

[80]*Ibid.*, p. 104.

[81]Burgon, *The Revision Revised*, p. 264.

[82]G. D. Kilpatrick, "The Greek New Testament Text of Today and the *Textus Receptus*," *The New Testament in Historical and Contemporary Perspective*, H. Anderson and W. Barclay, eds. (Oxford: Basil Blackwell, 1965), pp. 190-2. Cf. Bousset, TU, vol. 11 (1894), pp. 97-101, who agreed with Hort on only one of the eight.

[83]Lake, p. 68.

[84]Victor of Antioch for Mark 8:26, 9:38 and 9:49; Basil for Mark 9:38 and Luke 12:18; Cyril of Alexandria for Luke 12:18; Augustine for Mark 9:38.

[85]Zuntz, *The Text*, p. 12. I have not knowingly misrepresented Zuntz, or Colwell, Metzger, Aland, etc., in quoting from their works. I take it that Colwell does reject Hort's notion of genealogy, that Aland does reject Hort's notion of recensions, that Zuntz does reject Hort's notion of "Syrian" conflation, and so on. However, I do not mean to imply and it should not be assumed that any of these scholars would entirely agree with my statement of the situation at any point, and they certainly do not agree (as far as I know) with my total position.

[86]Westcott and Hort, p. 91.

[87]Lake, p. 53.

[88]Metzger, *Chapters*, p. 21.

[89]J. Geerlings and S. New, "Chrysostom's Text of the Gospel of Mark," *Harvard Theological Review*, XXIV (1931), 135.

[90]*Ibid.*, p. 141.

[91]Hoskier, *Codex B*, I, ii-iii.

[92]Zuntz, *The Text*, p. 152.

[93]Metzger, "Explicit References in the Works of Origen to Variant Readings in N.T. MSS.," *Biblical and Patristic Studies in Memory of Robert Pierce Casey*, ed. J. N. Birdsall and R. W. Thomson (New York: Herder, 1963), p. 94.

[94]Burgon, *The Traditional Text*, pp. 100, 121.

[95]To be precise, the Greek text used by the English Revisers in 1881 is meant here, or rather those places where it differs from the TR.

[96]Westcott and Hort, p. 114.

[97]Burgon, *The Traditional Text*, p. 99.

[98]*Ibid.*, p. 117.

[99]Hoskier, *Codex B*, I, 426-7.

[100]Burgon, *The Traditional Text*, pp. 99-101.

[101]Burgon, *The Causes of the Corruption*, pp. 2-3.

[102]E. Miller, *A Guide to the Textual Criticism of the New Testament* (London: George Bell and Sons, 1886), p. 53.

[103]Burgon, *The Traditional Text*, pp. ix-x. Miller's experiment pitted the Received Text against the Greek text pieced together by the body of revisers who produced the English Revised Version of 1881, which Miller aptly styles the "Neologian." He used Scrivener's *Cambridge Greek Testament* of 1887 which gives the precise Greek text represented by the E.R.V. but prints in black type the places that differ from the Received Text. Miller limited the investigation to the Gospels. He said that he discarded doubtful quotations and mere matters of spelling, that in doubtful cases he decided against the *Textus Receptus*, and that in the final tabulation he omitted many smaller instances favorable to the *Textus Receptus* (*Ibid.*, pp. 94-122).

[104]Kenyon, *Handbook*, pp. 321-2.

[105]Burgon, *The Traditional Text*, p. 116.

[106]Kenyon, *Handbook*, pp. 322-3.

[107]*Ibid.*, p. 323.

[108]*Ibid.*

[109]Supported by Barnabas (5), Justin M. (Apol. i. 15), Irenaeus (III. v.2), Origen (Comment. in Joh. xxviii. 16), Eusebius (Comment. in Ps. cxlvi), Hilary (Comment. in Matt. ad loc.), Basil (De Poenitent. 3; Hom. in Ps. xlviii. 1; Epist. Class. I. xlvi. 6). The evidence cited in footnotes 109-116 was taken from Burgon, *The Traditional Text*.

[110]Supported by Gospel of Peter (5), Acta Philippi (26), Barnabas (7), Irenaeus (Pp. 526, 681), Tertullian, Celsus, Origen, Eusebius of Emesa, ps-Tatian, Theodore of Heraclea, Ephraem, Athanasius, Acta Pilati.

[111]Supported by Gospel of Nicodemus, Acta Phillipi, Apocryphal Acts of the Apostles, Eusebius (ad Marinum, ii. 4), Gregory Nyss. (De Christ. Resurr. I. 390, 398), Gospel of Peter.

[112]Supported by Irenaeus (III. xvi. 3), Origen, Porphyry, Eusebius, Titus of Bostra.

[113]Supported by Irenaeus (III. x. 4), Origen (c. Celsum i. 60; Selecta in Ps. xlv.; Comment. in Matt. xvii.; Comment. in Joh. i. 13), Gregory Thaumaturgus (De Fid. Cap. 12), Methodius (Serm de Simeon. et Anna), Apostolic Constitutions (vii. 47; viii. 12), Diatessaron, Eusebius (Dem. Ev. pp. 163, 342), Aphraates (i.

180, 385), Jacob-Nisibis, Titus of Bostra, Cyril of Jerusalem (P. 180), Athanasius, Ephraem (Gr. iii. 434).

[114]Supported by Hegesippus (Eus. H.E. ii. 23), Marcion, Justin, Irenaeus (c. Haer. III. xviii. 5), Archelaus (xliv), Hippolytus (c. Noet. 18), Origen (ii. 188), Apostolic Constitutions (ii. 16; v. 14), Clementine Homilies (Recogn. vi. 5; Hom. xi. 20), ps-Tatian (E.C. 275), Eusebius (canon x), Hilary (De Trin. 1. 32), Acta Pilati (x. 5), Theodore of Heraclea, Athanasius (i. 1120), Titus of Bostra, Ephraem (ii. 321).

[115]Supported by Marcion (ad loc.), Justin M. (ii. 240, 762), Clement Alex. (p. 174), Tertullian (i. 455), Diatessaron, Athanasius (i. 644), Cyril of Jerusalem (iv. 1108), Gregory Nyss. (i. 624).

[116]Supported by Irenaeus (c. Haeres. IV. xiv. 1), Clement Alex. (Paed. i. 8), Cyprian (pp. 235, 321), Diatessaron, Eusebius (De Eccles. Theol. iii. 17—bis; c. Marcell. p. 292), Hilary (Pp. 1017, 1033), Basil (Eth. ii, 297), Caelestinus (Concilia iii. 356).

[117]Again we are faced with the question-begging of Hort and many subsequent writers. Irenaeus, for instance, is arbitrarily declared to be a witness to the "Western text-type" and then any reading he has is thereupon declared to be "Western." Even if we granted the existence of such entities as the "Western" and "Alexandrian" text-types (for the sake of the argument), if the requirement were imposed that only those readings which are supported by a *majority* of the witnesses assigned to a text-type may be claimed for that text-type then the number of "Western," "Alexandrian," and "Caesarean" readings would shrink *drastically*. By contrast, the number of "Byzantine" readings would remain about the same.

[118]E. F. Hills, *The King James Version Defended!* (Des Moines: The Christian Research Press, 1956), p. 73.

[119]Lake, p. 72.

[120]J. W. Burgon, *The Last Twelve Verses of the Gospel According to Saint Mark* (Ann Arbor, Mich.: The Sovereign Grace Book Club, 1959), p. 55. This reprint of Burgon's 1871 work contains an Introduction by E. F. Hills occupying pages 17-72.

[121]Taylor, p. 39.

[122]Of course this principle is also applied to the Greek MSS, with serious consequences. A recent statement by Metzger gives a clear example. "It should be observed that, in accord with the theory that members of f^1 and f^{13} were subject to progressive accommodation to the later Byzantine text, scholars have established the text of these families by adopting readings of family witnesses that differ from the Textus Receptus. Therefore the citation of the siglum f^1 or f^{13} may, in any given instance, signify a minority of manuscripts (or even only one) that belong to the family." (Metzger, *A Textual Commentary on the Greek New Testament* (companion to UBS3) p. xii.) Such a procedure misleads the user of the apparatus, who has every right to expect that the siglum will only be used when all (or nearly all) the members agree. A distorted view of the evidence is created—the divergence of f^1 or f^{13} from the "Byzantine" text is made to appear greater than it really is, and the extent of variation among the members is obscured. Greenlee's study of Cyril of Jerusalem (p. 30, see next footnote) affords another example. Among other things, he appeals to "the well-known fact that all the Caesarean witnesses are more or less corrected to the Byzantine

standard, but in different places, so that the groups must be considered as a whole, not by its [sic] individual members, to give the true picture." Would not the behavior of the individual MSS make better sense if viewed as departing from the Byzantine standard?

[123]I believe J. H. Greenlee's study of Cyril of Jerusalem is an example. *The Gospel Text of Cyril of Jerusalem* (Copenhagen: Ejnar Munksgaard, 1955).

[124]Burgon, *The Traditional Text*, pp. 97-8. I believe that Suggs tends to agree with Miller that the assimilating proclivity of medieval scribes can easily be overestimated ("The Use of Patristic Evidence," p. 140). The Lectionaries give eloquent testimony against the supposed assimilating proclivity. After discussing at some length their lack of textual consistency, Colwell observes: "Figuratively speaking, the lectionary is a preservative into which from time to time portions of the living text were dropped. Once submerged in the lectionary, each portion was solidified or fixed" (Colwell and Riddle, *Prolegomena to the Study of the Lectionary Text of the Gospels*, p. 17). Similarly, Riddle cites with favor Gregory's estimate: "He saw that as a product of the liturgical system they were guarded by a strongly conservative force, and he was right in his inference that the conservatism of the liturgy would tend frequently to make them media for the preservation of an early text. His analogy of the Psalter of the Anglican church was a good one" (*Ibid.*, pp. 40-41). Many of the lessons in the Anglican Prayer Book are much older than the AV but have never been assimilated to the AV. In short, we have good reason to doubt that medieval copyists were as addicted to assimilating the text as scholars such as Taylor would have us believe.

[125]Burgon, *The Last Twelve Verses*, p. 58. Sturz lists a number of further "Byzantine" readings that have had early Patristic support (Clement, Tertullian, Marcion, Methodius) and which now also have early Papyrus support (pp. 55-56). Here again it will no longer do to claim that the Fathers' MSS have been altered to conform to the "Byzantine" text.

[126]Zuntz, *The Text*, p. 55.

[127]Colwell, "The Origin of Texttypes," p. 132.

[128]Colwell, *What is the Best New Testament?*, p. 70.

[129]Burgon, *The Last Twelve Verses*, p. 50. (Hills wrote the Introduction.)

[130]*Ibid.*, p. 54.

[131]H. A. Sturz, *The Byzantine Text-Type and New Testament Textual Criticism* (Second Syllabus Edition; La Mirada, Cal.: Biola College Bookstore, 1972).

[132]Pp. 189-212. Sturz remarks that a number of readings (15 from this list) really should be considered as "distinctively Byzantine" but one or another so-called "Western" or "Alexandrian" witness also has them and so. . . .

Sturz draws the following conclusions from the evidence he presents: 1) "Distinctively Byzantine" readings are found in early papyri (p. 34). 2) Such readings are therefore early (p. 40). 3) Such readings cannot be the result of editing in the 4th century (p. 41). 4) The old uncials have not preserved a complete picture of the textual situation in the 2nd century (p. 41). 5) The "Byzantine" texttype has preserved some of the 2nd century tradition *not* found in the others. (p. 42). 6) The lateness of other "Byzantine" readings, for which early papyrus attestation has not yet surfaced, is now questionable (p. 43). 7) "Byzantine-Western" alignments go back into the 2nd century; they *must* be old (p. 49).

[133]P. 187. This means that the early Papyri vindicate "Byzantine" readings in 660 (or 885) places where there is significant variation. One might wish that Sturz had also given us the figures for "distinctively Western" and "distinctively Alexandrian" readings, but how are such expressions to be defined? Where is an objective definition for "Western reading," for example?

[134]Westcott and Hort, p. 21.

[135]*Ibid.*, p. 25.

[136]*Ibid.*, p. 286.

[137]Fee, "Modern Text Criticism and the Synoptic Problem," *J. J. Griesbach: Synoptic and Text-Critical Studies 1776-1976*, ed. B. Orchard and T.R.W. Longstaff (Cambridge: University Press, 1978), p. 156.

[138]Colwell, "The Greek New Testament," p. 37.

[139]Colwell, "External Evidence," p. 4.

[140]*Ibid.*, p. 3.

[141]Burgon, *The Traditional Text*, p. 67.

[142]Burgon, *The Revision Revised*, p. 251.

[143]Burgon, *The Traditional Text*, p. 66.

[144]Fee, *Papyrus Bodmer II.*

[145]Westcott and Hort, p. 235.

[146]Actually, a look at a good apparatus or at collations of MSS reveals that the "Byzantine" text-type is frequently shorter than its rivals. Sturz offers charts which show that where the "Byzantine" text with early papyrus support stands against both the "Western" and "Alexandrian" it adds 42 words and omits 36 words in comparison to them. The "Byzantine" comes out somewhat longer but the picture is not lopsided. Among the added words are 9 conjunctions and 5 articles but among the omitted are 11 conjunctions and 6 articles, which would make the "Byzantine" *less* smooth than its rivals. (Sturz, p. 184.)

[147]B. H. Streeter, *The Four Gospels: A Study of Origins* (London: Macmillan and Co., 1930), pp. 122-4. For a more recent discussion of critical activity at Alexandria, see W. R. Farmer, *The Last Twelve Verses of Mark* (Cambridge: Cambridge University Press, 1974), pp. 13-22.

[148]*Ibid.*, p. 131. I am aware that Kenyon and others have criticized Clark's treatment of this maxim, but I believe that it has sufficient validity to be worth taking into account.

[149]Burgon, *The Causes of the Corruption*, p. 156.

[150]Vaganay, pp. 84-5.

[151]Kilpatrick, p. 196.

[152]Colwell, "Scribal Habits," p. 378.

[153]*Ibid.*, p. 380.

[154]*Ibid.*, p. 383.

[155]*Ibid.*, p. 387.

[156]*Ibid.*, pp. 376-7.

[157]Vaganay, p. 86.

[158]Metzger, *The Text*, p. 195.

[159]*Ibid.*, p. 196.

[160]To anyone who feels that we are obligated to explain the origin of any or every peculiar variant reading, even if found in only one or two copies—especially if the copies happen to be B, Aleph or one of the papyri—Burgon calls attention to the far greater correlative obligation. "It frequently happens that the one remaining plea of many critics for adopting readings of a certain kind, is the inexplicable nature of the phenomena which these readings exhibit.

'How will you possibly account for such a reading as the present,' (say they,) 'if it be not authentic?' . . . They lose sight of the correlative difficulty:—How comes it to pass that the rest of the copies read the place otherwise?" (*The Causes of the Corruption*, p. 17.)

[161]Zuntz, *The Text*, p. 36.

[162]Salmon, pp. 33-4.

[163]S. Hemphill, *A History of the Revised Version* (London: Elliot Stock, 1906), pp. 49-50.

[164]Colwell, "External Evidence," p. 2. The application is mine. Colwell would perhaps not have agreed with it.

[165]My critics have graciously called attention to some genuine weaknesses in my treatment of this topic in the first edition. For this second edition the section has been rewritten and considerably enlarged.

[166]Metzger, *A Textual Commentary*, p. xx.

[167]Jakob Van Bruggen, *The Ancient Text of the New Testament* (Winnipeg: Premier, 1976), p. 30.

[168]*Ibid.* Cf. E. F. Hills, "Harmonizations in the Caesarean Text of Mark," *Journal of Biblical Literature*, 66 (1947), 135-152.

[169]Kilpatrick, p. 193.

[170]Van Bruggen, pp. 30-31.

[171]*Ibid.*, pp. 31-32.

[172]P. Walters, *The Text of the Septuagint. Its Corruptions and their Emendation*, ed. D. W. Gooding (Cambridge: University Press, 1973), p. 21. (Cited by Van Bruggen.)

[173]Van Bruggen, pp. 32-3.

[174]*Ibid.*, p. 33.

[175]Burgon, *The Traditional Text*, p. 67.

[176]Fee, "A Critique of W. N. Pickering's *The Identity of the New Testament Text*: A Review Article," *The Westminster Theological Journal*, XLI (Spring, 1979), p. 411.

[177]I owe the material in the above discussion to Maurice A. Robinson. It is taken from a much fuller response to Fee which he has submitted for publication.

[178]This discussion is adapted from Van Bruggen, pp. 33-34.

[179]I suspect that a thorough check will reveal that it is the "Western" text that leads all others in harmonization, not the "Byzantine." This discussion is adapted from Van Bruggen, p. 34.

[180]Fee, "A Critique," pp. 411-12.

[181]I owe the material used in the above discussion to Robinson. It is taken from his thorough and masterful response to Fee, which has been submitted for publication.

[182]Hort's characterization is similar to contemporary descriptions of Koine Greek in New Testament times.

That there was such a simple and plain style of Greek writing and speaking as is found in the Byzantine text, and that stems from the earliest New Testament times, is attested by non-biblical sources. Such sources as the non-biblical papyri and the Discourses of Epictetus, the Stoic philosopher, attest this style. In addition, there is a formal delineation of what the plain style ought to be, which dates approximately from the time in which the New Testament was being written. *Demetrius, On Style*, names "the plain style" . . . as one of four which he describes and discusses. Parts of his treatment of this subject tend to remind one of descriptions of the Koine of the Hellenistic period and the kind of Greek supposed to characterize the New Testament. . . .

. . . .

In spite of the known existence of such a plain style as set forth by Demetrius and found in Epictetus, there were those in the early period of the Church and its writings who scoffed at the plain style and spoke contemptuously of it as it is found in the Scriptures. One of these was the pagan Celsus, who sought to refute the Christian faith in a literary attack penned sometime between 161-180 A.D. Origen indicates that Celsus ridiculed the Scriptures by holding them up to unfavorable comparison with the writings of the philosophers in places where there seemed to be some parallel (Sturz, pp. 82-83).

[183]H. F. von Soden, *Die Schriften des Neuen Testaments* (2 Vols.; Gottingen: Vandenhoeck und Ruprecht, 1911), Vol. 1, part ii, pp. 1456-1459 (cf. 1361-1400), 1784-1878.

[184]Kilpatrick, *Op. Cit.*

[185]Hoskier, *Codex B*, Vol. I. I fail to see how anyone can read this work of Hoskier's with attention and still retain a high opinion of Codices B and Aleph.

[186]Elliott, pp. 241-3.

[187]Kilpatrick, p. 205.

[188]Burgon, *The Revision Revised*, p. 293.

[189]Kenyon, *Handbook*, pp. 324-5.

[190]Colwell, "The Origin of the Texttypes," p. 137.

[191]F. C. Grant, "The Citation of Greek Manuscript Evidence in an Apparatus Criticus," *New Testament Manuscript Studies*, ed. M. M. Parvis and A. P. Wikgren (Chicago: The University of Chicago Press, 1950), pp. 90-1.

[192]J. Geerlings, *Family E and Its Allies in Mark* (Salt Lake City: University of Utah Press, 1967), p. 1.

[193]Kenyon, *Handbook*, p. 325.

[194]Hodges, p. 42. For a further discussion of the problems confronting the "process" view see the section headed "*Objections*" in Appendix C.

[195]Metzger, *The Text*, (2nd ed., 1968), p. 212. In 1972 he wrote "Whether it really was Lucian . . .," so he may now be retreating from that position. "Patristic Evidence and the Textual Criticism of the New Testament," *New Testament Studies*, XVIII (1972), p. 385.

[196]Burgon, *The Revision Revised*, pp. 276-77.

[197]A. Voobus, *Early Versions of the New Testament* (Stockholm: Estonian Theological Society in Exile, 1954), p. 100.

[198]*Ibid.*, pp. 100-102.

[199]Burgon, *The Last Twelve Verses*, p. 56.

[200]Clark, "Today's Problems," p. 162.

[201]Epp, p. 403.

[202]*Ibid.*, p. 401.

[203]Colwell, "The Greek New Testament with a Limited Apparatus," p. 37. This theme pervades his "Hort Redivivus."

[204]Aland, "The Present Position," p. 731.

[205]Westcott and Hort, p. 40.

FOOTNOTES

[206]Epp, pp. 391-2.

[207]Clark, "Today's Problems," p. 161.

Chapter 5

[1]Z. C. Hodges, "A Defense of the Majority Text" (unpublished course notes, Dallas Theological Seminary, 1975), p. 4.

[2]Colwell, *What is the Best New Testament?*, p. 53.

[3]Westcott and Hort, p. 9. Cf. p. 7. It is clear that Hort regarded the "extant literature" as representative of the textual picture in the early centuries. This gratuitous and misleading idea continues to be an important factor in the thinking of some scholars today.

[4]For a statement of my presuppositions see Appendix A.

[5]I am aware that it could be Prov. 3:12 (LXX) rather than Heb. 12:6. Clement quotes from both books repeatedly throughout the letter, so they are equal candidates on that score. But, Clement agrees verbatim with Hebrews while Proverbs (LXX) differs in one important word. Further, the main point of Clement's chapter 56 is that correction is to be received graciously and as from the Lord, which is also the point of Heb. 12:3-11. Since Clement evidently had both books in front of him (in the next chapter he quotes nine consecutive verses, Prov. 1:23-31) the verbatim agreement with Hebrews is significant. If he deliberately chose the wording of Hebrews over that of Proverbs, what might that imply about their rank?

[6]I have used the translation done by Francis Glimm in *The Apostolic Fathers* (New York: Cima Publishing Co., Inc., 1947), belonging to the set, *The Fathers of the Church*, ed. Ludwig Schopp.

[7]J. V. Bartlet says of the formulae of citation used in Barnabas to introduce quotations from Scripture, "the general result is an absolute doctrine of inspiration," but he is unwilling to consider that II Peter is being used. Oxford Society of Historical Research, *The New Testament in the Apostolic Fathers* (Oxford: Clarendon Press, 1905), pp. 2, 15.

[8]See footnote 6.

[9]See footnote 6.

[10]I have used the translation in Vol. I of *The Ante-Nicene Fathers*, ed., A. Roberts and J. Donaldson (Grand Rapids: Wm. B. Eerdmans Publishing Co., 1956).

[11]I have used the translation by E. R. Hardy in *Early Christian Fathers*, ed., C. C. Richardson (Philadelphia: The Westminster Press, 1953).

[12]See footnote 10.

[13]*Ibid.* His careful study of the early Christian literary papyri has led C. H. Roberts to conclude: "This points to the careful and regular use of the scriptures by the local communities" (*Schweich Lectures 1977*, p. 25). He also infers from P. Oxy. iii. 405 that a copy of Irenaeus' *Adversus Haereses*, written in Lyons, was brought to Oxyrhynchus within a very few years after it was written (*Ibid.*, pp. 23, 53), eloquent testimony to the extent of the traffic among the early churches.

[14]*Ibid.*, except that Richardson is the translator here.

[15]Taken from G. D. Barry, *The Inspiration and Authority of Holy Scripture* (New York: The McMillan Company, 1919), p. 52.

[16]*Ibid.*, p. 53.

[17]*Prescription against Heretics*, 36. I have used the translation done by Peter Holmes in Vol. III of *The Ante-Nicene Fathers*.

[18]Metzger, *The Text*, p. 21.

[19]*Prescription against Heretics*, 36, using Holmes' translation.

[20]The implications of all this deserve further comment. The Aegean region included Antioch, the apostle Paul's home base from which he set out on his missionary journeys to the Aegean area. "Antioch was the third city of the empire, a city with an independent and proud spirit; and something of this same independent spirit no doubt was part of its heritage as the 'Mother of all the Gentile churches' " (Sturz, p. 76. Cf. M. C. Tenney, *New Testament Survey* [Grand Rapids: Eerdmans, 1961], p. 253). Glanville Downey, in *A History of Antioch in Syria, from Seleucus to the Arab Conquest* (Princeton: Princeton University Press, 1961), pp. 304ff, "calls attention to the influence that the church at Antioch exerted over the whole area of Syria" (Sturz, p. 76).

The rise of the so-called "school of Antioch" is a further relevant consideration. Beginning with Theophilus, a bishop of Antioch who died around 185, the Antiochians began insisting upon the literal interpretation of Scripture, a position that hardened progressively in opposition to the so-called "school of Alexandria" as it went into orbit with its allegorical interpretation of Scripture. The point is that a literalist is obliged to be concerned about the precise wording of the text since his interpretation or exegesis hinges upon it.

It is reasonable to assume that this "literalist" mentality would have influenced the churches of Asia Minor and Greece and encouraged them in the careful and faithful transmission of the pure text that they had received. It is not unreasonable to suppose that the Antiochian antipathy toward the Alexandrian allegorical interpretation of Scripture would rather indispose them to view with favor any competing forms of the text coming out of Egypt. Similarly the Quarto-deciman controversy with Rome would scarcely enhance the appeal of any innovations coming from the West.

(It is interesting to note that C. H. Roberts, in a recent scholarly treatment of the Christian literary papyri of the first three centuries [*Schweich Lectures 1977* (published by the British Academy)], seems to favor the conclusion that the Alexandrian church was weak and insignificant to the Greek Christian world in the second century [pp. 42-43, 55-57].)

The use of such designations as "Syrian," "Antiochian," and "Byzantine" for the Majority Text reflects its general association with that region. I know of no reason to doubt that the "Byzantine" text is in fact the form of the text that was known and transmitted in the Aegean area from the beginning. Although we have been repeatedly reminded that Chrysostom was the first Father to use the "Byzantine" text, mention is very seldom made of the relevant circumstance that he is the earliest Antiochian Father "whose literary remains are extensive enough so that their New Testament quotations may be analyzed as to the type of text they support" (Sturz, p. 57).

In sum, I believe that the evidence clearly favors that interpretation of the history of the text which sees the normal transmission of the text as centered in the Aegean region, the area that was best qualified, from every point of view, to transmit the text, from the very first. The result of that normal transmission is the "Byzantine" text-type. In every age, including the second and third centuries, it has been the traditional text.

[21]In writing this section I benefitted from the collaboration of Zane Hodges.

FOOTNOTES

[22]I have carefully avoided introducing any argument based on the providence of God because not all accept such argumentation and because the superiority of the Traditional Text can be demonstrated without recourse to it. Thus, I believe the argument from statistical probability given above is valid as it stands. However, while I have not argued on the basis of Providence, I wish the reader to understand that I personally do not think that the preservation of the true text was so mechanistic as the discussion above might suggest. From the evidence previously adduced, it seems clear that a great many variant readings (perhaps most of the malicious ones) that existed in the second century simply have not survived—we have no extant witness to them. We may reasonably conclude that the early Christians were concerned and able watchdogs of the true text. I would like to believe that they were aided and abetted by the Holy Spirit. In that event, the security of the text is considerably greater than that suggested by probability alone, including the proposition that none of the original wording has been lost.

[23]Burgon, *The Revision Revised*, pp. 323-4.

[24]Colwell, "The Origin of Texttypes," p. 138.

[25]F. H. A. Scrivener, *A Plain Introduction to the Criticism of the New Testament*, fourth edition edited by E. Miller (2 Vols.; London: George Bell and Sons, 1894), II, 264.

[26]G. D. Kilpatrick, "The Transmission of the New Testament and its Reliability," *The Bible Translator*, IX (July, 1958), 128-9.

[27]Zuntz, *The Text*, p. 11.

[28]Kilpatrick, "Atticism and the Text of the Greek New Testament," *Neutestamentliche Aufsatze* (Regensburg: Verlag Friedrich Pustet, 1963), pp. 129-30.

[29]Cf. Burgon, *The Revision Revised*, p. 323.

[30]One might speak of a P^{45}, W eddy or a P^{75}, B eddy for example.

[31]Although I have used, of necessity, the term "text-type" throughout the book, I view the Majority Text as being much broader. It is a textual tradition which might be said to include a number of related "text-types," such as von Soden's K^a, K^i, and K^l. I wish to emphasize again that it is only agreement in error that determines genealogical relationships. It follows that the concepts of "genealogy" and "text-type" are irrelevant with reference to original readings—they are only useful (when employed properly) for identifying spurious readings.

[32]I am not prepared to defend the precise figures used, they are *guesses*, but I believe they represent a reasonable approximation to reality. I heartily agree with Colwell when he insists that we must "rigorously eliminate the singular reading" ("External Evidence," p. 8) on the altogether reasonable assumption (it seems to me) that a solitary witness against the world cannot possibly be right.

[33]Sturz, *Op. Cit.*

[34]The readings, with their supporting MSS, are as follows:

ὄ - D

ω - 061

ὄς ϑεος - one cursive and one lectionary

ὄς - ℵ, 33, 442, 2127, three lectionaries

ϑεος - A, C^vid, F/G^vid, K, L, P, Ψ, over 300 cursives and lectionaries (including four cursives that read ὁ ϑεος and one lectionary that reads ϑεου).

227

It will be observed that my statement differs from that of the UBS text, for example. I offer the following explanation.

Young, Huish, Pearson, Fell, and Mill in the seventeenth century, Creyk, Bentley, Wotton, Wetstein, Bengel, Berriman, and Woide in the eighteenth, and Scrivener as late as 1881 all affirmed, upon careful inspection, that Codex A reads "God." For a thorough discussion please see Burgon, who says concerning Woide, "The learned and conscientious editor of the Codex declares that so late as 1765 he had seen traces of the Θ which twenty years later (viz. in 1785) were visible to him no longer" (*The Revision Revised*, p. 434. Cf. pp. 431-36). It was only after 1765 that scholars started to question the reading of A (through fading and wear the middle line of the *theta* is no longer discernible).

Hoskier devotes Appendix J of *A Full Account* (the appendix being a reprint of part of an article that appeared in the *Clergyman's Magazine* for February 1887) to a careful discussion of the reading of Codex C. He spent three hours examining the passage in question in this MS (the MS itself) and adduces evidence that shows clearly, I believe, that the original reading of C is "God." He examined the surrounding context and observes, "The *contracting-bar* has often vanished completely (I believe, from a cursory examination, more often than not), but at other times it is plain and imposed in the same way as at 1 Tim. iii.16" (Appendix J, p.2). See also Burgon, *Ibid.*, pp. 437-38.

Codices F/G read O̅C̅ wherein the contracting-bar is a slanting stroke. It has been argued that the stroke represents the aspirate of ὅς, but Burgon demonstrates that the stroke in question never represents breathing but is invariably the sign of contraction and affirms that "ὅς is *nowhere* else written O̅C̅ in either codex" (*Ibid.*, p. 442. Cf. pp. 438-42). Presumably the cross-line in the common parent had become too faint to see. As for cursive 365, Burgon conducted an exhaustive search for it. He not only failed to find it but could find no evidence that it had ever existed (*Ibid.*, pp. 444-45).

The three significant variants involved are represented in the ancient uncial MSS as follows: O, OC, and O̅C̅, meaning "which," "who," and "God" respectively. In writing "God" a scribe's omitting of the two lines (through haste or momentary distraction) would result in "who." Codices A, C, F, and G have numerous instances where either the cross-line or the contracting-bar is no longer discernible (either the original line has faded to the point of being invisible or the scribe may have failed to write it in the first place). For both lines to fade away, as in Codex A here, is presumably an infrequent event. For a scribe to inadvertently omit both lines would presumably also be an infrequent event, but it must have happened at least once, probably early in the second century and in circumstances that produced a wide ranging effect.

The collocation "the mystery . . . who" is even more pathologic in Greek than it is in English. It was thus inevitable, once such a reading came into existence and became known, that remedial action would be attempted. Accordingly, the first reading above, "the mystery . . . which," is generally regarded as an attempt to make the difficult reading intelligible. But it must have been an early development, for it completely dominates the Latin tradition, both versions and Fathers, as well as being the probable reading of the Syr^P and Coptic versions. It is found in only one Greek MS, Codex D, and in no Greek Father before the fifth century.

FOOTNOTES

Most modern scholars regard "God" as a separate therapeutic response to the difficult reading. Although it dominates the Greek MSS (97 percent), it is certainly attested by only two versions, the Georgian and Slavonic (both late). But it also dominates the Greek Fathers. Around A.D. 100 there are possible allusions in Barnabas, "Ἰησους . . . ὁ υἱος του Θεου τυπω και εν σαρκι φανερωθεις" (Cap. xii), and in Ignatius, "Θεου ανθρωπινως φανερουμενου" (Ad Ephes. c. 19) and "εν σαρκι γενομενος Θεος" (Ibid., c. 7). In the third century there seem to be clear references in Hippolytus, "Θεος εν σωματι εφανερωθη" (Contra Hæresim Noeti, c. xvii), Dionysius, "Θεος γαρ εφανερωθη εν σαρκι" (Concilia, i. 853a) and Gregory Thaumaturgus, "και εστιν Θεος αληθινος ὁ ασαρκος εν σαρκι φανερωθεις" (quoted by Photius). In the 4th century there are clear quotes or references in Gregory of Nyssa (22 times), Gregory of Nazianzus, Didymus of Alexandria, Diodorus, the Apostolic Constitutions, and Chrysostom, followed by Cyril of Alexandria, Theodoret, and Euthalius in the fifth century, and so on (Burgon, Ibid., pp. 456-76, 486-90).

As for the grammatically aberrant reading, "who," aside from the MSS already cited, the earliest version that clearly supports it is the gothic (fourth century). To get a clear Greek Patristic witness to this reading pretty well requires the sequence μυστηριον ὁς εφανερωθη since after any reference to Christ, Savior, Son of God, etc. in the prior context the use of a relative clause is predictable. Burgon affirmed that he was aware of no such testimony (and his knowledge of the subject has probably never been equalled) (Ibid., p. 483).

It thus appears that the "Western" and "Byzantine" readings have earlier attestation than does the "Alexandrian." Yet if "which" was caused by "who," then the latter must be older. The reading "who" is admittedly the most difficult, so much so that to apply the "harder reading" canon in the face of an easy transcriptional explanation for the difficult reading seems unreasonable. As Burgon so well put it:

> I trust we are at least agreed that the maxim "proclivi lectioni præstat ardua," does not enunciate so foolish a proposition as that in choosing between two or more conflicting readings, we are to prefer that one which has the feeblest external attestation,—provided it be but in itself almost unintelligible? (Ibid., p. 497).

35For further discussion see the final pages of Appendix C.

Chapter 6
1Burgon, The Traditional Text, p. 40.
2Zuntz, The Text, pp. 6-7.
3Oliver, pp. 312-3.
4Colwell, "Hort Redivivus," p. 157.
5Clark, "The Manuscripts of the Greek New Testament," p. 3.
6Colwell, "Scribal Habits," pp. 378-9.
7Ibid., pp. 374-6.
8Ibid., p. 387.
9Ibid., pp. 374-6.
10I am probably being unfair to the scribe who produced P75—some or many of those errors may have been in his exemplar. The fact remains that whatever their origin P75 contains over 400 clear errors and I am trying by the suggested

experiment to help the reader visualize how poor these early copies really are.

[11]Colwell, "Scribal Habits," pp. 374-6.

[12]*Ibid.*, p. 376.

[13]*Ibid.*, p. 383.

[14]Zuntz, *The Text*, p. 18.

[15]*Ibid.*, p 212.

[16]*Ibid.*, p. 252.

[17]H. C. Hoskier, "A Study of the Chester-Beatty Codex of the Pauline Epistles," *The Journal of Theological Studies*, XXXVIII (1937), 162.

[18]Zuntz, *The Text*, p. 157.

[19]Aland, "The Significance of the Papyri," p. 333.

[20]Burgon, *The Traditional Text*, p. 84.

[21]Burgon, *The Revision Revised*, pp. 30-1.

[22]Westcott and Hort, p. 243.

[23]Kenyon, *Handbook*, p. 308.

[24]Scrivener, *A Plain Introduction*, I, 120.

[25]Westcott and Hort, p. 233.

[26]Scrivener, *A Plain Introduction*, I, 130. Cf. Rendel Harris, *A Study of the Codex Bezae* (1891).

[27]Westcott and Hort, p. 149.

[28]Burgon, *The Traditional Text*, pp. 185-90.

[29]Zuntz, *The Text*, p. 252.

[30]Lake, Blake and New, p. 349. D. A. Carson offers the following response to this suggestion: "The answers to this ingenious theory are obvious: (1) If only one copy were made before the exemplar was destroyed, there would never be more than one extant copy of the Greek New Testament! (2) If several copies were made from one exemplar, then either (a) they were not all made at the same time, and therefore the destruction of the exemplar was not a common practice after all; or (b) they were all made at the same time. (3) If the latter obtains, then it should be possible to identify their sibling relationship; yet in fact such identification is as difficult and as precarious as the identification of direct exemplar/copy manuscripts. This probably means we have lost a lot of manuscripts; and/or it means that the divergences between copy and exemplar, as between copy and sibling copy, are frequently difficult to detect. (4) Why are there *no* copies of the Byzantine text before about A.D. 350, and *so many* [emphasis Carson's] from there on? This anomaly, it might be argued, demonstrates that the practice of destroying the exemplar died out during the fourth century" (*The King James Version Debate*, Grand Rapids: Baker Book House, 1979, pp. 47-48).

Perhaps it is fortunate that Lake is no longer available for comment upon this extraordinary statement. If I may presume to answer for him, it seems to me apparent that what Lake found was the end of the line, the last generation of copies. Neither Lake nor anyone else has suggested that only one copy would be made of any exemplar, but after a life of use and being copied a worn and tattered MS would be destroyed. Carson's point (4) is hard to believe. Lake, Blake, and New were looking at minuscule MSS, probably none earlier than the tenth century—they had to be copied from something, and it is a fact that Lake and company found no "parents." Carson offers no explanation for this *fact*. And what are we to understand from his strange remark about "Byzantine" MSS before and after A.D. 350? There are none from the fourth century, two partially so from the fifth, and a slowly expanding stream as one moves up through the succeeding centuries. It is only when we come to the minuscule era that we find "so many." A. Dain (*Les manuscrits*, Paris, 1949, pp. 111-20) explains why. "L'exemplaire translitteré, soigneusement écrit et solidement relié, devenait le point de départ de la tradition ultérieure. Les vieux modèles de papyrus ou de parchemin, sans doute très usés, qui avaient servi à sa confection n'offraient plus aucun intérêt. Ils étaient normalement abandonnés ou détruits" (p. 115). Apparently there was an organized movement to "transliterate" uncial MSS into minuscule form or script. Note that Dain agrees with Lake that the "well used" exemplars were then destroyed. What if those exemplars were ancient "Byzantine" uncials?

C. H. Roberts takes a similar view for the early church. "It was a Jewish habit both to preserve manuscripts by placing them in jars . . . and also to dispose of defective, worn-out, or heretical scriptures by burying them near a cemetery, not to preserve them but because anything that might contain the name of God might not be destroyed. . . . It certainly looks as if this institution of a morgue for sacred but unwanted manuscripts was taken over from Judaism by the early Church" (p. 7). Note that the effect of this practice in any but an arid climate would be the decomposition of the MSS.

[31]Van Bruggen, p. 24.

[32]*Ibid.*, p. 25.

[33]Burgon, *The Traditional Text*, p. 47.

[34]S. Lake, *Family II and the Codex Alexandrinus (Studies and Documents V)* (London: Christophers, 1936).

[35]Van Bruggen, pp. 26–27.

[36]*Ibid.*, p. 29. Cf. Eusebius, *Historia Ecclesiastica* VIII, II, I.4 and F.H.A. Scrivener, *A Plain Introduction*, pp. 265-66.

[37]Roberts, p. 8.

[38]Another consideration suggests itself—if, as reported, the Diocletian campaign was most fierce and effective in the Byzantine area, the numerical advantage of the "Byzantine" text-type over the "Western" and "Alexandrian" would have been reduced, giving the latter a chance to forge ahead. But it did not happen. The church, in the main, refused to propagate those forms of the Greek text.

[39]T. H. Horne, *An Introduction to the Critical Study and Knowledge of the Holy Scriptures*, 4th American edition (4 vols.; Philadelphia: E. Little, 1831), vol. II, p. 217. I am indebted to Maurice Robinson for calling this material to my attention.

[40]Colwell, "External Evidence," p. 3.

[41]*Ibid.*, p. 4.

[42]The fact that the transcriber of P75 copied letter by letter and that of P66 syllable by syllable (Colwell, "Scribal Habits," p. 380) suggests strongly that neither one knew Greek. When transcribing in a language you know you copy phrase by phrase, or at the very least word by word. P66 has so many nonsensical readings that the transcriber could not have known the meaning of the text. Anyone who has ever tried to transcribe a text of any length by hand (not

THE IDENTITY OF THE NEW TESTAMENT TEXT

typewriter) in a language he does not understand will know that it is a taxing and dreary task. Purity of transmission is not to be expected under such circumstances.

[43]Burgon, *The Revision Revised*, pp. 16-8.

[44]Cf. Zuntz, *The Text*, p. 157.

Chapter 7

[1]Burgon, *The Traditional Text*, p. 29. I acknowledge with alacrity my considerable indebtedness to Dean Burgon, especially for arousing me to look at the *evidence*, but my treatment of the various "notes" is not identical to his.

[2]Sturz, pp. 67-70.

[3]Burgon, *The Traditional Text*, pp. 107, 255-6.

[4]Anyone who offers a conjectural emendation in the face of such attestation is claiming that his authority is greater than that of all the witnesses combined— but since such a person is not a witness at all, does not and cannot know what was written, his authority is zero.

[5]Westcott and Hort, p. 45.

[6]Lake, Blake and New, pp. 348-9.

[7]Burgon, *The Traditional Text*, pp. 46-7.

[8]Cf. Epp, "The Claremont Profile Method for Grouping New Testament Minuscule Manuscripts," *Studies in the History and Text of the New Testament in Honor of Kenneth Willis Clark, Ph.D. (Studies and Documents*, 29) ed. B. L. Daniels and M. J. Suggs (Salt Lake City: University of Utah Press, 1967), pp. 27-38.

[9]Burgon, *The Traditional Text*, pp. 50-1. Anyone who has been taught that Burgon followed "mere number" will perceive that there is more to the story than that.

[10]Cf. Streeter, p. 148; Tasker, "Introduction to the Manuscripts of the New Testament," *Harvard Theological Review*, XLI (1948), 76; Metzger, *The Text*, p. 171; Clark, "The Manuscripts of the Greek New Testament," p. 3.

[11]Burgon, *The Traditional Text*, p. 52.

[12]*Ibid.*, p. 59.

[13]It seems to me to be frankly impossible that an original reading should have absolutely disappeared from the knowledge of the Church for over a millenium and then pop up magically in the twelfth century.

[14]Westcott and Hort, p. 275; Zuntz, *The Text*, p. 84.

[15]Burgon, *The Traditional Text*, p. 58.

[16]"How ill white hairs become a fool and jester!" (Shakespeare's *King Henry IV*, part 2, Act V, Scene V, about line 50).

[17]Burgon, *The Traditional Text*, p. 62.

[18]Burgon, *The Revision Revised*, pp. 77-8.

[19]Burgon, *The Traditional Text*, p. 65.

[20]Colwell, "Scribal Habits."

[21]Cf. Burgon, *The Revision Revised*, p. 339.

Chapter 8

[1]When all the evidence is in I believe the *Textus Receptus* will be found to differ from the Original in something over a thousand places, most of them being very minor differences, whereas the critical texts will be found to differ

232

FOOTNOTES

from the Original in some five thousand places, many of them being serious differences.

[2]I have an answer, but it will have to appear under separate cover.

[3]Aland, "The Significance of the Papyri," pp. 330-1.

[4]E. C. Colwell, *et. al.*, "The International Greek New Testament Project: a Status Report," *Journal of Biblical Literature*, LXXXVII (1968), 192, note 13.

[5]The present state of our knowledge (or ignorance) is such that we are left with between 150 and 200 places where we are not sure which of two competing readings should be followed.

[6]K. Aland, "The Greek New Testament: its Present and Future Editions," *Journal of Biblical Literature*, LXXXVII (1968), 183-4.

[7]Hodges may be reached at the Dallas Theological Seminary, 3909 Swiss Ave., Dallas, TX 75204. He will be very happy to hear from anyone interested in furthering the quest for the definitive Text.

[8]Burgon, *The Causes of the Corruption*, p. 286. Although I have used the expressions "Byzantine Text" and "Majority Text" throughout the book as an aid to understanding, I prefer "Traditional Text." (As used in this book the three expressions are synonymous.) The term "Byzantine" is not only pejorative, to many, it also fosters the notion that the Traditional Text was confined to that area. The term "Majority" fosters the continuing misimpression that the defense of the Traditional Text is predicated solely on "number" and "counting." By "Traditional" I mean that in every age, from the apostolic to the nineteenth century, the text-form in question (the Greek text only) was the one that the church in general recognized, used, and transmitted.

Appendix A

[1]Metzger is typical: "Burgon's argument was basically theological and speculative." (*The Text*, p. 135.) See also Greenlee, p. 81; Harrison, p. 73; Vaganay, p. 172; Sturz, p. 24; Paul McReynolds, *Journal of Biblical Literature*, XCIII (1974), 481; etc.

[2]Burgon, *The Traditional Text*, pp. 11-12.

[3]I believe that the theological implications of the degree and manner of the preservation of the Text are far-reaching indeed, but I feel that to discuss them here might distract attention from the main purpose of the book.

Appendix B

[1]J. O'Callaghan, "Papiros neotestamentarios en la cueva 7 de Qumran?" *Biblica*, LIII (1972), 91-100. 7Q5 is dated at around 50 A.D.

[2]M. Baillet, "Les manuscrits de la Grotte 7 de Qumran et le N.T." *Biblica*, LIII (1972), 508-516. Baillet was one of the two editors of the *editio princeps* that presented the 7Q fragments to the scholarly world in 1962.

[3]K. Aland, "Neue Neutestamentliche Papyri III," *New Testament Studies*, XX (July, 1974), 358-76.

[4]O'Callaghan, "Notas sobre 7Q tomadas en el 'Rochefeller Museum' de Jerusalén," *Biblica*, LIII (1972), 519-21.

[5]*Ibid.*, p. 523.

[6]Baillet, p. 511.

[7]O'Callaghan, "Notas," p. 524.

[8]O'Callaghan, "El cambio δ>τ en los papiros biblicos," *Biblica*, LIV (1973), 415-16.

[9]My discussion of P[9] is based on O'Callaghan, "Notas," pp. 528-30.

[10]One might even be inclined to join F. F. Bruce in his flight of the imagination (*Eternity*, June, 1972, p. 33, last paragraph).

Appendix C

[1]This appendix is an edited abstract from "A Defense of the Majority-Text" by Zane C. Hodges and David M. Hodges (unpublished course notes, Dallas Theological Seminary, 1975) used by permission of the authors.

[2]His statement is: *"The Greek Vulgate–The Byzantine or Alpha testtype–had its origin in no such single focus as the Latin had in Jerome"* (italics in the original). E. C. Colwell, "The Origin of Texttypes of New Testament Manuscripts," *Early Christian Origins*, p. 137.

[3]*Ibid.*, p. 136. Cf. our discussion of this view under "Objections."

[4]Cf. F. G. Kenyon, *Handbook to the Textual Criticism of the New Testament*, pp. 324ff.

[5]Kurt Aland, "The Significance of the Papyri for Progress in New Testament Research," *The Bible in Modern Scholarship*, p. 342. This is the most scientifically unobjectionable name yet given to this text form.

[6]*Ibid.*, p. 344.

[7]*Ibid.*, pp. 330ff.

[8]B. F. Westcott and F. J. A. Hort, *The New Testament in the Original Greek*, II, 45.

[9]By "error (b)" we mean, of course, an error made in another place in the text being transmitted from the autograph. We do *not* mean that "error (b)" has been substituted for "error (a)." Hence, while copies 5-6-7 contain "error (a)," they also contain the original autograph reading which is the rival to "error (b)."

[10]The key words here are "relatively" and "comparatively." Naturally, individual members of the Majority text show varying amounts of conformity to it. Nevertheless, the nearness of its representatives to the general standard is not hard to demonstrate in most cases. For example, in a study of one hundred places of variation in John 11, the representatives of the Majority text used in the study showed a range of agreement from around 70 percent to 93 percent. Cf. Ernest C. Colwell and Ernest W. Tune, pp. 28, 31. The uncial codex Omega's 93 percent agreement with the *Textus Receptus* compares well with the 92 percent agreement found between P[75] and B. Omega's affinity with the TR is more nearly typical of the pattern one would find in the great mass of minuscule texts. High levels of agreement of this kind are (as in the case of P[75] and B) the result of a shared ancestral base. It is the divergencies that are the result of a "process" and not the reverse.

A more general, summary statement of the matter is made by Epp, ". . . the Byzantine manuscripts together form, after all, a rather closely-knit group, and the variations in question within this entire large group are relatively minor in character." (Eldon Jay Epp, "The Claremont Profile Method for Grouping New Testament Minuscule Manuscripts," p. 33.)

[11]After describing the vicissitudes which afflicted the transmission of the

Vulgate, Metzger concludes: "As a result, the more than 8,000 Vulgate manuscripts which are extant today exhibit the greatest amount of cross-contamination of textual types." (*Text of the New Testament*, p. 76.) Uniformity of text is always greatest at the source and diminishes—rather than increases—as the tradition expands and multiplies. This caveat is ignored by the "process" view of the Majority text.

Appendix D

[1]The title and basic format for this appendix I owe to William G. Pierpont and use with his permission. I have, however, almost tripled the number of examples and the editorial comments are mine. The principal sources for the added examples are H. A. Sturz (*The Byzantine Text-Type*) and Maurice A. Robinson (unpublished paper). Peter J. Johnston has contributed significantly to the statements of evidence. Perhaps this appendix will serve as a partial response to a criticism that was frequently directed at the first edition of this book, namely that it lacked any actual examples of textual problems to illustrate the practical outworkings of the approach I advocate. A fuller response should be available in early 1981 when Thomas Nelson Inc. publishes the critical edition of the Traditional (Majority) Text of the New Testament being prepared by Zane Hodges, Arthur Farstad, and others (including myself).

[2]For a complete statement of what I mean by "discourse structure," see my book, *A Framework for Discourse Analysis* (Dallas: Summer Institute of Linguistics and University of Texas at Arlington, 1980).

[3]Metzger, *The Text*, p. 136. To my astonishment, D. A. Carson appears to still be of this opinion so recently as 1979. In his critique of the first edition of this book (*The King James Version Debate*, Grand Rapids: Baker, "Appendix") he declares that "textual scholars hold that a primary feature of the Byzantine text-type is its tendency to conflate readings" (p. 110) and speaks of "the Byzantine tradition in its mature conflated form" (p. 112). The reader is now in some position to form his own opinion on this subject.

[4]I am aware that the mechanism at work, especially in the Gospels, was probably harmonization in many/most cases rather than conflation. Since both mechanisms produce secondary readings the basic thrust of this appendix is not altered by a choice between them. I am also aware that I cannot *prove* conflation or harmonization in any instance, but then, of course, neither could Hort, and neither can anyone else.

Appendix E

[1]Jakob Van Bruggen is professor of New Testament exegesis at the Reformed Theological College in Kampen, The Netherlands. The material in this appendix comes from an unpublished lecture first given in Dutch. With the exception of a few stylistic changes, the translation into English sent to me by Dr. Van Bruggen is reproduced verbatim and with his permission.

Critics of the first edition have pointed out, appropriately, that my discussion of "harmonization" was weak. I include this appendix as a partial response to such criticisms. I believe it justifies two conclusions: Many apparent harmonizations may reasonably be interpreted in other ways, and the "Alexandrian" and "Western" texts may be said to be just as guilty of harmonizing as the "Byzantine" text.

References

Aland, Kurt, "The Greek New Testament: its Present and Future Editions," *Journal of Biblical Literature*, LXXXVII (1968).

———. "Neue Neutestamentliche Papyri III," *New Testament Studies*, XX (July, 1974).

———. "The Present Position of New Testament Textual Criticism," *Studia Evangelica*, ed. F. L. Cross and others. Berlin: Akademie—Verlag, 1959. Pp. 717-31.

———. "The Significance of the Papyri for Progress in New Testament Research," *The Bible in Modern Scholarship*, ed. J. P. Hyatt. New York: Abingdon Press, 1965. Pp. 325-46.

———. *Synopsis Quattuor Evangeliorum*. Stuttgart: Wurttembergeshe Bibelanstalt, 1964.

Aland, Kurt, Black, Matthew, Metzger, Bruce M., and Wikgren, Allen (eds.). *The Greek New Testament*, New York: American Bible Society, 1966.

Aland, Kurt, Black, Matthew, Martini, Carlo M., Metzger, Bruce M., and Wikgren, Allen (eds.). *The Greek New Testament*, 3rd ed. New York: United Bible Societies, 1975.

Anderson, H. and Barclay, W. (eds.). *The New Testament in Historical and Contemporary Perspective*. Oxford: Basil Blackwell, 1965.

Aune, D. E. (ed.). *Studies in New Testament and Early Christian Literature*. Leiden: E. J. Brill, 1972.

Baillet, M. "Les manuscrits de la Grotte 7 de Qumran et le N. T." *Biblica*, LIII (1972).

Barry, G. D. *The Inspiration and Authority of Holy Scripture*. New York: The Macmillan Company, 1919.

Birdsall, J. N. *The Bodmer Papyrus of the Gospel of John*. London, 1960.

———. "The Text of the Gospels in Photius," *Journal of Theological Studies*, VII (1956).

Birdsall, J. N. and Thomson, R. W. (eds.). *Biblical and Patristic Studies in Memory of Robert Pierce Casey*. New York: Herder, 1963.

Black, Matthew. *An Aramaic Approach to the Gospels and Acts*. Oxford: Oxford University Press, 1946.

Burgon, John William. *The Causes of the Corruption of the Traditional Text of the Holy Gospels.* Arranged, completed, and edited by Edward Miller. London: George Bell and Sons, 1896.

———. *The Last Twelve Verses of the Gospel According to S. Mark,* Ann Arbor, Michigan: The Sovereign Grace Book Club, 1959.

———. *The Revision Revised.* London: John Murray, 1883.

———. *The Traditional Text of the Holy Gospels Vindicated and Established.* Arranged, completed, and edited by Edward Miller. London: George Bell and Sons, 1896.

Burkitt, Francis C. *Evangelion da-Mepharreshe.* 2 vols. Cambridge: Cambridge University Press, 1904.

Buttrick, George A. and others (eds.). *The Interpreter's Dictionary of the Bible.* 4 vols. New York: Abingdon Press, 1962.

Carson, D. A. *The King James Version Debate.* Grand Rapids: Baker Book House, 1979.

Clark, K. W. "The Effect of Recent Textual Criticism upon New Testament Studies," *The Background of the New Testament and its Eschatology,* ed. W. D. Davies and D. Daube. Cambridge: The Cambridge University Press, 1956. Pp. 27-51.

———."The Manuscripts of the Greek New Testament," *New Testament Manuscript Studies,* ed. M. M. Parvis and A. P. Wikgren. Chicago: The University of Chicago Press, 1950. Pp. 1-24.

———. "The Theological Relevance of Textual Variation in Current Criticism of the Greek New Testament," *Journal of Biblical Literature,* LXXXV (1966).

———. "Today's Problems with the Critical Text of the New Testament," *Transitions in Biblical Scholarship,* ed. J. C. R. Rylaarsdam. Chicago: The University of Chicago Press, 1968.

Colwell, Ernest Cadman. "Biblical Criticism: Lower and Higher," *Journal of Biblical Literature,* LXVII (1948), 1-12.

———. "The Complex Character of the Late Byzantine Text of the Gospels," *Journal of Biblical Literature,* LIV (1935), 211-21.

———. "External Evidence and New Testament Criticism," *Studies in the History and Text of the New Testament,* eds. B. L. Daniels and M. J. Suggs. Salt Lake City: University of Utah Press, 1967.

———. "Genealogical Method: Its Achievements and its Limitations," *Journal of Biblical Literature,* LXVI (1947), 109-33.

———. "The Greek New Testament with a Limited Critical Apparatus: its Nature and Uses," *Studies in New Testament and Early Christian Literature,* ed. D. E. Aune. Leiden: E. J. Brill, 1972.

———. "Hort Redivivus: A Plea and a Program," *Studies in Methodology in Textual Criticism of the New Testament,* E. C. Colwell. Leiden: E. J. Brill, 1969.

———. "The Origin of Texttypes of New Testament Manuscripts," *Early Christian Origins,* ed. Allen Wikgren. Chicago: Quadrangle Books, 1961. Pp. 128-38.

———. "Scribal Habits in Early Papyri: A Study in the Corruption of the Text," *The Bible in Modern Scholarship,* ed. J. P. Hyatt. New York: Abingdon Press, 1965. Pp. 370-89.

———. "The Significance of Grouping of New Testament Manuscripts," *New Testament Studies*, IV (1957-1958), 73-92.

———. *Studies in Methodology in Textual Criticism of the New Testament*. Leiden: E. J. Brill, 1969.

———. *What is the Best New Testament?* Chicago: The University of Chicago Press, 1952.

Colwell, Ernest Cadman and Riddle, Donald W. (eds.). *Studies in the Lectionary Text of the Greek New Testament: Volume I, Prolegomena to the Study of the Lectionary Text of the Gospels*. Chicago: The University of Chicago Press, 1933.

Colwell, E. C. and Tune, E. W. "The Quantitative Relationships between MS Text-Types," *Biblical and Patristic Studies in Memory of Robert Pierce Casey*, ed. J. N. Birdsall and R. W. Thomson. Freiberg: Herder, 1963.

Colwell, E. C. *et. al.* "The International Greek New Testament Project: a Status Report," *Journal of Biblical Literature*, LXXXVII (1968).

Cross, F. L. and Others (eds.). *Studia Evangelica*. Berlin: Akademie—Verlag, 1959.

Dain, A. *Les Manuscrits*. Paris, 1949.

Daniels, B. L. and Suggs, M. J. (eds.). *Studies in the History and Text of the New Testament in Honor of Kenneth Willis Clark, Ph.D.* (*Studies and Documents*, 29). Salt Lake City: University of Utah Press, 1967.

Davies, W. D. and Daube, D. (eds.). *The Background of the New Testament and its Eschatology*. Cambridge: The Cambridge University Press, 1956.

Downey, Glanville. *A History of Antioch in Syria, from Seleucus to the Arab Conquest*. Princeton: University Press, 1961.

Elliott, J. K. *The Greek Text of the Epistles to Timothy and Titus*. (*Studies and Documents*, 36). Salt Lake City: University of Utah Press, 1968.

Epp, E. J. "The Claremont Profile Method for Grouping New Testament Minuscule Manuscripts," *Studies in the History and Text of the New Testament in Honor of Kenneth Willis Clark, Ph.D.* (*Studies and Documents*, 29), ed. B. L. Daniels and M. J. Suggs. Salt Lake City: University of Utah Press, 1967.

———. "The Twentieth Century Interlude in New Testament Textual Criticism," *Journal of Biblical Literature*, XCIII (1974).

Estrada, David and White, William, Jr. *The First New Testament*. Nashville: Thomas Nelson, 1978.

Farmer, W. R. *The Last Twelve Verses of Mark*. Cambridge: Cambridge University Press, 1974.

Fee, G. D. "A Critique of W. N. Pickering's *The Identity of the New Testament Text*: A Review Article," *The Westminster Theological Journal*, XLI (Spring, 1979).

———. "Modern Text Criticism and the Synoptic Problem," *J. J. Griesbach: Synoptic and Text-Critical Studies 1776-1976*, ed. B. Orchard and T.R.W. Longstaff. Cambridge: University Press, 1978.

———. *Papyrus Bodmer II* (P[66]): *Its Textual Relationships and Scribal Characteristics*. Salt Lake City: University of Utah Press, 1968.

———. "Rigorous or Reasoned Eclecticism—Which?," *Studies in New Testament Language and Text*, ed. J. K. Elliott. Leiden: E.J. Brill, 1976.

Geerlings, J. *Family E and its Allies in Mark.* Salt Lake City: University of Utah Press, 1967.

Geerlings, Jacob and New, Silva. "Chrysostom's Text of the Gospel of Mark," *Harvard Theological Review,* XXIV (1931), 122-42.

Goulburn, Edward M. *Life of Dean Burgon,* 2 vols. London: John Murray, 1892.

Grant, F. C. "The Citation of Greek Manuscript Evidence in an Apparatus Criticus," *New Testament Manuscript Studies,* ed. M. M. Parvis and A. P. Wikgren. Chicago: The University of Chicago Press, 1950. Pp. 81-94.

Grant, Robert M. "The Bible of Theophilus of Antioch," *Journal of Biblical Literature,* LXVI (1947), 173-96.

———. *A Historical Introduction to the New Testament.* New York: Harper and Row, 1963.

Greenlee, J. H. *The Gospel Text of Cyril of Jerusalem.* Copenhagen: Ejnar Munksgaard, 1955.

———. *Introduction to New Testament Textual Criticism.* Grand Rapids: Wm. B. Eerdmans Publishing Co., 1964.

———. "Some Examples of Scholarly 'Agreement in Error'," *Journal of Biblical Literature.* LXXVII (1958), 363-64.

Harrison, Everett F. *Introduction to the New Testament.* Grand Rapids: Wm B. Eerdmans Publishing Co., 1964.

Hemphill, S. *A History of the Revised Version.* London: Elliot Stock, 1906.

Hills, E. F. "Harmonizations in the Caesarean Text of Mark," *Journal of Biblical Literature,* LXVI (1947), 135-52.

———. *The King James Version Defended!* Des Moines, Iowa: The Christian Research Press, 1956.

Hodges, Zane Clark. "A Defense of the Majority Text." Unpublished course notes, Dallas Theological Seminary, 1975.

———. "The Ecclesiastical Text of Revelation—Does it Exist?" *Bibliotheca Sacra,* CXVIII (1961), 113-22.

———. "The Greek Text of the King James Version," *Bibliotheca Sacra,* CXXV (October-December, 1968).

Horne, T. H. *An Introduction to the Critical Study and Knowledge of the Holy Scriptures.* 4th American ed. 4 vols. Philadelphia: E. Little, 1831.

Hort, Arthur Fenton. *Life and Letters of Fenton John Anthony Hort.* 2 vols. London: Macmillan and Co., Ltd., 1896.

Hoskier, Herman C. *Codex B and its Allies.* 2 vols. London: Bernard Quaritch, Ltd. 1914.

———. *Concerning the Text of the Apocalypse,* 2 vols. London: Bernard Quaritch, Ltd., 1929.

———. *A Full Account and Collation of the Greek Cursive Codex Evangelium 604.* London: David Nutt, 1890.

———. "A Study of the Chester-Beatty Codex of the Pauline Epistles," *The Journal of Theological Studies,* XXXVIII (1937), 149-63.

Hutton, Edward Ardson. *An Atlas of Textual Criticism.* London: The Cambridge University Press, 1911.

Hyatt, J. Philip (ed.). *The Bible in Modern Scholarship.* New York: Abingdon Press, 1965.

REFERENCES

Kenyon, Frederick G. *Handbook to the Textual Criticism of the New Testament.* 2nd ed. Grand Rapids: Wm B. Eerdmans Publishing Co., 1951.

————. *Recent Developments in the Textual Criticism of the Greek Bible.* London: Oxford University Press, 1933.

Kilpatrick, G. D. "Atticism and the Text of the Greek New Testament," *Neutestamentliche Aufsatze.* Regensburg: Verlag Friedrich Pustet, 1963.

————. "The Greek New Testament Text of Today and the *Textus Receptus,*" *The New Testament in Historical and Contemporary Perspective,* ed. H. Anderson and W. Barclay. Oxford: Basil Blackwell, 1965.

————. "The Transmission of the New Testament and its Reliability," *The Bible Translator,* IX (1958), 127-36.

Klijn, A. F. J. *A Survey of the Researches into the Western Text of the Gospels and Acts; part two 1949-1969.* Leiden: E. J. Brill, 1969.

Lake, Kirsopp. *The Text of the New Testament.* 6th ed. revised by Silva New. London: Rivingtons, 1959.

Lake, Kirsopp, Blake, R. P., and New, Silva. "The Caesarean Text of the Gospel of Mark," *Harvard Theological Review,* XXI (1928), 207-404.

Lake, Silva. *Family II and the Codex Alexandrinus (Studies and Documents V).* London: Christophers, 1936.

Metzger, Bruce Manning. *Chapters in the History of New Testament Textual Criticism.* Vol. IV of *New Testament Tools and Studies,* ed. B. M. Metzger. Grand Rapids: Wm. B. Eerdmans Publishing Co., 1963.

————. *The Early Versions of the New Testament.* Oxford: Clarendon Press, 1977.

————. "The Evidence of the Versions for the Text of the N.T.," *New Testament Manuscript Studies,* ed. M. M. Parvis and A. P. Wikgren. Chicago: The University of Chicago Press, 1950. Pp. 25-68.

————. "Explicit References in the Works of Origen to Variant Readings in N. T. MSS.," *Biblical and Patristic Studies in Memory of Robert Pierce Casey,* ed. J. N. Birdsall and R. W. Thomson. New York: Herder, 1963. Pp. 78-95.

————. *Historical and Literary Studies.* Vol. VIII of *New Testament Tools and Studies,* ed. B. M. Metzger. Grand Rapids: Wm. B. Eerdmans, 1968.

————. "Patristic Evidence and the Textual Criticism of the New Testament," *New Testament Studies,* XVIII (1972).

————. "St. Jerome's Explicit References to Variant Readings in Manuscripts of the New Testament," *Text and Interpretation: Studies in the New Testament Presented to Matthew Black,* ed. Best and McL. Wilson. Cambridge: University Press, 1979.

————. *The Text of the New Testament,* London: Oxford University Press, 1964.

————. *A Textual Commentary on the Greek New Testament.* London: United Bible Societies, 1971.

Miller, Edward. *A Guide to the Textual Criticism of the New Testament.* London: George Bell and Sons, 1886.

Nestle, Erwin and Aland, Kurt. *Novum Testamentum Graece.* 24th ed. Stuttgart: Privilegierte Wurttembergische Bibelanstalt, 1960.

New International Version of the New Testament. Grand Rapids: Zondervan Bible Publishers, 1973.

O'Callaghan, J. "El cambio δ>τ en los papiros biblicos," *Biblica*, LIV (1973).

———. "Notas sobre 7Q tomadas en el 'Rochefeller Museum' de Jerusalén," *Biblica*, LIII (1972).

———. "Papiros neotestamentarios en la cueva 7 de Qumran?" *Biblica*, LIII (1972).

Oliver, H. H. "Present Trends in the Textual Criticism of the New Testament," *The Journal of Bible and Religion*, XXX (1962), 308-20.

Oxford Society of Historical Research, *The New Testament in the Apostolic Fathers*, Oxford: Clarendon Press, 1905.

Parvis, Merrill M. "The Nature and Task of New Testament Textual Criticism," *The Journal of Religion*, XXXII (1952), 165-74.

———. "The Need for a New *Apparatus Criticus* to the Greek New Testament," *Journal of Biblical Literature*, LXV (1946), 353-69.

———. "Text, NT.," *The Interpreter's Dictionary of the Bible*. 4 vols. New York: Abingdon Press, 1962. Pp. 594-614.

Parvis, Merrill M. and Wikgren, A. P. (eds.). *New Testament Manuscript Studies*. Chicago: The University of Chicago Press, 1950.

Pickering, W. N. *A Framework for Discourse Analysis*. Dallas: Summer Institute of Linguistics and University of Texas at Arlington, 1980.

———. " 'Queen Anne . . .' and all that: a Response," *Journal of the Evangelical Theological Society*, XXI (June, 1978), 165-67.

Revised Standard Version. London: Thomas Nelson and Sons Ltd., 1952.

Richardson, C. C. (ed.). *Early Christian Fathers*. Philadelphia: The Westminster Press, 1953.

Riddle, Donald W. "Fifty Years of New Testament Scholarship," *The Journal of Bible and Religion*, X (1942), 136-40, 183.

Rist, Martin. "Pseudepigraphy and the Early Christians," *Studies in New Testament and Early Christian Literature*, ed. D. E. Aune. Leiden: E. J. Brill, 1972.

Roberts, A. and Donaldson, J. (eds). *The Ante-Nicene Fathers*. Grand Rapids: Wm. B. Eerdmans Publishing Co., 1956.

Roberts, C. H. *Schweich Lectures 1977*. London: British Academy, 1977.

Rylaarsdam, J. C. R. (ed.). *Transitions in Biblical Scholarship*. Chicago: The University of Chicago Press, 1968.

Salmon, George. *Some Thoughts on the Textual Criticism of the New Testament*. London: n.p., 1897.

Schopp, Ludwig (ed.). *The Apostolic Fathers*. New York: Cima Publishing Co., Inc., 1947.

Scrivener, F. H. A. *A Plain Introduction to the Criticism of the New Testament*. 4th ed. edited by E. Miller. 2 vols. London: George Bell and Sons, 1894.

———. (ed.). *The New Testament in the Original Greek, together with the Variations Adopted in the Revised Version*. Cambridge: Cambridge University Press, 1880.

Soden, Hermann F. von. *Die Schriften des Neuen Testaments*. 2 vols. Göttingen: Vandenhoeck und Ruprecht, 1911.

Streeter, Burnett H. *The Four Gospels: A Study of Origins*. London: Macmillan and Co., 1930.

Sturz, H. A. *The Byzantine Text-Type and New Testament Textual Criticism*.

REFERENCES

Second Syllabus Edition; La Mirada, Cal.: Biola College Bookstore, 1972.

Suggs, M. J. "The Use of Patristic Evidence in the Search for a Primitive New Testament Text," *New Testament Studies*, IV (1957-1958), 139-47.

Tasker, R. V. G. (ed.). *The Greek New Testament*. Oxford: Oxford University Press, 1964.

———. "Introduction to the Manuscripts of the New Testament," *Harvard Theological Review*, XLI (1948), 71-81.

Taylor, R. A. "Queen Anne Resurrected? A Review Article," *Journal of the Evangelical Theological Society*, XX (December, 1977), 377-81.

Taylor, Vincent. *The Text of the New Testament*. New York: St. Martin's Press Inc., 1961.

Tenney, M. C. *New Testament Survey*. Grand Rapids: Eerdmans, 1961.

Thiessen, Henry C. *Introduction to the New Testament*. Grand Rapids, Michigan: Wm. B. Eerdmans Publishing Co., 1955.

Tischendorf, Constantinus. *Novum Testamentum Graece*. 8th ed. 2 vols. Lipsiae: Giesecke and Devrient, 1869-72.

Turner, C. H. "Historical Introduction to the Textual Criticism of the New Testament," *Journal of Theological Studies*, (Jan. 1910).

Vaganay, Leo. *An Introduction to the Textual Criticism of the New Testament*. Translated by B. V. Miller. London: Sands and Co., Ltd., 1937.

Van Bruggen, Jakob. *The Ancient Text of the New Testament*. Winnipeg: Premier, 1976.

———. *The Future of the Bible*. Nashville: Thomas Nelson, 1978.

Vööbus, Arthur, *Early Versions of the New Testament*. Stockholm: Estonian Theological Society in Exile, 1954.

Walters, P. *The Text of the Septuagint. Its Corruptions and their Emendation*, ed. D. W. Gooding. Cambridge: University Press, 1973.

Westcott, Brooke Foss and Hort, Fenton John Anthony. *The New Testament in the Original Greek*. 2 vols. London: Macmillan and Co., 1881.

Wikgren, Allen. "Chicago Studies in the Greek Lectionary of the New Testament," *Biblical and Patristic Studies in Memory of Robert Pierce Casey*, ed. J. N. Birdsall and R. W. Thomson. New York: Herder, 1963. Pp. 96-121.

——— (ed.). *Early Christian Origins*. Chicago: Quadrangle Books, 1961.

Williams, Charles S. C. *Alterations to the Text of the Synoptic Gospels and Acts*. Oxford: Basil Blackwell, 1951.

Zuntz, Gunther. "The Byzantine Text in New Testament Criticism," *Journal of Theological Studies*, XLIII (1942), 25-30.

———. *The Text of the Epistles*. London: Oxford University Press, 1953.

INDEX

About the Author

Wilbur N. Pickering, the son of missionary parents, has worked extensively in linguistics for the past twenty years. He is associated with the Wycliffe Bible Translators, and much of his work has been among the Apurinã tribe in Brazil, the country of his birth.

He received his B.A. in English Literature from Bryan College, Th.M. in Greek Exegesis from Dallas Theological Seminary, and M.A. and Ph.D. in Linguistics from the University of Toronto.

Dr. Pickering and his wife, Ida Lou, make their home in Pennsylvania when they are in the United States. They have two children, Candace Sinapa and Karis Irene.